The
Annotated
Arch

The Annotated Arch

A CRASH COURSE IN THE HISTORY OF ARCHITECTURE

Carol Strickland, Ph.D.

Book Designer: Barbara Cohen Aronica
Photographic Researcher: Toby Greenberg
Managing Editor: Patty Brown
Editor: Amy Handy

A John Boswell Associates Book

**Andrews McMeel
Publishing**

Kansas City

To Sid, Alison, and Eliza—my foundation and my peaks

In memory of Meg Colclough
&
Sidney and Margaret King Strickland

Thanks to the superb team who produced this book: idea man, John Boswell; project manager, Patty Brown; book designer, Barbara Cohen Aronica; photo researcher, Toby Greenberg; editor, Amy Handy; and illustrators, Luci Betti, whose work appears on pages 5, 6, 7, 9, 11, 14, 17, 19, 20, 22, 24, 32, 34, 35, 39, 46, 49, 58, 64, 71, 86, 87, 88, 90, 105, 162, and Ken Scaglia, for the reuse of his drawing on page 12.

01 02 03 04 05 TWP 10 9 8 7 6 5 4 3 2 1

Library of Congress Cataloging-in-Publication Data

Strickland, Carol.
    The annotated arch : a crash course in the history of architecture / Carol Strickland;
  book designer, Barbara Cohen Aronica ; photographic researcher, Toby Greenberg ;
  managing editor, Patty Brown ; editor, Amy Handy.
        p. cm.
    "A John Boswell Associates book."
    Includes index.
    ISBN 0-7407-1024-9
    1. Architecture—History.   I. Handy, Amy.   II. Title.

NA200.S77 2001
720'.9—dc21
                                                            00-046877

CONTENTS

PHOTO CREDITS

INTRODUCTION:
THE ELEMENTS OF ARCHITECTURE

TWO FOR THE SEESAW. Tracing the history of architecture from the Stone Age to the Space Age is a tall order. Through thousands of years of bricks and mortar, two motifs—evolution and revolution—invariably recur. While some architects respect the status quo, others rock the foundation.

Ancient Greeks and Romans set the fundamentals in stone. From then on, architects disposed to revere the past revived and embellished the Classics. In more forward-thinking periods, rebels busted loose from Greco-Roman rules. These insurgents designed buildings owing little to convention, bowing only to the individual imagination.

Besides these cycles of continuity versus innovation, another back-and-forth trend constantly appears. Styles alternate between plain-Jane and fancy-schmancy. Greek temples were simple; ensuing Roman buildings, ornate. Gothic architecture was complex and mysterious; succeeding Renaissance designs were purely rational. Most sensationally, High Victorian structures were overlaid with froufrou. Modernism stripped buildings bare.

For eons, styles in architecture have tended to revile and overthrow immediate forebears, while respecting and resuscitating long-departed ancestors. In olden days, styles lasted for centuries before reaction set in. In today's high-velocity culture, the quest for novelty causes turnover within a decade.

TECHNO-TECTURE. An important sidelight in the history of architecture is the story of engineering advances, making new building forms possible. From the keystone arch pioneered by the Romans to cantilevered slabs jutting over a cascade in Frank Lloyd Wright's Fallingwater, discoveries in technology allowed daring structural departures. Architecture is a unique art form that combines art and science, beauty and utility.

Nave, Amiens Cathedral, Amiens, France, by Robert de Luzarches, 1288
Soaring vertical lines, tall openings of bays, and horizontal moldings create a rhythm of rapid progression, sweeping the eye inexorably from entrance to altar.

Nave, San Andrea, Mantua, Italy, by Leon Battista Alberti, designed 1470
Segmented bays (each in a proportionate ratio to the central crossing square) and starkly geometrical forms of the church interior make for a regular beat marked by mathematics and reason.

AUTOBIOGRAPHY OF THE HUMAN RACE.
More than an account of technical know-how or individual genius, the story of architecture is also the story of human history. Buildings that rise to the status of public monuments are social artifacts. In material and immaterial ways, they reveal much about the philosophical, religious, and political values of society.

The critic John Ruskin wrote, "All architecture proposes an effect on the human mind, not merely a service to the human frame." More than shelter from the storm, architecture has symbolized reigning mental and moral concepts. Great buildings are ideas made tangible.

Pyramids, by virtue of their massiveness, suggest the Egyptian yen for permanence and immortality. The Parthenon, with its balance of vertical and horizontal lines, represents the Golden Mean, or ideal equilibrium of Greek philosophy. The dominant vertical lines of Gothic cathedrals illustrate the heavenward aspirations of the medieval mind.

Architectural masterpieces are also the most durable components of our cultural heritage, leaving, in Longfellow's words, "footprints on the sands of time." When first erected, however, structures now rated revolutionary were seen as visual provocation. Truly original architecture forces viewers to reassess preconceived notions. When Prince Charles called one proposal for a radical building a "monstrous carbuncle," he initiated a debate that still rages today. Really innovative architecture is so controversial, it could start a barroom brawl.

HOW TO ANALYZE ARCHITECTURE.
Understanding these implications involves some knowledge of the social and political background of an era, which this book will supply. (The book confines itself to extraordinary, rather than vernacular, architecture, focusing on the Western tradition.)

Judging a building's artistic merit involves understanding how architects manipulate elements of design. What makes architecture excellent is the handling of factors like detail, craftsmanship, materials, proportion, function, surface color and texture, relation to site, space, and light.

In the 1990s, signature architects engaged in "star wars"—style wars among "starchitects" who produced read-it-from-a-mile-away buildings that trumpet their trademark techniques. Assessing excellence is more than identifying a style or architectural fad.

Contemporary architect Hugh Newell Jacobsen has said, "If anyone thinks this isn't theater, they're nuts. But if it looks like theater, you've blown it." Basic facets of architecture—shape, scale, manipulation of light, form, and proportion—define a masterpiece more than flashy appliqué of shtick motifs.

Three qualities that Architecture with a capital *A* must embody are function, structure, and beauty. The function, or purpose and use of a building, is shown in the floor plan, a diagram of the horizontal layout of rooms. Structure, or how a building is supported, is illustrated in the section, or vertical slice through a building's stories. Beauty is best demonstrated in an elevation drawing, which shows exterior or interior elements as if one were facing the building.

In terms of sound structure, a building must support two types of load: "dead" load (the static weight of materials and structural members like floors, roof, walls) and "live" load (dynamic forces acting on the structure generated by wind, traffic, seismic tremors, the movement of occupants).

"Architectural art begins physical and ends psychological," according to James F. O'Gorman in *ABC of Architecture*. Physical components like structure and function are relatively easy to assess. The psychological effects of a building involve more art than science and are trickier to discern. To gauge architectural aesthetics requires consideration of the following.

RHYTHM.

Architects set up a pattern of rhythmic repetition of elements like solids and voids, walls and windows, projecting or receding parts. Placement of columns on a facade or arches in an arcade, for example, was usually regular and symmetrical during the Renaissance and syncopated in the Mannerist period.

Consider the exceedingly tall, narrow bays lining a Gothic cathedral's nave. The interval between bays is so reduced, with slender piers punctuating high, pointed-arch openings, that one perceives the bays as a flickering rhythm of voids progressing from entrance to altar.

The horizontal moldings separating different layers of the elevation (arcade, triforium, clerestory) also sweep the eye down the length of the nave toward the altar. The architecture is a perfect analogy for the church's function, which is to serve as a framework for processions culminating at the apse.

In contrast, the rhythm of Renaissance churches is more measured and deliberate— static more than dynamic. Each bay is a mathematical unit, a subdivision of the square under the crossing. Regular shapes—such as squares, octagons, or circles with domes—predominate. The spectator can comprehend the layout rationally. A feeling of structural clarity pervades Renaissance churches, such as those by Palladio or Alberti. It's all a matter of rhythm. Divine mystery sets the heart racing in Gothic cathedrals, while in stately Renaissance churches, the steady ticktock of human reason prevails.

Pennsylvania Academy of Fine Arts, Philadelphia, by Frank Furness, 1871–76
Furness exaggerated load-bearing structure through sturdy columns and flattened arches that seem compressed by extreme weight. He heaped on ornament to enrich the surface visually and contrasted colors and textures, making this an ultimate example of High Victorian Gothic complexity. The abundant surface detail and rusticated stone base add to the sense of weightiness.

Villa Savoye, Poissy, France, by Le Corbusier, 1928–31
The unadorned, monochrome surface and elevation off the ground on thin stilts give this structure an almost weightless aspect. The open ground floor, continuous bands of windows, and perforations in the second- and third-story walls further decrease the impression of mass, sculpting an architecture of space and linear planes.

LINE. Before the first skyscraper (the Tower of Babel), even before Jacob raised up his stone pillow to create a pillar in the Old Testament, vertical lines of monuments like Stonehenge have been linked to human yearning toward the divine and an afterlife. The Gothic cathedral, with its soaring vertical lines, illustrates most graphically the idea of uplift and striving for ascent to a heavenly realm.

In contrast, symbolism connected with horizontal lines is earthbound. Frank Lloyd Wright, inventor of the low-slung Prairie House, criticized the modern tendency "to tip everything in the way of human occupation or habitation up edgewise instead of letting it lie comfortably flatwise with the ground." Horizontal lines—like the prone position of sleep—imply shelter, stasis, security. Wright's earth-hugging Prairie Houses, with their horizontally cantilevered porch roofs, represent contentment with home, hearth, and the natural (rather than supernatural) world.

Diagonal lines best convey a sense of movement. Exploited most obviously in Baroque churches and the slanting lines of twentieth-century Deconstructivist buildings, diagonals imply action and energy.

SCALE. Scale refers to a building's size in relation to the human body, as well as to its surroundings. Architects manipulate scale to make a building seem cozy or overwhelming. In the buildings lining Michelangelo's Campidoglio, he used the giant order of pilasters stretching over several stories to achieve a sense of vast scale. The columns in the hypostyle hall of the Egyptian Temple of Amon at Karnak are hugely oversized in relation to the human body. Their enormousness humbles the human ego before the god Amon. In his Post-Modern Portland Building, Michael Graves inflated the scale of architectural elements like a keystone to make the building seem imposing and grandiose.

LIGHT. Light (natural or artificial, interior or external) clarifies and defines the form of a building. It can also provide visual delight and highlight meaning, focusing the eye on important points. In Baroque churches, architects like Bernini created theatrical lighting effects through hidden spotlights to heighten emotional impact. In Le Corbusier's modern masterpiece, the chapel at Ronchamp, shafts of colored light pierce the dark interior over altars.

Light through stained glass in Gothic cathedrals softens the stone walls and adds an otherworldly effect. A beam of sunlight falling from the overhead oculus in the Pantheon travels across the surface of the interior, illuminating statues in niches and changing in intensity and color as the day progresses.

Light also determines one's perception of texture and form, creating both a physiological effect and a psychological mood. In the strong light of southern climates, moldings and ornamental detail are needed as relief, to articulate and animate a facade with shadow. Light also creates a circle of intimacy and warmth—a feeling of well-being—or of hostile glare.

TEXTURE. Texture can create an effect of solidity and stability. In Renaissance palaces, the bottom floor was constructed of rusticated stone to suggest a firm foundation and impenetrable defenses. Higher floors were formed from smooth ashlar blocks, with the joints hardly perceptible, to represent the refinement of the living area.

The most blatant recent use of textural effects was in Paul Rudolph's Yale Art and Architecture Building, an icon of the Brutalist style, which looks as aggressive as it sounds. Rudolph specified an exterior of corrugated cement, a corduroy surface made of an aggregate of crushed rock and concrete. "Abrasive" doesn't begin to describe the sharp, ridged surface, which was literally cutting edge.

Optical texture also exploits the contrasting qualities of hard versus soft surfaces. At Versailles, the movement of gushing fountains and softness of greenery counter the stone palace's rigid symmetry.

COLOR. Color can be used to differentiate various parts of a building, as in bands of contrasting stone that separate stories or wings. Warm colors on the red-orange end of the spectrum evoke a more heated emotional response, while blue-green colors are perceived as restful and calming. Byzantine churches with their vivid mosaics, Muslim and Moorish mosques with brightly glazed ceramic tiles, and Post-Modern, highly colored buildings all use color for different effects. In Charles Moore's Piazza d'Italia, with its mustard yellows and deep oranges, color spritzes up the semiclassical colonnade with jazzy zest.

ORNAMENT. Style warriors have fired their most furious salvos on the subject of ornament. Victorian John Ruskin proclaimed ornament "the principal part of architecture," while the Modernist Adoph Loos countered with, "Ornament is crime."

Among the many purposes of ornament are to emphasize structure, embellish the surface with visual detail, model light and shadow, add human scale, and delight the eye. Ornament can even serve practical aims, as in the Gothic gargoyles that function as downspouts. Louis Sullivan used ornament to articulate both the structure and the function of parts of his skyscrapers. In Romanesque churches, sculptured ornament served a didactic purpose—teaching illiterate worshipers homilies of church doctrine.

ACOUSTICS. Buildings are perceived not just with the eyes but through multiple senses. The New Mexico architect Antoine Predock tries to engage all the senses. He plants herbs and flowers to scent the air near his buildings, and uses the sound of water to draw one deeper into the interior.

Buildings use hard surfaces (like marble and mosaics) to reflect sound and create "live" acoustics. Soft surfaces (like sound-absorbing fabrics and upholstery) make spaces seem "dead" acoustically and provide a quiet atmosphere.

Winston Churchill said, "We shape our buildings, and afterwards our buildings shape us." This reciprocity was certainly true for the development of Western music, which was directly influenced by the form of church buildings.

Gregorian chants developed because of the extended reverberation period of notes in the long naves covered with hard surfaces in the early Christian basilicas. Gabrieli invented polyphonic music to exploit echoes bounced between multiple choirs in the San Marco basilica in Venice. Bach's complex cantatas were made possible by the acoustics of St. Thomas church in Leipzig.

SITE. Buildings can contrast with their settings (natural or man-made) or enhance and blend in with their surroundings (called "contextual" or "organic" design). Wright's Fallingwater seems to grow naturally from its site, even using local limestone laid in rough-textured strata to

(above) Fallingwater, Bear Run, Pennsylvania, by Wright, 1937–39

simulate rocky ledges. (Wright contrasted this craggy base with the smooth concrete of his balconies.)

Anasazi cliff dwellings in the American Southwest take maximum advantage of climate through siting. At Mesa Verde, the village was tucked under the recesses of a cliff, which provided shade at noon in the broiling summer. In winter, the low-slanting sun penetrated the backs of the houses to warm them.

Basilica of San Marco, Venice, Italy, 976–1094, interior

Schröder House, Utrecht, Netherlands, by Rietveld (1888–1964), 1924

Modernist buildings are the antithesis of harmonious melding with a site. They sit like alien spacecraft, bristling with self-consciousness as an *objet d'art* amid their conventional neighbors. Rietveld's cubist Schröder House in Utrecht is at the end of a row of old-fashioned brick dwellings. It looks as out of place as a Martian in a mall.

SPACE. Space can seem static, as in the segmented compartments of Romanesque churches and isolated rooms of Victorian homes. Or it can interpenetrate, as in Japanese villas like the Katsura pavilions, where sliding partitions minimally divide the whole. Interior-exterior spatial flow is another trait of Japanese architecture, which twentieth-century architects like Wright borrowed.

Space can also appear either positive or negative, depending on whether it is defined by enclosing walls (a void wrapped in a shell, or positive space) or as a hollowed-out solid or space between two masses (negative space). Convex forms generally convey an impression of mass, while concave shapes evoke a feeling of space. Americans have tended to focus on positive space, while Japanese philosophy considers voids just as evocative.

WEIGHT AND MASS. Different periods have placed varying value on weight and mass as attributes of architecture. In the Victorian era, American architect Frank Furness designed some of the chunkiest buildings ever. Not that their tonnage was actually greatest, but they appeared compressed like Atlas hefting the globe, bulging from the force of gravity. Furness used strongly contrasting forms, scale, color, rugged textures, and solid materials to express this sense of tension and vigor.

Conversely, Gothic architects took great pains to deny the bonds of earth, creating the thinnest piers to support the highest vaults. Le Corbusier, too, sought to disguise weight and emphasize space in his masterpiece, the Villa Savoye. A smooth finish, such as Corbu used, generally appears light, while large stone blocks, such as Furness employed, seem heavy. The Villa Savoye rests on slim stilts, making it almost seem to levitate, as if it were an immaterial composition of weightless planes. Without a cornice, gutters, or ornament, the villa looks flat, nearly two-dimensional.

Byodo-in Temple: Phoenix Hall, Kyoto, Japan, 1053

Architecture is much more than the sum of these singular parts. It's an art of interdependence, where separate elements interact with the time, place, materials, technology, economy, and individual genius.

Goethe called architecture "frozen music." Sounding all the notes from high to low on the scale of human invention, architecture preserves the best-loved tunes of civilization.

The Annotated Arch

Ancient World: The Building Blocks

If walls could talk, they'd tell the story of the human race. From prehistory to the present, architecture shows human character, ambition, and values set in stone.

Remarkably early, human beings reached beyond pure utility. Whether constructing in mud, wood, brick, stone, marble, or concrete, they erected shelters and shrines meant to impress. Motives for these grand buildings were diverse. Most often, tombs and towers filled political, religious, or military needs. Just as frequently, a ruler's vanity propelled buildings far beyond necessity into the realm of aesthetics.

The story of ancient architecture begins with the first dwellings of the Neolithic Age, when hunter-gatherers settled down in communities to grow food and tend domestic animals. Once people mingled in villages, their urge to show off flowered. Stone monoliths sprouted like wild poppies across the landscape of Western Europe.

After Mesopotamia invented the city, huge piles of sun-baked brick, or ziggurats, rose. Along the Nile, stone pyramids proclaimed life everlasting for the pharaohs (the word *pharaoh* comes from the Hebrew for "great house"). In the New World of Meso-america, steep pyramids climbed to the sky, and in the Near and Far East, architecture of sumptuous ornament developed. In Greece and Rome, architecture—like civilization itself—achieved classic status, becoming Architecture with a capital *A*.

Ruins and archeologists' theories give us only a hazy view of ancient architecture. But just as the arch opened up ceiling vaults, technology, coupled with imagination, opened up new vistas for the roof above our heads.

WORLD HISTORY		ARCHITECTURE
	B.C.E.	
Grain domesticated for agriculture	c. 11,000	
Paleo-Indians cross Bering Strait to Alaska	c. 10,000	
	c. 7500	Jericho walls constructed
Bronze Age, marked by bronze tools	c. 3200–1050	
	c. 3000	Earliest features of Stonehenge built
Earliest Meso-american cultures appear	c. 3000–2000	
	c. 2630	Oldest dressed-stone structure built (Saqqara pyramid)
	c. 2550–2470	Pyramids at Giza constructed
	c. 2100	Ziggurat of Ur built
	c. 1900–1200	Palaces constructed in Crete
Mycenaean influence expands	c. 1350–1250	
Moses leads Jews out of Egypt, receives Ten Commandments	c. 1230	
Fall of Troy	c. 1200	
Iron tools developed	c. 1050	
First Olympiad held	776	
Legendary founding of Rome	753	
Homer composes *The Iliad* and *The Odyssey*	c. 750	
Japanese Empire founded	600	
	565	Buddha born; temple architecture developed
Roman Republic founded	509	
Persian wars fought	490–479	
	447–432	Parthenon constructed in Athens
Peloponnesian War fought	431–404	
Socrates dies	399	
Life of Alexander the Great	356–323	
Macedonians defeat Greeks; Hellenistic age begins	338	
	c. 350	Epidaurus theater constructed in Greece
Rome is master of Italian peninsula	275	
	c. 221	Great Wall of China construction begins
Ptolemy theorizes earth is center of universe	c. 150	
Greece becomes Roman province	146	
Julius Caesar assassinated	44	
Mark Antony and Cleopatra defeated	31	
End of Republic, Roman Empire begins	27	
Jesus born	c. 4	
	C.E.	
Jesus crucified	c. 30	
Buddhism introduced in China	58	
Fire consumes much of Rome	64	
Romans destroy Jerusalem	70	
	c. 70–80	Colosseum built in Rome
Eruption of Vesuvius destroys Pompeii	79	
Roman Empire reaches greatest extent	c. 98–117	
	122–27	Hadrian builds wall in northern England
	c. 164	Earliest Mayan monuments built
	c. 212–16	Baths of Caracalla built
Christian martyrs persecuted	c. 250	
Christian faith legalized	312	
Constantine moves imperial capital to Byzantium	324	
Council of Nicea decrees even women have souls	325	
Constantine (first Christian emperor) dies	337	
Goths sack Rome	455	

PREHISTORIC ARCHITECTURE: ROCK OF AGES

As soon as human beings emerged from caves to live in huts, two basic drives—aggression and religion—dictated the forms of the first permanent architecture.

The ancient city of Jericho (in modern Jordan) was built 9,300 years ago surrounded by a wall of rough stone blocks to repel marauding enemies. Remnants of the wall, 14 feet high and 10 feet thick, still stand. Its most impressive feature was a tower more than 25 feet tall, presumably to spot approaching invaders. These defensive fortifications tell us that, from the end of the last Ice Age, large-scale warfare was a fact of human existence.

Judging from other early relics, the flip side of the coin of human nature was spirituality. Neolithic monuments created 6,500 years ago had nothing to do with a practical matter like survival. The massive stone formations scattered across western Europe, from Spain to Scandinavia, were erected with incredible effort to meet emotional and spiritual needs.

STONEHENGE: IF STONES COULD TALK. Built over the course of a thousand years, possibly from as early as 3000 B.C.E., Stonehenge sprang from both rational and irrational concepts. The stones' site is linked to precise astronomical observation. Arranged in concentric circles around an inner horseshoe shape, on the Summer Solstice (the longest day of the year), the sun rises exactly over the apex of the Heel Stone. One theory considers the group a giant stone computer—about as hard as hardware can get—to predict solar and lunar eclipses.

More than a passive sundial, however, Stonehenge was almost certainly used for ritual religious practices. At its center is an altar, with the tallest stone (28 feet high) behind it.

Stonehenge, Wiltshire, England, c. 3000–1500 B.C.E., aerial view
This monument may have been a solar calendar to predict the seasons, instructing ancient people when to plant crops.

More than 900 stone circles, called *cromlechs,* have been identified across the British Isles, but Stonehenge's construction is the most sophisticated. In its earliest incarnation, workers, using bone antlers, dug a circular trench (or henge) in the white chalk bedrock. A break in the circle faces a tall sandstone pillar, called the Heel Stone, outside the ring. In the center of the ditch, a double ring of bluestones was placed. These rocks weigh up to five tons each and were quarried hundreds of miles away in the mountains of Wales.

At a later date, five sets of megaliths (from the Greek *megas*= great and *lithos*=stone) were arranged in a U shape, with the open end facing sunrise. These huge, 40-ton stones were combined in threes to make trilithons, in a post-and-lintel setup. An outer round of thirty 15-foot-high megaliths was once a continuous circle of trilithons. Lintels fit together end to end in tongue-and-groove joints to form a smoothly curved arc.

Stonehenge exemplifies basic principles of all architecture. Its creators understood the fundamental element of support and load, where vertical pillars bear the weight of horizontal crossbeams. The monument clearly owes a debt to wood construction, for the stones are linked with a carpenter's mortise-and-tenon joints. (On top of each upright is a projecting knob of stone that fits into a matching notch in the lintel.)

Prehistoric structures demonstrate a fundamental characteristic of architecture. Monuments play symbolic and practical roles.

NEOLITHIC CONSTRUCTION TECHNIQUE

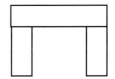

Post and Lintel. The post-and-lintel system of construction uses vertical supports spanned by horizontal beams. The heavier the load (beam), the stronger the supports.

Carnac, France, stone alignments, third millennium B.C.E., aerial view
Around Carnac on the Atlantic coast of France, an army of more than 10,000 granite slabs marches toward the sea over an area of nearly 5 square miles. The avenues of 12-foot-tall stones are arranged in ten to thirteen straight rows called alignments. No one knows why these megaliths were erected.

HOW THEY DID IT. For a people who lacked bronze or iron tools and the wheel, the amount of work involved is nearly inconceivable. With only the crudest picks, these determined Neolithic workers quarried and shaped boulders weighing up to 50 tons. They transported the stones by barge or sled, probably dragged by large crews on log rollers. A team gradually levered the slabs into a vertical position and planted them in holes. Raising the huge, 7-ton lintels up 20 feet to the shoulders of the standing stones was done in stages. By prying the ends up and inserting timber beneath, they added layer after layer of logs to make an ascending palette. After they reached the height of the top and shoved the lintel sideways onto the uprights, the elevating scaffold was removed.

No one quite understands how our primitive ancestors pulled off such a feat. The secret is likely the limitless time and labor devoted to construction. The "how" we can begin to grasp. The "why" remains a mystery.

STONED SENTINELS

Stone alignments, Carnac, c. 4500 B.C.E.

Myths abound to explain the origin of these rocky rows. In one, the slabs are Roman soldiers, petrified by a local saint. New Age sorcerers consider them Stone Age landing lights to guide extraterrestrial visitors. They are not, as another explanation would have it, connected to the Druids, who came along two thousand years later and preferred worshipping in oak groves.

In England, local people have not always been kind to their prehistoric legacy. At dusk, horses were said to shy at the giant stones and bolt down hills, so one notorious "Stone-killer" took it upon himself to knock down countless monoliths, smashing them with a sledgehammer.

For six or seven millennia the stones have stood the test of time. Daniel Defoe wrote in the seventeenth century, "All that can be learn'd of them is, That here they are."

MESOPOTAMIA:
THE DAWN OF CIVILIZATION

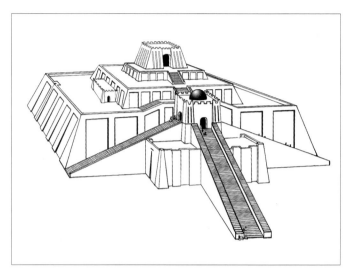

The natural resources they started with—mud and water—were not very promising. But what the ancient Mesopotamians constructed from such meager means was nothing short of a civilization. With mud bricks, they erected massive towers, the first monumental buildings designed with artistic intent. And on the arid plain between the Tigris and Euphrates Rivers (Mesopotamia means "between rivers"), in the area that is now Iraq, they founded the first cities.

Along the way, from about 4500 B.C.E. to 539 B.C.E. (when the Persian king Cyrus seized Babylon to end the Mesopotamian Empire), they developed writing, invented the wheeled vehicle, studied the stars, wrote epic poetry, and compiled the first legal code.

Mesopotamia is most celebrated for inventing the city. When Europe was still scrabbling in the Neolithic dirt with stone and bone tools, Mesopotamia enjoyed what has to be called culture. Their society was rolling in wealth derived from metal working, organized food production, and trade. The Greek historian Herodotus, a gadabout who left records of many sites he visited, said in about 450 B.C.E., "Babylon surpasses in splendor any city in the known world."

Ziggurat of Ur-Nammu at Ur-of-the-Chaldees, c. 2000 B.C.E., reconstruction drawing
The ziggurat form came into being inadvertently. Since new temples were built on the ruins of old, terraced levels grew successively higher until the stepped form became deliberate. Each block was smaller than the one below, and all were connected by monumental staircases. More than thirty ziggurats have been excavated.

SUMER: THE BEGINNING. Near the Persian Gulf in the area known as the Chaldees, early Sumerian culture developed, reaching its Golden Age around 3300 B.C.E. They had no timber or stone, which meant their buildings of unfired, sun-dried brick, mortared with earth, had a distressing tendency to dissolve. Not much is left. Yet, since brick is structurally weak, walls were made extra thick (up to 20 feet) and reinforced with buttresses, so parts of some buildings remain.

The major innovation of Mesopotamian architecture was the ziggurat, a tall, terraced tower with up to seven successively smaller stages, placed one on top of the other, and a temple at the summit. (Think of a square, multitiered wedding cake.)

One thing architecture makes clear is that size and grandeur are manifestations of power. Ziggurats trumpet the king's clout. They were conceived as artificial mountains, which the priest-king climbed to commune with the gods.

The Mesopotamians invented large-scale architecture, equating extreme height with political might. Their buildings were the first designed for aesthetic effect.

MARTIAL ART. As the king became more powerful, his royal palace became the most sumptuous monument. When Sargon II built a citadel at Khorsabad (c. 706 B.C.E.), his palace dominated the complex, intimidating potential foes. Remains of the mile-square city show muscle-flexing decor. In the throne room, larger-than-

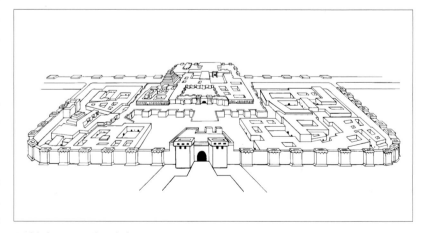

Citadel of Sargon II, Khorsabad, 742–706 B.C.E.
The capital built by Sargon II of Assyria occupied one square mile. The royal palace (center rear), with private temples and small ziggurat, dominates the city.

life alabaster relief sculptures of the king in his war chariot, triumphant atop a heap of enemy corpses and decapitated heads, made a ferocious wall treatment.

BABYLONIAN SPLENDOR: THE ZENITH.

The most famous ziggurat, the Tower of Babel, was supposedly 300 feet high. The Book of Genesis quotes King Nebuchadnezzar's order "to raise the top of the Tower that it might rival heaven." Herodotus described the tower as seven-layered, each level faced with glazed tiles of a different color. Twenty-six tons of gold furnishings and sculpture filled the interior of the temple.

Babylon (located 25 miles south of Baghdad) reached its peak of luxury from 605 to 562 B.C.E. The city is renowned for two of the most famous architectural achievements of antiquity—the Processional Way and Ishtar Gate. The vast processional avenue, 73 feet wide and paved with white limestone and pink marble, ran north to south through the city. On either side, colorful walls rose 23 feet high, decorated with glazed blue tiles and red and gold relief enamels of lions.

In Mesopotamia, we see the first phase of an urban revolution. Public structures such as streets, squares, walls, gates, temples, palaces, canals, homes, and shops—what we would call "mixed use" zoning today—served a population of perhaps 50,000. By 200 C.E., "that great city, that was clothed in fine linen, and purple, and scarlet, and decked with gold, and precious stones, and pearls," as Revelations puts it, was in ruins. Today all that's left is a mound of mud.

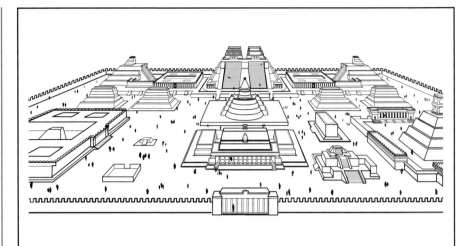

Tenochtitlan, Mexico, 1325–1521, reconstruction view
The Aztec City. In another era, another early civilization established a sophisticated urban civilization. In 1519, Montezuma's Aztec capital was the size of London. "Never will a city such as this one be discovered again," wrote a Spanish soldier. The Venice of Central America, Tenochtitlan was built on an island in the middle of a lake, with canals for thoroughfares. One palace held chambers built entirely of silver and gold.

Ishtar Gate, Babylon, c. 575 B.C.E. Reconstruction in Pergamon Museum, Berlin
The Ishtar Gate is the most magnificent remnant of the Oz-like extravaganza that was Babylon. The Mesopotamians introduced the use of colorful tiles as ornament. A veneer of blue enameled bricks adorns the four-story-high gates, with tiers of hundreds of almost life-size gold bulls and dragons.

EGYPT: ARCHITECTURE TO DIE FOR

An ancient Arab proverb goes, "All things dread Time, but Time dreads the Pyramids." Unfazed by erosion, pollution, or aging, the pyramids have endured for almost 5,000 years. They are the only example of the seven wonders of the ancient world still around today, and it's likely they'll remain at least several more millennia.

Ancient Egyptian civilization flourished for 3,000 years, from about 3100 B.C.E. to 30 B.C.E. It ended with a dramatic flourish when Cleopatra, last of the Ptolemies, pressed an asp to her bosom, choosing death rather than the dishonor of marching to Rome as prisoner. In the long interim between the rise and fall of Egypt, through the reign of thirty dynasties, the most notable buildings were religious and mortuary monuments, built of stone to last forever.

Among Egypt's contributions to architecture are: (1) the first large-scale, dressed stone buildings; (2) pure, geometric forms, such as the pyramid (the first abstract art); (3) invention of

Pyramids at Giza, Egypt, 2570–2500 B.C.E.
The pyramid's extreme simplicity and the stability of its geometric form reflect the concepts of permanence and eternity. After thousands of years, more than eighty pyramids still stand south of Cairo. Pared down to minimal form, they have the durability of bedrock.

the column, capital, cornice, pylon, and obelisk; and (4) fine craftsmanship, including carved bas-reliefs as an integral part of the aesthetic whole.

What's called the "grand monotony" of Egyptian landscape—the flat planes of the desert and repetitive cycles of ebb and flood of the Nile River—may have

Construction Secrets of the Pyramids

They had to clear and level the site, survey it for a perfect square base, and orient its sides precisely without a magnetic compass. Then they quarried millions of stones, transported them hundreds of miles, and lifted them to heights more than forty stories high using levers but no cranes or pulleys. They dressed the blocks with only stone and soft copper tools and fitted them together in exact masonry courses without mortar. And the work—carried out over decades—had to culminate in a perfect point at the peak. How did the Egyptians ever manage this epic undertaking?

One secret was that, for three months every year when the river flooded, no farming was possible. The pharaoh had a huge labor force at his disposal. They quarried stones, some up to 200 tons, at Aswan and floated them up the Nile on barges. They hauled the stones on huge earthen ramps that wrapped around the pyramid as it rose, then were removed after completion.

One mural shows a team of 172 men hauling a 60-ton statue, with an overseer marking rhythm for pulling and another dripping liquid on the ramp to lubricate it. The gilded capstone and mantle of limestone could have been applied from the top down and mortared into place above the substructure. A system of bronze mirrors reflected light to the interior of the pyramid so tunneling workers could create passages deep inside. After the coffin was placed in the heart of the pyramid, props were knocked away and giant blocks crashed down the corridor to seal the entrance.

Although this how-to theory is feasible, the biggest secret will probably never be solved. Why, if they were built as tombs, does the trio of pyramids at Giza contain no bodies or inscriptions? Enigmatically, the empty monuments are all dressed up with no place to go.

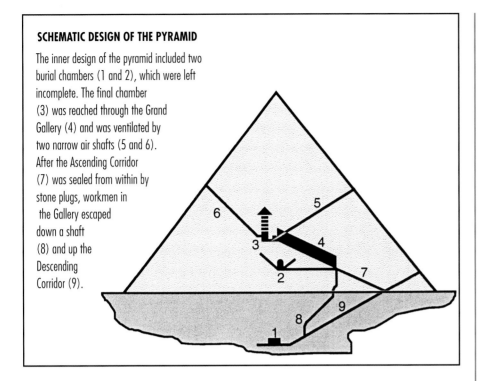

SCHEMATIC DESIGN OF THE PYRAMID

The inner design of the pyramid included two burial chambers (1 and 2), which were left incomplete. The final chamber (3) was reached through the Grand Gallery (4) and was ventilated by two narrow air shafts (5 and 6). After the Ascending Corridor (7) was sealed from within by stone plugs, workmen in the Gallery escaped down a shaft (8) and up the Descending Corridor (9).

shaped Egyptian style. Cultural conservatism finds a visual equivalent in linear works with an emphasis on mass and permanence. Looming over the sands, huge stone monuments rival in scale and ambition the river, desert, and mountains. It's as if their creators intended them to be not just objects in space but in the fourth dimension of time.

EVOLUTION OF PYRAMIDS: SOLID LIKE A ROCK.

The embryo of the revolutionary pyramid form originated with the mastaba, a flat-topped rectangular tomb. Resembling a bar of metal bullion with sides that slope inward toward the top (mastaba means "bench" in Arabic), the tomb was made first of mud-brick, then solid rock, with shafts and passages leading to a subterranean crypt.

The impetus for lavishing such effort on what was basically a grave came from Egyptian religion. Immortality depended upon adequately providing for the deceased. (They were convinced that you can take it with you.) Tombs were designed to protect

the mummified corpse and its possessions until the end of time.

STAIRWAY TO HEAVEN: THE STEPPED PYRAMID.

After mastabas, the next phase was the stepped pyramid of Zoser (c. 2700 B.C.E.), designed by the first known architect, Imhotep (see page 162). It consists of a receding stack of six stone mastabas rising to a height of 204 feet. Perhaps the form was intended as a concrete image of a staircase, which the departed king would ascend, as an inscription put it, "so that he may mount up to heaven thereby."

SUCCESS AT LAST.

Just about 100 years after the first Egyptian stepped pyramid, Cheops built the stunning Great Pyramid, which was joined at Giza by two others erected by his successors, Chephren and Mycerinus. Perfectly proportioned, each consisting of four equilateral triangles; they were originally encased in gleaming white limestone, with a gold capstone. To travelers in the desert, they seemed

like shafts of light made manifest.

The engineering involved in their construction was impressive. For the largest, or Great Pyramid, 2,300,000 blocks of granite and limestone, each weighing about two tons, or as much as an elephant, were stacked in 201 ascending tiers. The base, which covers 13 acres, or ten football fields, is an exact square, so level that one corner is only a fraction of an inch higher than its opposite corner. Each side is oriented precisely to a point of the compass.

Before its capstone was stripped away, the Great Pyramid stood 481 feet high and weighed $6\frac{1}{4}$ million tons. Hundreds of feet of stone are piled atop the burial chamber, cut into the middle of the edifice. To prevent the ceiling from collapsing under such weight, the architects created a partitioned ceiling, with layers of slabs weighing 400 tons in five separate compartments to relieve the stress. A triangular arch deflects the load into the mass of the pyramid itself.

More remarkable than their technology is the pure geometric form of the pyramids. The architects created an austere symbol of the concept of eternal life. The pyramid, the most stable geometric form, also serves as an abstracted image (like the obelisk) of rays emitted by the sun god Ra.

CAVEAT VISITOR

A note in the 1908 edition of the guidebook *Baedeker's Egypt* warned visitors to the pyramids: "Travelers who are in the slightest degree predisposed to apoplectic or fainting fits, and ladies travelling alone, should not attempt to penetrate into these stifling recesses."

TEMPLES. The pyramids were part of a linear ensemble of buildings, including a square-pillared temple near the Nile and a causeway leading to another temple at the base of the pyramid. The processional aspect of alternating open and closed spaces was paramount. After it was evident that pyramids could be looted by grave robbers, pharaohs began constructing temple complexes with tombs cut directly into cliffs.

KARNAK AND LUXOR: AMBIANCE OF OVERSTATEMENT.

In *The Iliad*, Achilles called Thebes "the hundred-gated city." Two temple compounds near Thebes were similarly profuse. Luxor and Karnak temples bristle with a plethora of fat carved columns, huge portals, and avenues lined with ram-headed sphinxes. Surfaces were covered with incised, painted hieroglyphics, like the tattooed man at a

Hypostyle Hall, Temple of Amon at Karnak, c. 1350–1280 B.C.E., "Touring Egypt" painting by Jacob Jacobs (1812–79)
The huge scale of the hall, crammed with bulbous columns, creates an effect of grandiosity. Sixteen rows of 134 columns, each column up to 12 feet thick and 69 feet tall, were densely painted with hieroglyphics.

Living with Landscape: Two Approaches

Abu Simbel, Egypt (c. 1301 B.C.E.); Mesa Verde, Colorado (c. 1200 C.E.); Taliesin West, Scottsdale, Arizona (1937–38) by Frank Lloyd Wright

How a structure relates to a site varies according to its builder's attitude. Some, like the Egyptians, sought to dominate the surroundings, while others—like the Pueblo Amerindians and the "organic architecture" of Frank Lloyd Wright—blended with the environment.

King Rameses II's temple at Abu Simbel, cut into 1,000-foot sandstone cliffs, was adorned with four massive statues of the king, each seven stories high. Instead of building a solid pyramid-mountain, he hollowed out a mountain and carved his image on its face.

In contrast, the pueblos of the American Southwest echo the form of the landscape. At Mesa Verde, 500 cliff dwellings housing 1,200 people nestled in the cliffs, a perfect example of symbiosis between architecture and topography.

Wright's studio/home, Taliesin West, seems an extension of its environment. Desert rubble incorporated into the masonry makes the structure and landscape almost a continuum. Its canted form reflects the angled profile of neighboring mountain ranges. "A struggle against nature never appealed to me," Wright wrote. "The struggle for and with nature thrilled me and inspired my work."

COLUMNS AND CAPITALS

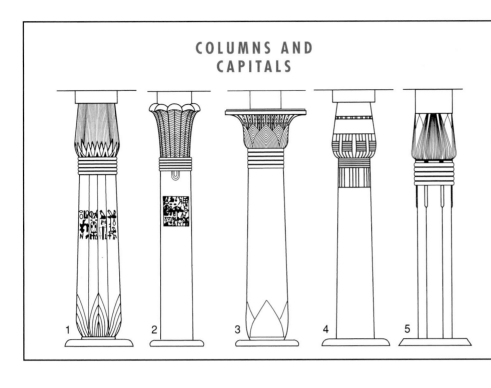

1　2　3　4　5

The Egyptians pioneered various fanciful forms of columns, all based on natural prototypes.

(1) Fluted columns resembled tied bundles of papyrus reeds. The tops, or capitals, of the columns were patterned on papyrus or lotus flowers, the symbols of, respectively, Lower and Upper Egypt.

(2) Tree-trunk pillars with palm leaves,

(3) papyrus flowers,

(4) closed papyrus buds, and

(5) tied bundles of lotus flowers were some of the shapes freely mixed in temple compounds.

circus. A forest of pillars clogged interior spaces. So ornate is the temple at Luxor that, when Napoleon's troops first spotted its ruins, the entire army, agape, halted spontaneously and grounded their arms to stare.

Built by successive pharaohs from about 1530 to 320 B.C.E., the complexes included enormous pylon gateways, colonnaded courtyards, hypostyle halls, and inner sanctums hiding gold-sheathed statues of the deity Amon. The series of spaces gradually became darker and more constricted as the interiors became more sacred and inaccessible to the public. The architecture mirrored the progression from earthly to supernatural realms and from life to afterlife.

Imposing pylons (146 feet high and 50 feet thick at the base), covered with painted reliefs, formed massive entrances and recurred at intervals in the processional. A peristyle (area surrounded by columns) court was open to the sky, with rows of lotus-topped columns and gigantic statues of the king at the sides. Most remarkable was Rameses II's Hypostyle Hall, a room crammed

with enormous, thick columns with papyrus-blossom capitals. Since the Egyptians lacked the arch, many supports were needed to support stone lintels. (Hypostyle means "resting on pillars" in Greek.)

The first clerestory windows at the top of the central nave walls admitted dim light, which increased the impression of claustrophobic seclusion. Colossal mass rather than refined aesthetics seems to have been the decorating aim.

Running the gamut from the pyramid's ultimate simplicity to the gaudy excess of late mortuary temples, Egyptian architecture had one common thread—an obsession with death and the need to house the immortal soul. The word for "temple" meant "house of death," but what the Egyptians really created were dwellings that would live forever.

The First Architect

Imhotep, designer of the stepped pyramid of Zoser, is history's first named architect. Like the multitalented Michelangelo and Leonardo in the Renaissance, he seems to have been a man for whom the word *versatile* was invented. Grand vizier (or counselor) to the king, Imhotep was also a great magician, priest, scholar, astronomer, and physician. Two hundred years after his death, he was worshipped as a god of medicine and learning. Constructing Zoser's tomb seems to have been a stepping-stone to fame for Imhotep. If inscriptions can be believed, the architect was a national hero—a sage, diplomat, economist, and poet. One wonders when he had time to supervise the stonecutters.

GREECE: THE CLASSICS

In his play *Antigone,* Sophocles describes humanity as the peak of creation. "Wonders are many on earth, and none is more wonderful than man. . . . There is nothing beyond his power. . . . Clever beyond all dreams the inventive craft that he hath." The ancient Greeks managed to prove him right. During the space of about fifty years, from 480 to 431 B.C.E., they invented democracy and philosophy and created sublime works of art in drama, sculpture, and architecture. The styles the Greeks originated are so universally admired, they've been imitated for 2,500 years, setting the standard in Western civilization for the meaning of "classic."

Greek culture is probably the first that seems remotely compatible with modern attitudes. Their value system revolved not around an autocratic ruler or unknowable deity, but around man—"the measure of all things," as the Athenian philosopher Protagoras put it. They modeled their Olympian gods, with all their strengths and flaws, on men and women. They thought people could seek truth and perfection through inquiry, debate, and striving for *arete,* or excellence.

DORIC ORDER: THE SYSTEM.

Whether in philosophy, mathematics, or science, the Greeks were geniuses at developing systems. The sculptor Polycleitos established a canon of ideal measurements for the body that produced statues of ideal beauty. Similarly, in architecture a system of "orders" defined the ideal proportions for all components of temples according to set mathematical ratios.

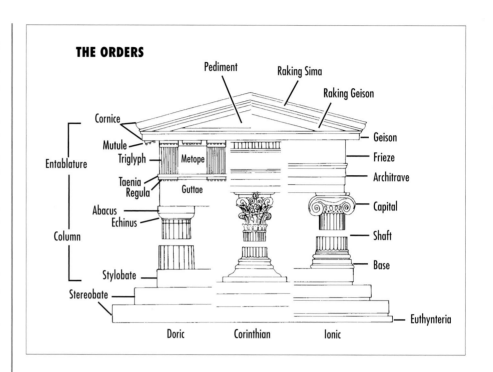

THE ORDERS

Pediment • Raking Sima • Raking Geison • Cornice • Mutule • Triglyph • Metope • Taenia • Regula • Guttae • Abacus • Echinus • Stylobate • Stereobate • Entablature • Column • Geison • Frieze • Architrave • Capital • Shaft • Base • Euthynteria

Doric • Corinthian • Ionic

The order was based on the diameter of a column, with other elements following from this measure.

The Doric order evolved in the late seventh century B.C.E. Columns (usually six across the front and rear of the temple) were four to six times as tall as the diameter of the shaft. Thirteen columns (the number at the front, doubled, plus one) surrounded each side. The entablature, or horizontal elements atop the columns, was one-fourth the height of a column. Each column was composed of many superimposed drums with twenty sharply cut flutes or vertical indentations. These ridges gave visual coherence and unity, not to mention flow, to the segmented columns.

The temple form is called "petrified carpentry," since the Greeks adapted techniques used in wooden construction when they switched to stone. The incised vertical bands in the entablature known as a triglyph (which means "three grooves") represents the ends of rafters, and guttae look like the wooden pegs they replaced. Decoration of the Doric temple emphasizes structure. Pillars were stocky and bulge slightly in the middle, almost as if compressed by the weight of their load.

This swelling halfway up the column is called entasis and is part of a system of refinements designed to bring individual temple parts into overall visual harmony. In a trick of optics, vertical elements seem to narrow as they rise, so architects increased the girth of tapering columns minutely (just $^{11}/_{16}$ inch in a 31-foot-tall column) to convey an impression of straight lines.

The basic Doric temple format was a rectangular marble structure, encircled by a double row of columns, with a portico at front and rear. A sculptured frieze in the pediments and metopes (the space between triglyphs) adorned the temple without detracting from the overall simplicity and unity of design. The temple was intended to be seen as a sculptural unit. Its small interior was not a place for public worship but housed the cult statue of a deity. Ceremonies took place outside.

THE PARTHENON: WORLD'S MOST PARFECT BUILDING.

The Doric style reached its zenith in the Parthenon, a marble temple dedicated to Athena, the patron goddess of Athens. Located at the highest point on the Acropolis, the 300-foot-high hill overlooking the city, the Parthenon was a shining symbol of the enlightened city-state under its most famous statesman, Pericles. Its perfect proportions and balance of architecture and sculpture make it not only the literal pinnacle of a superb group of Classical buildings but the ultimate symbol of architectural refinement.

Second Temple of Hera, Paestum, Italy, c. 450 B.C.E.
Paestum, founded in the late seventh century B.C.E., was a Greek colony 50 miles south of Naples. Its examples of early Doric architecture are the best preserved anywhere. This simple temple had two inner colonnades to support the roof around the cult statue. Entasis, or curved thickening of each column, is particularly evident. Made of local limestone, the building was originally covered with smooth stucco.

Today, only its skeleton remains. As late as 1687, when a direct hit by Venetian soldiers set off an explosion that brought down the roof and much of the structure, the Parthenon was still fairly intact. The next blow came around 1800, when Lord Elgin carted off most of the relief sculptures to the British Museum.

Today, one can only imagine the impression the temple made when it housed the nearly 50-foot-tall ivory statue of Athena, adorned with more than a ton of gold by the sculptor Phidias. Originally, 520 feet of sculpted figures formed a continuous marble frieze depicting the procession of horsemen and maidens to honor Athena (the first time ordinary mortals were so enshrined). Pediment sculptures that are the absolute summit of art represented the birth of Athena and her victory over Poseidon for sponsorship of Athens. Sculpted panels in ninety-two metopes showed serene, idealized figures of gods struggling with various foes like centaurs.

Parthenon, Athens, Greece, by Ictinus and Callicrates, 447–438 B.C.E.
Made of 20,000 tons of marble to house a huge statue of Athena, the Parthenon was designed by Ictinus (possibly incorporating the remains of a temple by Callicrates) and adorned with sculpture under the direction of Phidias. Even in ruins, it projects an image of clarity, precision, and logic.

HOW TO TELL THEM APART

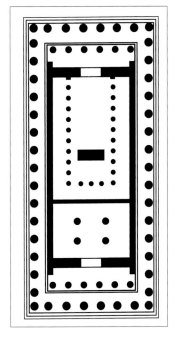

ATHENS—PARTHENON
447–438 B.C.E.

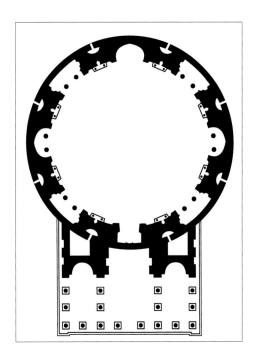

ROME—PANTHEON
118–128 C.E.

DETAIL	GREEK ARCHITECTURE	ROMAN ARCHITECTURE
BUILDING FORM	Temple	Basilica, amphitheater, baths
SHAPE	Rectangular	Circular, oval, complex
MATERIAL	Marble	Concrete
STRUCTURE	Post and beam	Arcuated with arch, vault, dome
DISTINGUISHING FEATURE	Column	Arch
EMPHASIS	Exterior sculptural form	Interior space, utility
CEILINGS	Low-pitched	Soaring
INTERIORS	Small, cramped	Vast
CITY CENTER	Agora, framed by stoas	Forum
SIZE	Based on human proportions	Huge
SPIRIT	Moderation	Ostentation

OPTICAL REFINEMENTS. Eight columns wide (101 feet) and seventeen columns long (228 feet), the Parthenon's form embodies the Greek ideals of harmony and balance. But this image of geometric precision, of equilibrium between vertical lift and horizontal load, results from countless small adjustments.

In fact, there is barely a straight line to be found. The swell of entasis overcomes the eye's tendency to make columns appear concave. (The organic bulge also keeps the austere geometry of the temple from appearing stiff.) To counteract the tendency to read long, straight lines as sagging in the middle, the platform, or stylobate, on which the columns stand rises slightly in the middle (two inches at front and rear, and four inches at the side colonnades). All parallel lines, such as the entablature, are similarly curved, in order to appear straight.

Nothing is truly perpendicular. Everything is slightly off, in order to appear straight-on. Columns lean forward, backward, or sideways to create the illusion of a true vertical. And since columns at the end of a row look thinner against the sky, these pillars are two inches thicker and clustered two feet closer to their neighbors. The metopes, which seem to be square, are actually oblong. Despite the seeming chaos of these adjustments, every dimension is proportionally derived from the diameter of a single column.

Temple to Athena Nike, Athens, by Callicrates, c. 448–421 B.C.E
One of the earliest surviving Ionic temples is the tiny temple to Athena Nike on the Acropolis. Its delicacy makes this temple a perfect example of Ionic style.

The Greeks were conservative in temple design, sticking to a basic format developed in wood structures. Yet they constantly refined the details until, in the Parthenon, they achieved a golden mean that has never been surpassed.

This unity of parts in service to a whole reflects the concept of a democratic city-state, which they also pioneered. As the playwright Euripides said of the Athenian principle of equality, "The whole folk year by year, in parity of service is our king." One definition of art is finding the perfect visual form for an idea. The Parthenon does that for the Golden Age of Greece.

IONIC ORDER. The Roman architectural historian Vetruvius wrote that Greek architecture was based on the human form and compared the Doric style to a sturdy male and the Ionic to a slender female form. Its signature element is the volute on an Ionic capital that looks like the rolled ends of a scroll. The shaft of each column is eight to nine times as high as its diameter, with twenty-four flutes. Ionic temples generally look more delicate than robust Doric temples.

An Ionic masterpiece on the Acropolis, created during Pericles' ambitious building program, is the Erechtheion (421–405 B.C.E.). A sloping site inspired the irregular, split-level design, with no continuous colonnade but four separate porticos and columns of different heights.

The shrine had to accommodate diverse hallowed areas, which explains why its floor plan departs from the Parthenon's pure symmetry. The temple shelters trident marks made when Poseidon smote a rock to bring forth a spring of sea water in his contest with Athena for the city's loyalty. (She won by causing an olive tree to sprout, which still grows by the Erechtheion.) The building also stands on the site of the former palace of a king of Athens and once even housed a den of snakes. Different levels and porches contain these separate sanctuaries. Elaborate ornamentation of friezes and filigree demonstrates the fine carving of Ionic style.

The Erechtheion's most striking element is its Porch of the Maidens. Six marble caryatids (named after the captive women of Caria in Asia Minor) support the load of the flat marble roof on their heads. Both sculpture and architecture work together for an effect of unity.

CORINTHIAN ORDER, HELLENISM. In the United States, mock Corinthian temples housing banks, courthouses, and schools dot the landscape. In Classical Greece, where "nothing to excess" was the credo, Corinthian columns were rare and used exclusively for interiors. The style's popularity arose during the Hellenistic period when Greek culture spread widely. The Romans were especially infatuated with embellishment and scattered Corinthian columns liberally throughout their empire.

Erechtheion, Athens, by Philokles, 421–405 B.C.E
Scrolled capitals on slim columns, a continuous frieze running around the building above the architrave, and an abundance of sculpted ornament (most notably, the caryatids) are typical Ionic elements in this shrine.

The hallmark of Corinthian is its distinctive capital, shaped like an inverted bell surrounded by acanthus leaves. According to Vetruvius, the Athenian sculptor Callimachus, while banqueting at Corinth, conceived the form when he spied a goblet surrounded by leaves. The style first appeared around the end of the fifth century. Its twenty-four-flute column is the tallest of the orders, with a height ten times the diameter of a column.

The first known Corinthian column is found inside the temple of Apollo Epicurius at Bassae (c. 420 B.C.E.). Surrounded by Ionic half-columns (engaged with the wall), the Corinthian capital is centrally located for maximum visual impact at the end of the cella, or interior room of the temple. A high-relief frieze surrounds the cella, featuring melodramatic battle scenes between agitated foes. The design shows the Hellenistic stress on applied ornament and theatrical effect, rather than the structural integrity that marks Classical architecture.

Alexander the Great died at the age of thirty-three, weeping that he had no more worlds to conquer. Having united the independent Greek city-states into one country and broadcast their beliefs throughout his empire, including Syria, Egypt, Asia Minor, and India, he did not live to see the Hellenistic style conquer native traditions. But conquer it did, and the culture of Greece—including its elaborate Corinthian style—was the rage in Alexander's vast empire and among his Roman successors.

The buildings associated with Hellenism relied on grandiose effects and monumental scale. They were rich in pictorial appeal, if not to say ostentation. As an example of imperial hubris, the architect Dinokrates proposed to Alexander nothing short of sculpting an entire mountain. In his vision of perfected nature, Mount Athos would be carved into the figure of a man holding a city in the palm of his hand. In the other hand, he would grasp an enormous vase to collect mountain streams cascading into the sea.

This project was not realized, but Hellenism did give the ancient world several of its seven wonders. The Pharos of Alexandria (279 B.C.E.) was the tallest lighthouse ever built, a 400-foot-high marble structure of four tapering stories. Another world-class wonder was the grandiloquent Mausoleum at Halicarnassus (349 B.C.E.). The monument was 150 feet high, its pyramidal roof supported by 36 columns. At the peak stood a marble chariot driven by sculptures of the departed king and his queen. Spectacle, display, and superhuman size replaced the restraint of Classical Greece.

Pergamon Altar, Pergamon Museum, Berlin, Germany, 164–156 B.C.E., reconstruction of the west side
Nearly 30 feet high, this massive marble structure features Ionic capitals, a 7-foot-tall frieze, and a 60-foot-wide staircase cutting into its plinth.

A textbook example of Hellenism is the marble Altar of Zeus at Pergamon. A U-shaped Ionic colonnade surrounds a showy staircase that is virtually a Niagara of flowing steps. A 400-foot-long frieze, with figures more than 7 feet high, wraps around the base of the altar. More than a hundred sculpted gods and giants grapple violently in a writhing tableau of rippling muscles.

CIVIC ARCHITECTURE. Classical Greeks cared little for fine palaces or adorning their modest homes. But they lavished infinite care on amenities to benefit the populace, like structures for transacting public affairs or for athletic contests. In participatory democracy, free male citizens ran the city-state, voting to approve expenditures, and they saw fit to spend more for art and public projects than any modern state.

The center of political, social, and commercial life was the *agora,* an open public square or marketplace where public debate and self-government transpired. Along the *agora* was the *stoa,* a covered walk consisting of a roofed colonnade with a back wall. Well before his fatal sip of hemlock for allegedly corrupting local youth, Socrates strolled along the Stoa of Zeus in Athens—one of his favorite spots for dialogues.

Later, Zeno and his colleagues' philosophy of Stoicism took its name from the stoa, where they worked out its main tenets in rambling discourse. The long galleries gave order to the open space of the agora but allowed freedom of movement, in a visual equivalent of the independence and interdependence that marked Athenian society.

Other public structures included the *bouleuterion* (a meeting hall with covered seating for 1,200 where affairs of state were settled), basilicas (courthouses), public baths, gymnasia, and stadia that accommodated up to 60,000 spectators.

Theater, Epidaurus, Greece, c. 350 B.C.E.
Greek theaters were built into hillsides. Fifty-five semicircular rows provide seating for 14,000 spectators at this theater, which is still in use.

One public structure still in use today is the amphitheater at Epidaurus. Built around 350 B.C.E. for 14,000 spectators, the semicircular outdoor theater consists of 55 tiers of steeply banked stone seats. Not only would political assemblies be held there, but religious festivals and plays by the likes of Sophocles, Euripides, or Aeschylus as well. From the circular orchestra, the acoustics are so perfect, one can literally hear a drachma drop in the highest seat.

The Roman historian Plutarch said of the Acropolis masterpieces, "Such is the bloom of perpetual newness, as it were, upon these works of Pericles, which makes them ever to look untouched by time." Just as the gilded spear tip of the colossal bronze statue of Athena on the Acropolis could be seen far out to sea, the architectural legacy of Greece radiates in influence across time and space. The works, Plutarch wrote, "were created in a short time for all time."

SITE LINES

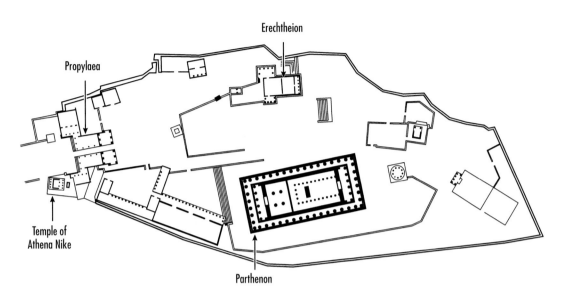

Erechtheion

Propylaea

Temple of
Athena Nike

Parthenon

An oddity of the Greek way was that individual buildings were often strictly symmetrical but the layout of an ensemble of buildings was purposely asymmetrical. On the Acropolis, each building presents itself as a unique sculptural unit, often located at an irregular angle to its neighbor.

This disalignment stands in sharp contrast to site plans of authoritarian states like pharaonic Egypt and imperial Rome. Strict bilateral symmetry in their complexes limits the freedom of the viewer, just as a centralized state controls experience and thought. Imperial Roman layouts fixed the sequence of perceptions to reduce choice.

The Greeks, who insisted on citizens' active role in government, incorporated their concept of individual freedom into site plans. Irregular placement forced viewers to move around a site according to their own volition. Site planning was a physical equivalent of how the Greek city-state operated. Individuals played a starring role within the larger whole.

Acropolis, Athens (c. 400 B.C.E.), general plan (above)

Trajan's Forum, Rome (98–117 C.E.), by Apollodorus of Damascus, plan (right)

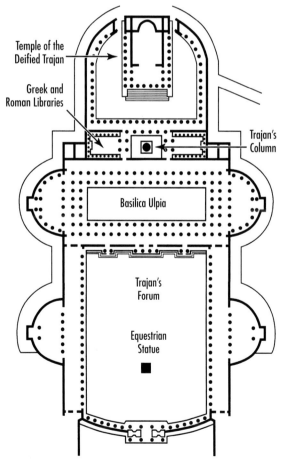

Temple of the
Deified Trajan

Greek and
Roman Libraries

Trajan's
Column

Basilica Ulpia

Trajan's
Forum

Equestrian
Statue

ROME: CONCRETE ACHIEVEMENTS

Philosopher Alfred North Whitehead wrote, "The Roman Empire existed by virtue of the grandest application of technology that the world had hitherto seen." This technology included engineering innovations like the arch, vault, and dome. For the first time, Roman builders spanned huge volumes of interior space, shaping an architecture of enclosed voids, not supporting mass. With the invention of concrete, they built increasingly daring forms, from baths to basilicas, on a vast scale.

Coupled with utilitarian construction triumphs like roads, bridges, and aqueducts, emperors stamped the concept of "Romanitas" on most of the known world. "Have style, will travel" was their calling card, as distinctive Roman buildings left a permanent imprint from the Thames to the Nile. Virgil quoted Jupiter in the *Aeneid,* "I have granted [the Romans] dominion, and it has no end."

From laws and government to modern necessities like indoor plumbing, hot water, heat, public lavatories, sewers, and stadium sports, Romans set the standard for civilization. Roman architecture played a missionary role. When forums, triumphal arches, or amphitheaters appeared, conquered territories entered the fold of Lex Romana.

THE SUPPORTING CAST. The essential ingredient of Roman building was the arch. Although Romans were smitten by "superior" Greek style and plastered conspicuous columns on facades, they abandoned the column as an actual structural support.

The arch and its progeny—the vault and the dome—revolutionized architecture. A stone lintel atop two columns rarely spans a distance as wide as 15 feet, but an arch can span 150 feet. Additionally, when its keystone is locked into place, the arch supports itself as well as immense loads on top. Combined with concrete, which could be cast in molds of any shape and scale, the arch allowed

Vaulting Ambition

ARCH. The basic building block of Roman architecture was the arch, which revolutionized the practice of architecture. Stone voussoirs shaped like wedges were supported by a wood framework called centering, removed after the keystone was in place.

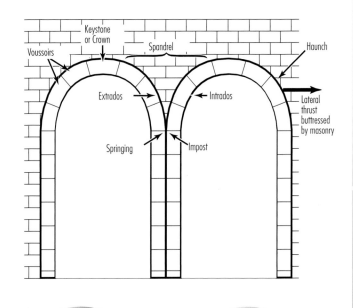

BARREL VAULT

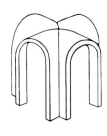

GROIN VAULT

BARREL VAULT. An arch extended in space forms a tunnel or barrel vault. Intersecting barrel vaults create a **GROIN OR CROSS-VAULT**. Romans combined the arch and vault with concrete to sustain large loads and enclose huge volumes of interior space.

DOME. An arch rotated in a circle generates a dome.

Romans to enclose enormous spaces and fully exploit the potential of these new forms and materials.

When an arch is extended in a straight line, or multiplied in depth, it becomes a barrel (or tunnel) vault. Such vaults provide a curved ceiling over two parallel walls and may be combined to form arcades (as in the Colosseum) supporting multiple tiers of superstructure. When two barrel vaults intersect at a right angle, the juncture forms a groin or cross-vault, which provides lunette windows for lighting at either end. An arch, rotated 360 degrees, creates a dome. By the first century B.C.E., the arch and vault were pervasive in Roman buildings.

Ancient concrete was not liquid but a viscous mixture of sand, lime, water, and aggregate. It was laid down in layers inside wooden or brick form work and solidified into a dense artificial stone that was light, strong, fireproof, and monolithic. Roman concrete walls and shells were always lined on both the exterior and interior with brick or a veneer of decorative stucco, fresco, mosaic, or marble. Purely ornamental columns, like olives dressing up a plain salad, adorned arches for a touch of Greek zest. The columns were generally engaged, or partially embedded in walls. When flattened and squared off, they are known as pilasters.

Exterior of the Pantheon, Rome, 18–128 C.E.
With its soaring rotunda, the Pantheon is the most beautiful of Roman buildings. In terms of engineering, it is a daring creation, since the dome exerts 5,000 tons of pressure on 20-foot-thick walls. The building's blend of enormous interior space, concrete construction, and traditional classical forms makes it the most imitated of Roman edifices.

THE PANTHEON. The supreme example of Roman structural ingenuity—and its aesthetic apogee—is the Pantheon. Built by the emperor Hadrian to replace an earlier temple by Agrippa, the Pantheon still stands, virtually unchanged for almost 1,900 years. Its dome was the widest until the nineteenth century. "The design not of a man but of an angel," Michelangelo said.

Interior of the Pantheon
Engraving by Francesco Piranesi

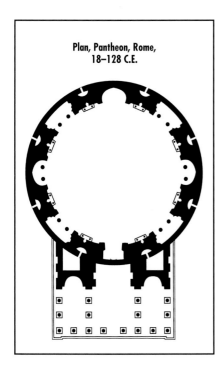

Plan, Pantheon, Rome, 18–128 C.E.

The design is a hybrid. Its pedimented porch and Corinthian columns are Greek, while the soaring rotunda—unsuspected from the outside—is pure Roman. This synthesis became the model for countless succeeding buildings, from St. Peter's in the Renaissance to designs by Palladio and Thomas Jefferson.

Five thousand tons of concrete shape the dome, but the content of the concrete varied to lighten the load as it ascended. Mixed with heavy basalt at the bottom, the layers contained porous, lightweight pumice at the top. The coffers, or recessed panels, of the dome also diminish in size and depth as the dome rises. This decrease creates a false perspective to make the dome seem even higher, while the coffering itself lightens the weight of the domed shell. The sole supports of the dome are sixteen barrel vaults channeling weight to eight piers, disguised by cosmetic columns.

A 30-foot-wide oculus (or round opening; the Latin word means "eye") at the apex of the dome is the only natural source of light inside. As the day progresses, a ray of sunlight travels across the interior, illuminating niches that formerly contained statues of Roman gods (the temple was dedicated to all the gods, or "pantheon"). A gilded bronze rosette was originally set inside each coffer to suggest stars in the heavens. The geometry and details of design create a cosmic symbol to match the purpose of the temple.

What makes the interior so pleasing to the eye is the perfect harmony of its proportions. The width of the dome (142 feet) is exactly equal to the height of the drum walls. If doubled, the hemispheric dome would form a sphere that filled the rotunda and touched the floor. Interior surfaces are also richly decorated with multicolor marbles and bronze. The floor, paved with disks and squares of marble, porphyry, and granite, reflects the coffered ceiling.

HADRIAN'S VILLA: THE ITALIAN VERSAILLES.

Fifteen miles outside Rome, near Tivoli, the creator of the Pantheon, Hadrian, built a 500-acre compound that rivals any royal residence in luxury and inventiveness. Scattered over seven miles were gardens, pavilions, palaces, theaters, temples, and baths of unprecedented fantasy. Even as ruins, the alternating convex and concave curves of the buildings ripple like the waters punctuating the grounds.

One innovation of Hadrian's villa, planned by the emperor himself, was the fusion of architecture and landscape. Flowing water in the form of canals, pools, fountains, and waterfalls was an integral part of the design, enlivening inanimate

The Canopus, Hadrian's Villa, Tivoli, Italy, c. 125–133 C.E.
Flat and arched sections of entablature alternate to link columns flanking a long canal at Hadrian's Villa, the emperor's version of Xanadu.

spaces with movement and sound. The design exploited the play of light as an expressive element. Walls waved in and out, creating shadows and highlights.

An architect, poet, painter, and mathematician as well as a brilliant statesman, Hadrian reigned from 117 to 138 C.E. Presiding over the zenith of Rome's wealth and geographic span, he personally inspected much of the Empire. His traveling entourage included surveyors, architects, decorators, and construction crews. He scattered Roman monuments throughout the Empire, leaving a legacy of mini Romes wherever he set up camp.

When the emperor built his dream retreat, he incorporated much of what he had seen during his travels. The Canopus, a long canal dug into an excavated valley, imitated an Egyptian resort he admired. Its bordering colonnade alternates flat and arched architraves to create a rising and falling rhythm. Caryatids, copied from the Acropolis, and Egyptian statues line the canal.

An example of Roman practicality is the underground network of service roads snaking beneath the grounds. In two miles of subterranean tunnels, carts and workers performed menial tasks. Underground depositories also provided cold storage for snow to refrigerate food and concoct cold drinks.

Besides libraries, dining halls, and barracks, Hadrian built his own private island surrounded by a circular moat. A tiny villa on the isle offered seclusion where he could study his beloved Greek texts or entertain visiting philosophers. As enlightened as he was, Hadrian could be touchy when it came to questions of style. The emperor who excelled at curvilinear lines designed the stubby Temple of Venus and Rome (135 C.E.) himself. When the famed architect Apollodorus of Damascus justly criticized its low-slung profile, Hadrian had him executed.

TRAJAN'S FORUM. Adjacent to the original Forum Romanum, which had become a hodgepodge of accumulated temples and arches, the emperor Trajan built the most extravagant imperial forum (see page 19). Trajan's ensemble encompassed more than 40,000 square feet and shows the empire's monumental aspirations. Planned by Apollodorus of Damascus, the entire composition, nearly one-third mile long, is an emblem of Rome's might and magnificence.

A huge colonnade set the tone at the entrance, with its central arch surmounted by a statue of the emperor in a chariot drawn by six horses. A courtyard with bilateral exedrae (or semicircular recesses) contained an equestrian statue of Trajan. Then a huge basilica, 400 feet long, cut crosswise from one side of the site to the other. Another court, bordered by twin libraries (one for Greek

Maison Carrée, Nîmes, France, c. 19 B.C.E.

This temple is the best-preserved example of Roman style. Its 12-foot-high podium, with steps only at the entrance, establishes the strict frontality of design. Among Roman buildings, temples were the most derivative from Greek prototypes, but they diverged from Greek models, which were set on a low platform and accessible from all sides. In Roman temples, the Corinthian columns are engaged at the sides and back, rather than freestanding.

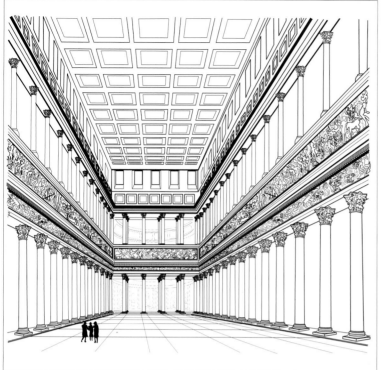

Basilica Ulpia, Trajan's Forum, Rome, Apollodorus of Damascus, 98–117 C.E., reconstruction drawing
The Roman basilica form was adopted as the model for later Christian churches. Oblong buildings with aisles and galleries and an apse on the longitudinal axis, basilicas first had flat, then vaulted ceilings.

scrolls, the other for Roman), contained the 125-foot-tall Trajan's Column. A continuous frieze spiraling 600 feet proclaimed Trajan's victories. (To level the column's site, a sloping hill was carved to a depth of the column's height.) Crowning the whole was a Temple of the Deified Trajan.

The rigid, symmetrical composition, with its right angles and linear progression, revealed the Roman mania for control and propaganda. Unlike the Greeks, who built structures oriented to the landscape and allowed spectators freedom of movement, Romans plowed right through natural obstacles and created a total design promoting their political agenda.

A later emperor allegedly admired Trajan's equestrian statue and remarked that he wanted one like it. His companion, a Persian prince, gestured toward the mind-boggling complex of Trajan's Forum and said, "Only if you have a stable like this, will you have a horse like that."

THE BASILICA: INFLUENTIAL FORM. Similar to a Greek stoa, the Roman basilica was a place of public assembly and commerce, as well as a hall of justice. In format, it was a roofed, large rectangle (its length twice the width) with aisles dividing the nave from side galleries. In a semicircular apse at the end opposite the entrance stood a tribunal to dispense justice.

Lit by clerestory windows (upper windows atop the nave), basilicas became increasingly lavish. Ceilings were covered in gilded bronze and floors with marble and porphyry. Growing ever more enormous, the basilicas replaced their original trabeated, timber-and-truss roofing with vast vaults springing from giant pilasters.

In order to distinguish Christian houses of worship from pagan temples, Constantine selected the basilica plan as a model. During the Middle Ages and Renaissance, this form proved immensely influential in cathedral design.

NERO: SIC SEMPER TYRANNIS

The emperor Nero, one of the nastiest villains of history, was also one of the most imaginative patrons of architecture. When a disastrous fire burned one-third of Rome, the historian Suetonius reported that Nero, "enraptured by what he called 'the beauty of the flames,' then put on his tragedian's costume and sang *The Fall of Ilium* from beginning to end." With so much clutter in the heart of the city cleared away, Nero built the gaudiest "country villa" possible. The precinct of 350 acres contained an artificial lake, landscaped parks, porticoes, pavilions, temples, and vineyards. At its center was the Domus Aureus, or Golden House. "True gentlemen always throw their money about," Nero explained.

The palace had a triple portico one mile long. A gilded bronze statue of Nero as sun god stood 120 feet tall outside. The palace was overlaid with gold, gems, and mother-of-pearl. Dining rooms had "fretted ceilings of ivory," Suetonius noted, "whose panels could turn and

shower down flowers and were fitted with pipes for sprinkling the guests with perfumes. The main banquet hall was circular and constantly revolved day and night, like the heavens." When his abode was complete, Nero said, "Good, now I can at last begin to live like a human being!"

Today, an underground wing of a hundred rooms remains of the Golden House. One domed, octagonal room lit by a central oculus attests to the originality of the design. Another room has a concrete slope where an interior waterfall cascaded down. Baths provided pools of salt water and sulphured water for soaking.

The hot tub didn't mellow Nero much. He not only murdered his mother and his wife, but he poisoned another claimant to the throne and initiated the persecution of Christians, during which Saints Peter and Paul died. Although he had ambitions to be a poet and an artist, a series of revolts caused him to commit suicide. Nero's last words were, "What an artist dies with me!"

DRAWING A BATH. Bathing to exercise and relax was a daily ritual for the Romans, but establishments like the mammoth Baths of Caracalla (c. 216 C.E.) offered far more than a soap bar and aerobics. Roman baths, which were a combination health club, school, and all-round recreation facility, were so extensive, one writer called them "provinces." Built to accommodate thousands and covering 50 acres, they divided into separate rooms for warm *(tepidarium)*, hot *(caldarium)*, and cold *(frigidarium)* bathing. Romans spent so much time immersed in water, there was even a special room where attendants rubbed them with oil to counter dry skin.

At its peak, when the population of ancient Rome was more than one million, the city consumed 200 million gallons of water a day. Not just baths, but fountains and maritime spectacles created demand for water that was filled by eleven aqueducts, bringing large volumes from faraway springs. Since pumps were primitive, Romans relied on gravity to transport water for distances up to 62 miles. Arched aqueducts spanning valleys kept it at a high level with a continuous gradual line of descent. Many of these aqueduct-bridges are in use today, more than 1,700 years later. The aqueduct at Segovia, Spain, still carries the town water supply.

Baths of Caracalla, Rome, c. 216 C.E., nineteenth-century engraving
In 354, there were 952 public baths in Rome. Many were complexes that included gymnasia, covered gardens, libraries, restaurants, shops, and museums, with venues for musical performances and lectures. Coffered ceilings, domed rotundas, statues, and walls covered with marble, mosaic, and alabaster made them more like spiffy spas than soggy locker rooms. Furnaces conducted heat through tile tubes to warm floors and walls, while boilers created hot water for bathing and steam.

Lifestyles of the Rich and Roman

Lavish dinner menus at a Roman banquet might include delicacies like pike livers, flamingo tongues, peacock brains, and sow udders (a special treat if the pigs have been fattened on figs). For the main course, guests appreciated complicated dishes like "Trojan pig"—a roast porker stuffed, like the Trojan horse, with miscellaneous creatures, like live quail.

Since the repast was fairly greasy, servants circulated with perfumed water to wash guests' fingers. Longhaired servant boys offered their shiny locks as towels for diners to dry their hands.

Eating went on forever, with well-paced trips to the *vomitorium* to purge before resuming the gluttony. Besides the main sport of marathon consumption of food and wine, guests entertained themselves with scintillating conversation.

The historian Plutarch recommended as dinner-party banter such crowd-pleasing topics as, "Why is fresh water better than salt water for washing clothes?" With dazzling dialogue like this, it's no wonder Romans enlivened the occasion with erotic dancing girls or light verses. Some thoughtful hosts even supplied attractive slaves for fondling.

THE AMPHITHEATER: BLOOD AND CIRCUSES.

The satirist Juvenal said that bread and circuses kept the populace content, since 20 percent of Romans were on the dole and inclined to be grumpy. Official holidays occupied nearly half the year, and emperors vied for public favor with gifts of grain and spectacles to divert citizens. In 65 B.C.E., Julius Caesar, "the people's patrician," organized a sort of Super Bowl with 320 pairs of gladiators. Twenty years later, he hosted a banquet, lasting several days, for 22,000 guests. New building forms, like amphitheaters and circuses, had to be developed for such large-scale entertainment.

An eighteenth-century prophecy said that the end of the Colosseum was bound to the end of Rome and the end of Rome to the end of the world. Fortunately, the Colosseum's sturdy structure still stands, an impressive monument to both the Romans' taste for sport and their skill at engineering. Built over an artificial lake created by Nero for his townhouse (the lake was used to flood the Colosseum for mock naval battles), the oval structure takes its name from a gargantuan statue of Nero called the Colossus, which once stood nearby.

In the Colosseum, gladiators fought each other or slaughtered animals such as bears, rhinoceroses, lions, ostriches, or giraffes. (The name *arena* comes from the Latin word for sand, which was spread over the wooden floor to absorb blood.) Sublevels of cages, counterweighted hoists for elevators, and ramps were used to store animals and bring them to the surface for their closeups.

Fifty thousand spectators sat on six tiers of seats supported by a structural brick and concrete facade of eighty arches on four levels. Originally the exterior was faced with a veneer of travertine, which was looted in succeeding centuries.

Colosseum (Flavian Amphitheater), Rome, c. 72–80 C.E.
The largest Roman amphitheater, the Colosseum could seat 50,000 at sports events. On a typical day, thousands of men and animals might be executed. More than 600 feet from end to end, with a travertine exterior, limestone facade, and covered with marble benches and statues, the Colosseum demonstrates both the brilliance and the brutality of ancient Rome.

New materials, techniques,

and building types stamped

the Roman seal on a vast empire.

UNDER THE VOLCANO: POMPEII

When the French writer Stendhal visited the ruins of Pompeii in 1817, he said he felt "transported back into the ancient world . . . face to face with antiquity." Buried under 30 feet of volcanic ash by the eruption of Mt. Vesuvius in 79 C.E., many structures of this prosperous resort town were preserved virtually intact, a time capsule of first-century life. Bodies of many of the 20,000 inhabitants were captured in positions of suffocation or flight.

At Pompeii, we see the typical villa layout, with houses built around a central atrium containing a catch basin for rain. Exterior colonnades, gardens, and fountains show the Roman appreciation of nature and the incorporation of landscape into home design. Among these rich summer estates were many with gilded beams inlaid with ivory, mosaic floors, and walls painted with fantasy scenes. The humble house of a wood-turner contained this inscription in a courtyard: "Lucrum gaudium" (Profit is joy).

Villa of the Mysteries, a ninety-room mansion, was set upon a hillside with a terrace overlooking the sea. Its frescoes in vibrant colors are among the wonders of ancient art.

House of the Vettii, Pompeii, Italy, third century B.C.E.

Pont du Gard, Nîmes, France, c. 25 B.C.E.
A marvel of engineering, the Pont du Gard aqueduct consists of three tiers of stone arches 160 feet high bringing water from 25 miles away. A single arch made of two-ton blocks spans the bed of a river.

Nature's Architects: Feathering a Nest

The animal world is bustling with busy home-makers. Prairie dogs dig tunnels, turret spiders pile up pentagonal towers of sticks, and trapdoor spiders seal their front doors with impenetrable barriers. Tailorbirds sew leaves together, while weaverbirds work in teams on 9-foot-tall, multifamily housing.

The most extravagant of all animal habitats is the Australian bower bird nest. The male spends his days creating a fanciful bachelor pad to attract a mate. The pigeon-sized bird builds elaborate structures on the forest floor from leaves, moss, and twigs. The nest is not a home, tweet home. It serves only as a locale for romantic trysts. The avian architect's goal is to lure a female and mate before she flies off to establish a nest for eggs elsewhere.

Decorating is the primary obsession. The drabber a bird's plumage, the more elaborate his digs, and the more likely to lure a female. The birds weave shells, berries, flowers, and silvery leaves into a complex bower. To outshine their rivals, some birds incorporate bright coins, spoons, scraps of aluminum foil, even a glass eye. If a gust of wind disturbs a twig's placement or a leaf withers, they immediately refurbish the nest.

These amorous architects even paint the walls with stain made from chewed berries, charcoal, and saliva, using a leaf as a paintbrush. The blue satin bower bird's favorite color is—naturally—blue, and he goes to great lengths to create the proper ambiance. Collecting blue feathers, berries, shells, and flowers, he adorns the walls with his favorite hue, turning the nest into a bird's-eye version of the house of blues.

(Wealthy families later stripped Roman ruins to furnish their palazzos. A saying goes, "What the Barbari [barbarians] dared not do was done by the Barberini.") Engaged columns rose through the orders, with Tuscan (the Roman form of Doric) on the ground floor, Ionic on the second level, Corinthian on the third, and Corinthian pilasters at the attic level. In terms of design, the ornamental columns framing structural arches and piers create a rhythm of alternating solid and void, straight and curved lines.

To shield spectators from the blazing sun, fifty-eight wooden masts around the top held aloft a huge awning. Scents were sprayed to overcome the stench of gore and garbage. Seventy-six gates served a network of efficient entrances and barrel-vaulted ramps in a design copied by football stadiums today. Used for animal games up to the year 523, the Colosseum is the largest of many similar stadiums built throughout the empire. At Arles and Nîmes, France, Roman amphitheaters are still used for bullfights.

Another means to keep the rowdy population cheerful was state sponsorship of chariot races. The Circus Maximus, built in a valley between two hills, was the largest race course. During the reign of Augustus, when it was also used as an amphitheater, 3,500 animals were slaughtered there. Three hundred thousand spectators could attend races at the 2,000-foot-long stadium—not always safely, for in the time of Diocletian when grandstands were made of wood, risers collapsed, killing 13,000.

To divert attention from such mishaps, emperors often indulged their fancies for glitz. Some carpeted the floor of the arena with shiny particles like powdered red lead, silvery mica, or green malachite. Dividing the track was a central spine, on which sat seven large carved eggs and seven stone dolphins. During the race, these statues were removed one by one to mark the number of laps. The Circus Maximus was used until 549. At the Piazza Navona in Rome, one can see the ghostly outline of a circus—once the Stadium of Domitian.

The Romans' flare for organization, coupled with their progressive architecture and diverse building types, extended Roman style through all the lands bordering the Mediterranean. All roads didn't really lead to Rome. It just seemed that way, since they built so many, so flawlessly. Roman streets were said to be "pulchrae, amplae, et rectae" (beautiful, wide, and straight). Built of four layers, advancing inexorably straight ahead regardless of terrain, the roads facilitated a cross-fertilization that made Greco-Roman culture dominant.

Triumphal arches, plastered with Greek columns, celebrated the exploits of Roman generals and emperors. They were built as permanent replacements for temporary arches through which victorious armies marched, laden with booty and captives. The laurel-wreathed emperor rode a chariot at the head, lauded by adoring crowds in the streets of Rome but with a slave to whisper in his ear, "Remember, you are only a mortal." True enough, but Roman architecture has proved well-nigh immortal.

THE ANNOTATED ARCH

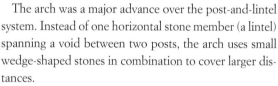

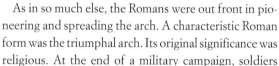

Arches come in many shapes—curved like a horseshoe or the handle of a basket—and profiles: rounded or pointed. Its shape virtually defines a style. A pointed arch equals Gothic architecture, while rounded signals Romanesque. What they have in common is their ingenious way of spanning an opening.

The arch was a major advance over the post-and-lintel system. Instead of one horizontal stone member (a lintel) spanning a void between two posts, the arch uses small wedge-shaped stones in combination to cover larger distances.

As in so much else, the Romans were out front in pioneering and spreading the arch. A characteristic Roman form was the triumphal arch. Its original significance was religious. At the end of a military campaign, soldiers were encouraged to pass under an arched "magic door" to siphon off their aggression, taming them for civilian life. Later, triumphal arches were a monumental gateway through which emperors paraded during victory marches. From the first century B.C.E., these arches were erected in stone, richly sculpted, as portals or commemorative monuments.

Built throughout the Roman empire, triumphal arches were of two types: a single archway, like the Arch of Titus in Rome (c. 82 C.E.), or a three-part structure, with two smaller arches flanking one large arch. These arches were revived during the Italian Renaissance and were again popular in the eighteenth and nineteenth centuries. The largest is the Arc de Triomphe in Paris by Chalgrin (1806–35).

A fantastic version of the Moorish horseshoe arch is found in the scalloped arcade of the Great Mosque. More than 500 slender columns support arches striped with red and white stones. Multiple tiers of arches seem to billow up like spinnakers.

Romanesque is a style of the round arch, as the interior of St. Sernin makes clear. Square bays defined by round arches divide Romanesque churches into distinct modules.

Filippo Brunelleschi's loggia in his Renaissance Foundling Hospital shows extraordinary delicacy. Each arch generates lateral forces that require buttressing, but when arches are linked in an arcade, each supports its neighbor, so columns can be slender and elegant.

Peter Eisenman's facade of the Wexner Center for the Visual Arts is a textbook example of Deconstructivism. He slices a tower in two vertically and uses a nonfunctional, truncated arch to indicate fragmentation and instability in the contemporary world.

Clockwise from lower left: Great Mosque, Cordoba, Spain, 786–987; Church of Saint-Sernin, Toulouse, France, 1077–1125; Arch of Constantine, Rome, 312–15 C.E.; Foundling Hospital, Florence, Italy, by Brunelleschi, 1419–24; Wexner Center for the Visual Arts, Ohio State University, Columbus, by Eisenman, 1989.

The Middle Ages: Church and State

The Middle Ages didn't exist as a distinct period until a Renaissance scholar invented the term to cover the thousand years between the glories of Rome and the Renaissance. He considered the medieval period (roughly 500–1500) a black hole between two stars of civilization. Only later did more objective historians acknowledge the Middle Ages' achievements, although most grant that the years 500–800 were truly Dark Ages in Western Europe, beset by constant invasions and warfare.

Meanwhile, in what was known as the Eastern Roman Empire, in Byzantium (or Constantinople), Roman law and administration continued, mixed with Greek language and culture. Beginning in the late fourth century, while barbarians in the West were slaughtering each other with regularity, Byzantine builders constructed a sophisticated civilization that lasted a millennium. Once crusaders caught a glimpse of these shining cities, Western Europe began sprucing up, too.

With the rise of monasteries and feudalism after 850, culture started to bloom. Travel and trade increased, spurred by pilgrimages and the Crusades. A widespread revival of large-scale building, sponsored mostly by the church, took off. From 900 to 1200, massive Romanesque churches and castles were erected.

After 1200, cities grew rapidly and nations took form. Technological and engineering advances, in harmony with religious ideology, produced the Gothic cathedrals that are the marvels of the West. Almost each town in every country vied to build the highest, most grandiose church to honor its patron saint.

The English critic John Ruskin said, "Great nations write their autobiographies in three manuscripts, the book of their deeds, the book of their words and the book of their art. Not one of these books can be understood unless we read the two others, but of the three the only trustworthy one is the last."

During the Middle Ages, the deeds were bloody and violent, the words were excessively pious, and the art was gilded (Byzantine), solid (Romanesque), or ethereal (Gothic). The autobiography of medieval architecture is ultimately a story of state pride in stone churches, built to live happily ever after.

WORLD HISTORY		ARCHITECTURE
Anglo-Saxons conquer England	449	
Emperor deposed in Rome; Western Roman Empire falls	479	
Benedictine monastic order founded	529	
	532	Hagia Sophia Basilica in Constantinople begun
Semilegendary Briton King Arthur killed in battle	537	
	550	Golden era of Byzantine art
Buddhism firmly established in Japan	575	
Pope Gregory the Great increases power of Catholic Church	590–604	
First use of decimal in math, India	595	
St. Augustine reestablishes Christianity in England	596	
	607	Horyu-ji temple completed in Japan (oldest surviving wooden building)
"Burning water" (petroleum) used in Japan	615	
Life of Mohammed	570–632	
	625	First Ise shrine built in Japan
French and German split into separate languages	636	
	705	Great Mosque built in Damascus
Muslims begin conquest of Spain	711	
Charles Martel defeats Arabs to check expansion	732	
Gregorian music sung in churches in France, Germany, England	750	
Charlemagne ascends Frankish throne	768	
	796	Palatine Chapel built by Charlemagne
	800	Machu Picchu built in Peru
Magyar hordes invade Central Europe	c. 890	
Feudal system begins	c. 900	Romanesque style develops
Benedictine Abbey of Cluny founded	910	Classic Maya architecture ends
Vikings settle in Normandy	911	
Otto I of Germany establishes Holy Roman Empire	936	Anasazi build Mesa Verde cliff dwellings
	976	Basilica of San Marco begun in Venice
	990	Mosque of Cordoba built (begun 785)
Gunpowder developed in China; Lief Ericson discovers America	c. 1000	
	1050	Wave of church building begins
	1063	Pisa Cathedral built
	1050–1350	Peak years for castle construction
William the Conqueror establishes Norman rule in England	1066	
	1078	Tower of London begun
	1093	Earliest use of rib vaulting, Durham Cathedral
First Crusade launched	1096	
First university founded in Bologna, Italy	1119	Work on Angkor Wat begins
	1137–44	Gothic style invented at St.-Denis, France
Second Crusade loses territory in Palestine, Syria	1147–49	
	1163	Notre-Dame Cathedral begun in Paris
	1194	Construction of present Chartres begun
Richard the Lion Heart dies	1199	
Francis of Assissi establishes Franciscan order of beggar-monks	1209	
Mongol leader Genghis Khan invades China	1211	
Magna Carta grants rights to English citizens	1215	
	1246	La Sainte-Chapelle erected in Paris
Inquisition begins using instruments of torture	1252	
Marco Polo travels to China	1271	
Crusades end	1291	
	1309	Doge's Palace built on earlier site in Venice
Dante writes *Divine Comedy* in Italy	c. 1310–20	
First cannons used	c. 1327	Aztecs found city of Tenochtitlan
100 Years' War between England and France starts (ends 1453)	1337	
Black Death (bubonic plague) kills 75 million, one-third of population of Western Europe	1348–49	
	1386	Work begins on Milan Cathedral
Chaucer publishes *Canterbury Tales*	1387	

BYZANTINE SPLENDOR

In his *Meditations,* Roman emperor Marcus Aurelius (121–180) recognized the slump into which his dissipated nation had fallen. "Toys and Fooleries at home, wars abroad," he wrote. "Sometimes terror, sometimes torpor or stupid sloth: this is thy daily slavery."

By the third century, the Empire was even more in the dumps. The military, the economy, and its general esprit took a nosedive. Public dole and spectacle—bread and circuses—were no longer enough, and dissatisfaction with the pagan state religion was rampant. To fill the void, Christianity signed up converts, becoming the official religion in 394. New buildings reflected the grandeur of this imperial status. For the next thousand years, church structures dominated the rolls of great architecture.

Once Rome and the western empire were in ruins, the center of gravity shifted eastward. As waves of Germanic tribes like Huns, Goths, and Vandals sacked and pillaged, the era of barbarism known as the Dark Ages prevailed. Yet in the East, Constantinople enjoyed a radiant age, blooming with opulent churches and palaces that would later stun the Crusaders.

In 330, Constantine (the first Christian emperor) relocated the capital of the empire to Byzantium, which he modestly renamed Constantinople. (Never one to hide his light, Constantine also promoted himself as the thirteenth apostle.) Until it fell to the Turks in 1453, this dazzling city was the chief locus of culture in Europe. The Byzantine Empire's high mark crested during the reign of Justinian (527–65). For the next 900 years, the empire survived but gradually waned in size. Its influence waxed, however, as the chief repository of the classic tradition.

The shift from Greco-Roman to Byzantine style mirrored a religious change of heart. Under paganism, architectural design stressed external appearance, just as the state religion required outward conformity but no sincere conviction. Similarly, Roman temples were all exterior show, with no interior happenings. (Ceremonies took place outside, in front of temples.)

Old Basilica of St. Peter, Rome, c. 330, plan
The first church of St. Peter, torn down in 1505 to build the current domed cathedral, used a simple basilica format. Its long nave and double aisles led to a transept placed at one end, with a central apse. An atrium and central fountain outside the building formed a forecourt.

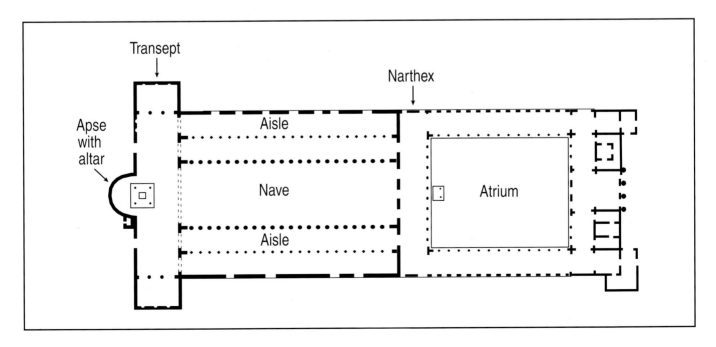

In Christianity, the emphasis was the opposite—on inner conversion, and new church forms spent all their visual capital on buildings' interiors. Even the philosopher Plotinus admitted, "Ugly is that which has no soul." Inside Byzantine monuments, the solid Roman trappings of worldly power melted away to insubstantial color, light, and air.

BYZANTINE STYLE.

Two forms of church structures evolved to serve the new religion.

First, in Rome, a long, rectangular hall called a basilica was the typical form, as at the original St. Peter's (319–29) and Sant' Apollinaire Nuovo (490) in Ravenna. This format, adapted directly from the Roman meeting hall, included colonnades of pillars forming one or two narrow aisles on the sides and a timber-trussed roof. At one end of the longitudinal axis, attention focused on a semicircular apse with an altar. A wide central aisle, or nave, was lit by high clerestory windows.

Plain on the outside, basilicas were a sparkling light show inside. Walls shimmered with gold and colored-glass mosaics. No surface was left unadorned. Marble inlays, frescoes, and painted and carved stucco sculpture animated walls, floors, and ceilings. It was like being swallowed by a kaleidoscope.

Second, principally in the East, a domed, central-plan church format predominated. Called *martyria* because they originally enshrined martyrs' relics or burial grounds, these structures, when used for church services, combined the basilica's horizontal axis with the vertical accent of a dome. They were frequently built on a Greek cross plan (with two arms of equal length crossing under a central dome) and could be round, octagonal, or square on the outside.

San Vitale, Ravenna, Italy, c. 526–47
This centralized church, a perfect example of Byzantine style, shines with glass and gold-cube mosaics.

The common element of the two plans was their urge to dematerialize a building's structure. In contrast to Roman secular values, which sought comfort in the here-and-now, Christianity stressed salvation in an afterlife. In early Christian architecture, an otherworldly atmosphere created by lavish interior decoration promoted this emphasis on the hereafter.

Byzantine style fused Oriental, especially Persian, and Hellenic motifs. From the East, it borrowed a colorful, lush mood, a central plan, symbolic decoration full of geometric patterns, and an appeal to the emotions. From Roman and Greek precursors, Byzantine architecture adopted the basilica layout, columns, vaulting techniques, arches, and soaring ceilings. The combination was an original style bent on inducing a mystical experience. As an image of heaven, the church interior was intended to be transporting.

MOSAICS: SPARKLE GALORE.

The city of Ravenna is frozen in a Byzantine time warp. From about 404, when it became the Western capital of the Empire, to 751 when Byzantine rule lapsed, the city was graced with more mosaics per square inch than any locality on earth. Sant' Apollinaire in Classe (c. 532–49), the Mausoleum of Galla Placidia (c. 425), and the Neone Baptistery (450) are a few shrines still aglitter with golden light.

The octagonal San Vitale (c. 526–47) is one of the least altered of all Byzantine buildings. Its marble, stucco, and—above all—mosaics in green, white, blue, and gold flow over the faceted walls to enliven spaces and weave together major and minor chambers. The figures of saints, apostles, and Christ seem to swell and ebb as they march across walls and up toward the heavens. The apex is a mosaic Redeemer in the chancel vault. Colors observe a strict hierarchy, with apostles and lesser lights appearing on a background of celestial blue. Christ rates the supreme backdrop of gold.

HAGIA SOPHIA: THE PINNACLE. For more than a thousand years, from 330 to 1453, Constantinople was the epitome of architectural glory, but it hit its peak early with a domed basilica, Hagia Sophia (pronounced ah-YEE-ah So-FEE-ah), built by Justinian in 532–37. The 107-foot diameter of its 180-foot-high dome is only 8 feet less than St. Paul's in London, but it's not size that makes this church a masterpiece. It's how all structural supports are hidden to give the effect of mass suspended on beams of light.

The historian Procopius noted that the dome "seems somehow to float in the air on no firm basis. . . . [It] seems not to rest on solid masonry" and "by reason of the seeming insecurity of its composition [is] altogether terrifying."

With such a giant structure of mystifying internal complexity, how did its architects achieve this weightless effect? Well, for one thing, Anthemios of Tralles and Isidorus of Miletus weren't architects but mathematicians. Justinian, to celebrate his victory over rioting masses, which left 30,000 dead in the streets, commissioned the temple to project the power of church and empire. Since most structures at the time were fairly conservative, he hired two intellectuals who specialized in geometry and the theory of vaulting.

Probably only geometricians could have designed this daunting edifice, in which arches open up into apses, domes into semidomes, and all vectors seem to funnel into space. Only nonarchitects who never encountered practical mishaps would have dared dream up such a support system. At one point, their courage failed and they told Justinian the structure wouldn't hold up. Keep going with the giant arches, he said, until they meet and support each other. His confidence paid off. Hold up it did

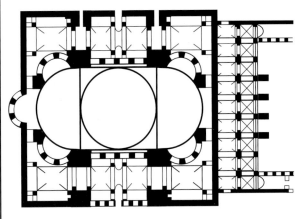

Hagia Sophia (Holy Wisdom), by Anthemios of Tralles and Isidorus of Miletus, Istanbul, Turkey, plan
The church consists of a 230-foot by 250-foot rectangle enclosing a 100-foot square with four huge piers at each corner. The piers support four massive arches across the sides of the square, which, with pendentives, support the round dome. Twin half-domes extend beneath the arches to double the length of the nave. Each half-dome rests on three arches, with small half-domed apses at the two corners and a chancel. Peripheral aisles and galleries surround the nave.

Hagia Sophia, 532–37
For a thousand years, this building was the model for Byzantine churches. (Minarets are a later addition.)

Hagia Sophia, nave interior
Two teams of 5,000 workers competed to build the eastern and western sections, pushing construction at such a pace, the basilica was completed in five years. The layout combined longitudinal and centralized form, with screens of columns to create multiple layers of experience. The mystic interior, encrusted with color and pattern and irradiated by light, launched the era of Byzantine architecture.

(until an earthquake in 558 necessitated replacing the dome).

Built in about five years, the building is as much a feat of engineering as a work of art. Support for the dome rests on four 70-foot-high piers hidden by colonnaded screens and four vast round arches. Between them are 60-foot-wide pendentives, or concave rounded triangles, which effect the transition from a square base to a round bed for the dome.

The artful part of this scheme derives from a ring of forty round windows at the base of the dome, piercing the substructure with a band of light. The dome seems without visible support, "suspended on a golden chain from heaven," as one viewer wrote. Catching the light from every angle, rays of sunlight irradiate the inside of the building, reflected from the gold-sheathed ceiling and marble walls and floor.

Screened aisles and galleries around the rotunda not only conceal the dome's supports, they create contrast between the central illumination and dark antechambers. The whole exerts a profound emotional impact, induced by light and color. Dome and pendentives are covered with mosaics with a gold-leaf background, and lower levels are sheathed in multicolored marble. Columns of green marble and red porphyry add to the rich effect.

As opposed to classical architecture, with its formal clarity and static right angles, the Hagia Sophia is all curves that intersect, as if in motion. The twin half-domes beneath the great arches split into small half-domed apses at their corners. Spaces are ambiguous and seem to mutate. Procopius noted that parts seem to float off, and one's vision constantly shifts from one detail to the next. Four levels high, the scale expands and swells as one approaches the center. When Justinian entered the fin-

ished church, he strode alone to stand under the great dome and declared, "Solomon, I have surpassed thee." Today, Solomon's temple is gone and the Hagia Sophia is sorely reduced after Crusaders carted off its treasures. Muslims later converted it to a mosque, whitewashing many mosaics and stripping the gilded vaulting.

Sweeping and bold as its interior still is, the exterior is an unassuming amalgam of plastered brick masses. Minarets were added after it became a mosque, further complicating its profile.

What remains is that great levitating dome, its foot dissolved in light. Color and pattern similarly dissolve wall surfaces. Lacelike carved marble on the walls dematerializes their solid substance. The scale, like the ethereal effect, is godlike rather than human. The form is one with its purpose: to uplift through an image of heaven.

IN THE PROVINCES. For a thousand years, Byzantine style pioneered in Constantinople exerted a powerful influence throughout Europe. In Venice, Italy, the Basilica of San Marco is an extravaganza of Byzantine magic. Although the exterior is overlaid with later Gothic touches, the interior preserves the domed, Greek-cross plan. The layout is a faithful replica of Justinian's Church of the Holy Apostles (536–50), which no longer exists in Constantinople.

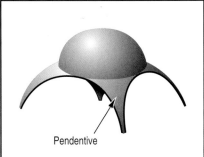

Pendentive

Pendentive. A concave form of masonry in the shape of inverted triangular vaulting rises from two walls of a square to form the base of a circular dome. Since a pendentive seems to rest on one small point, its supporting function appears insubstantial. It looks as if it hangs from the dome but actually supports it.

The church was begun around 830, intended to display the remains of the apostle Mark, which had been spirited away from Alexandria by Venetian merchants. It houses miscellaneous plunder, since trading ships were charged with bringing home loot to embellish the edifice. Among the booty are four Roman gilded-bronze horses, stolen from the hippodrome in Constantinople during the fourth crusade in 1204.

Napoleon called San Marco square (the piazza outside the church) "the greatest salon of Europe." The British aesthete John Ruskin called the church itself "a vision" and "a treasure heap." With more than 45,000 square feet of mosaics cover-

---

Cult of the Carts

When the cathedral at Chartres was being built, a revivalist religious movement swept the populace. People of all social classes thronged to help, hoping to gain salvation by their efforts. Twelfth-century nobles and peasants strapped themselves in traces like draft animals and dragged carts loaded with enormous limestone blocks from quarry to town. Laboring in profound silence, more than 1,000 people at a time pulled slowly and painfully. A contemporary chronicler described the wonder that "kings, princes, mighty men of the world puffed up with honors and riches, men and women of noble birth, should bind bridles upon their proud and swollen necks and submit themselves to wagons which, after the fashion of brute beasts, they dragged with their loads . . . to build churches." Miracles were said to occur daily. The abbot of Mont-St.-Michel said of the cart-hauling phenomenon: "Who did not see it, will never see the like."

San Marco, interior view
Glowing color and gold-sheathed vaulting dissolve surfaces to create an earthly vision of heaven. Forty thousand square feet of gold-inlaid mosaics and 500 plundered pillars of jasper, porphyry, and marble adorn the interior. Above the altar is an enamel and gold screen encrusted with hundreds of pearls, garnets, amethysts, emeralds, and rubies. Ruskin called it "a vision . . . delicate as ivory."

Basilica of San Marco, Venice, Italy, 976–1094
Although the exterior is overlaid with Gothic details, San Marco is Byzantine in its floor plan, extensive marble inlays, and gold-ground mosaics. It was built to house the body of the apostle Mark, stolen by a merchant of Venice from Alexandria, Egypt.

Cathedral of St. Basil the Blessed, Moscow, Russia, 1555–60
The onion dome is a variation of Byzantine style used in Russia until the twentieth century.

ing the walls and floor, it's very easy to understand why tourists rave.

Surfacing interior vaults and five domes is enough gold-ground mosaic to render the whole a glowing tent of religious art. On the outside, elaborate stone tracery and five vaulted doorways, separated by a cluster of colonnettes and topped with rounded gables and lunettes, diverge from the usual sober Byzantine exterior. Three levels of semicircular shapes on the facade rise to circuslike peaks and spires on the roof. With its voluptuous aura of Oriental mystery, San Marco is a unique example of Byzantine splendor.

In Russia, Byzantine style outlived the demise of Constantinople. Although Russians liked exterior flourishes more than did straightforward Byzantine architects, they imported the modular, domed church from the Middle East, along with Eastern Orthodox Christianity in 988.

One thing was in need of drastic change. In northern climates, the shallow Byzantine dome tended to collapse under the weight of winter snows. The characteristic bulging onion dome, which is a signature of Russian architecture, came into being to shed heavy snow.

On St. Basil's Cathedral in Red Square (1555–60), nine flamboyant domes create a fantasy effect atop a traditional cross-in-square plan. The multicolor tiled surfaces—more busy than Byzantine—inordinately pleased Ivan the Terrible, who commissioned the church to mark a victory. Legend has it the tsar was so enchanted, he ordered his architect's eyes put out to avoid the prospect of any other church rivaling this creation.

HOW TO TELL THEM APART

	Byzantine	**Romanesque**	**Gothic**
WHERE:	Constantinople, northern Italy	Western Europe	France, northern Europe
WHEN:	330–1453	1030–1200	1140–1500
MAJOR BUILDING FORM:	Church	Church, castle	Cathedral, university, guild hall
PLAN:	Cross-in-square capped with domes	Compartmentalized, cruciform	Unified interior
SUPPORT:	Pendentives and piers	Sturdy piers, thick walls	Piers, flying buttresses
HALLMARK:	Dome	Round arch, barrel vault	Pointed arch, rib vault
DECOR:	Lavish inside, plain outside; mosaics	Stone sculpture	Sculpture, stained glass
EFFECT:	Mysterious	Massive, segmented	Soaring, vertical, skeletal
INSPIRATION:	Heaven	Roman construction	Heavenly light
GOAL:	To arouse emotion, transport	To accommodate pilgrims	To impress, uplift

ROMANESQUE: A MIGHTY FORTRESS

In the history of Western architecture, the five centuries between the fall of Rome around 479 and the millennium were mostly blank. Under the depredations of illiterate barbarian tribes bent on destruction, monumental architecture didn't decline; it all but disappeared. Then, after the thousand-year anniversaries of the birth of Christ and the crucifixion (1033), when the world did not end in flames and the Second Coming as many expected, Europe regained its verve. From about 1000 to 1200, two forms of buildings proliferated: castles and churches. Whether built for military or religious purposes, both forms were weighty piles of stone, their massive walls not only for structural support but defense.

With the exception of the Eastern Byzantine Empire, the refined culture achieved by Rome had vanished during the Dark Ages (500–800). In Western Europe, civilized amenities like roads, law, sanitation, and running water were a distant memory. But enough fragments of Rome remained in crumbling triumphal arches and amphitheaters dotting the landscape. When architecture revived, it was these ancient monuments that medieval architects imitated, adapting Roman vaulting techniques and the basilica plan. In the nineteenth century, critics called the style Romanesque—the first coherent, international style to appear in Western Europe after a lapse of five hundred years.

Since warfare constantly threatened, all buildings were strongholds, fortified for security. With thick walls and small windows, both religious and secular architecture had a fortresslike appearance. Other Romanesque traits were a modular system of construction, with interiors divided into squarish bays, and fat piers supporting round arches and barrel vaults. Romanesque architecture varied considerably in different locales, according to the diverse climates, traditions, and materials of France, Italy, Spain, England, and Germany.

Mont-Saint-Michel, Normandy, France, 1024–84
This Benedictine abbey is a rare surviving example of a wooden-roofed, Romanesque church. (Since interiors were lit by candles and torches, timber construction was prone to catch fire, giving rise to stone vaulting elsewhere.) Built on a rocky islet, the abbey is cut off from the mainland at high tide. Its inaccessible location was considered conducive to a life of asceticism. The Cistercian monk St. Bernard of Clairvaux (1090–1153) was so devoted, he refused to lift his eyes to a sunset, fearful its beauty would distract his thoughts from God. The motto of monastic life was "Ora et Labora" (prayers and work). Since their treasuries were subject to theft, churches were built, in Martin Luther's words, like *eine feste Burg* (a mighty fortress).

ROMANESQUE CHURCHES: PILGRIM'S PROGRESS. Around 1050, the monk Ralph Glaber described the upsurge in church building: "Shortly after the year 1000, all Christian peoples were seized with a great desire to outdo one another in magnificence. It was as if the very world had shaken itself, and, casting off her old garments, was clothing herself everywhere in a white robe of churches."

A general religious fervor, increasing prosperity of monasteries, and the cult of pilgrimages spurred this upswell of construction. Between 1050 and 1350 in France alone, eighty cathedrals, five hundred large churches, and tens of thousands of parish churches were erected.

Nave, Mont-Saint-Michel
The nave wall is constructed in three layers, rising from the ground floor to a tribune gallery to clerestory windows. Round-arched openings—a hallmark of Romanesque style—create different horizontal zones, in contrast to the strong vertical lines of half-columns from floor to ceiling that divide the nave into regular bays.

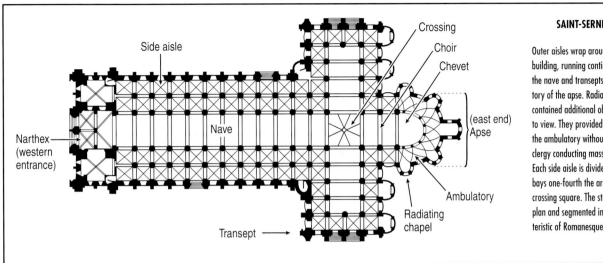

SAINT-SERNIN, PLAN

Outer aisles wrap around the entire building, running continuously beside the nave and transepts to the ambulatory of the apse. Radiating chapels contained additional objects for pilgrims to view. They provided extra stops along the ambulatory without interfering with clergy conducting mass in the nave. Each side aisle is divided into square bays one-fourth the area of the central crossing square. The strongly geometric plan and segmented interior are characteristic of Romanesque architecture.

The largest was the French abbey of Cluny, seat of the most influential monastic order. Founded in 910, Cluny and its successive churches were called by a scholar "the greatest creation of the Middle Ages." Not only did monasteries preserve ancient and medieval learning in their libraries, they were virtual utopian communities. At Cluny, the church held thousands, twelve hundred monks slept in the dormitory, and there were twelve bathhouses and fountains fed by running water through underground pipes. A library, refectory, cloistered court, and service buildings like barns, brewery, and mill were standards at a monastery. The sumptuous abbey church of Cluny, torn down in 1810 by antireligious mobs after the French Revolution, had a 600-foot-long nave, multiple towers, fifteen chapels, lavish interior sculpture and frescoes, and a choir for three hundred monks.

A HANK OF HAIR AND A PIECE OF BONE. Chaucer described a fourteenth-century pilgrimage in his *Canterbury Tales:* "from every shire's end/Of England to Canterbury they wend/The holy blessed martyr for to seek." He was describing a mass phenomenon that set thousands on road trips, wending their way from one church to the next where they paid homage to saints' relics, like skulls, a splinter of the True Cross, or a spot of Christ's blood. These remains, housed

Church of Saint-Sernin, Toulouse, France, 1077–1119
A cruciform shape with altar at the east end and main door at the west is typical of Romanesque churches. The entrance is divided into a three-part facade, with each portal indicating the internal division into nave and side aisles. Chapels radiate off the rear apse. (The Gothic tower over the central crossing was a later addition.)

Nave, Saint-Sernin
Compound piers define bays and rise to meet the barrel vault over the nave, banded with transverse arches. The size and grandeur of Romanesque churches were vital to their message, as were the Gregorian chants that bounced off stone vaults, filling the space with celestial music. The English writer Joseph Addison (1672–1719) said, "By opening the mind to vast conceptions they fit it for the conception of God."

Basilica of San Miniato al Monte, Florence, Italy, 1062–c. 1200
Crisp geometric patterns of marble veneer on the exterior and echoes of classical temple shape show the reliance of Italian Romanesque on ancient Roman models.

Cathedral, Pisa, Italy (architect, Boschetto), 1063–1350; Bell Tower, 1174–1271; Baptistry (architect, Dioti Salvi), 1153–1265
This trio of buildings is united by the pattern of white marble arcades facing their exteriors. On the central-plan Baptistry, only the lower arcade is Romanesque.

in jeweled reliquaries, were thought to work miracles. Crippled pilgrims on crutches often camped out awaiting a cure.

Elaborate sanctuaries to house relics rose along the pilgrims' routes, and their popularity as tourist attractions dictated a church's interior form. Since hordes of pilgrims venerating the shrines interfered with daily offices by clergy, the solution was to create a loop for circulation ringing the nave. The rectangular basilica format evolved into two quadrant-vaulted side aisles outside a barrel-vaulted nave. At the east end, a large, semicircular apse behind the altar was supplied with an ambulatory (a walkway around the perimeter) and radiating chapels (smaller apses, each displaying treasure). Linked to aisles around the nave and transept, the ambulatory separated pilgrims from monks and allowed both groups to go about their business without traffic jams. The transept (or horizontal crossing arm) was moved toward the center of the church, creating a strongly cruciform shape.

The Church of Saint-Sernin in Toulouse, France, is a typical abbey church on the pilgrimage path. Thick walls support the barrel vault over the nave, and two side aisles are topped by a second-story gallery called a tribune. Compound piers running from floor to ceiling divide the interior vertically into bays. This articulation into components is further emphasized where the shafts meet transverse arches beneath the barrel vault.

To remedy the lack of light in early Romanesque church interiors (due to thick walls and few windows), churches like Autun Cathedral (1120–30) added a third story to the elevation. Atop the tribune were clerestory windows lighting the nave. Registers of the three-level elevation are separated by a horizontal cornice, which directs the eye down the length of the nave toward the altar. Gradually, as Romanesque approached the succeeding Gothic era, larger windows pierced church walls, and clusters of linear forms visually broke up the stone masses.

ITALIAN ROMANESQUE: LOCAL QUIRKS. Italy never completely embraced the Romanesque style. Its version was a hybrid of European and classical forms. Even from one city-state to another, styles varied. Church architecture in the Lombard region and its cities like Pavia and Milan differed from buildings in Tuscan cities like Florence and Pisa. This local flavor is hardly surprising. Not until 1870 did Italy unite as one country. Cities were fiercely chauvinistic, especially in their architecture, which was seen as evidence of superior culture. The word for local chauvinism, *campanilismo,* derives from the name for a bell tower, or campanile, which towered over a city and rang out its claim to fame.

The basilica of San Miniato al Monte in Florence shows classical influence. Five arches springing from Corinthian capitals frame three doors of the lower level of the facade. The shape of upper levels refers to the portico of an antique temple front, and geometric patterns of green-on-white marble resemble inlaid veneers in ancient Roman buildings.

The triad of marble buildings on the green in Pisa forms one of the most perfect compositional groupings since Trajan's Forum. Unified by their graceful exterior arcading, the domed baptistry, bell tower, and cathedral were built over hundreds of years but share the same decorative features of color, texture, pattern, and materials. Sharply scalloped arcs repeat in regular rhythm on all three buildings of the group, regardless of their differing shapes.

ENGLISH INNOVATION: THE RIB VAULT. The Vikings or Norsemen (later called Normans) settled in France and accepted Christianity. Not content to dominate northwest France, they sailed across the Channel under William the Conqueror and added England to their domain in 1066. Until 1200, Norman rulers solidified their kingdom, building castles and churches across England and Wales. The English Romanesque style is often called Norman, as William the Conqueror's legacy.

Nave, Durham Cathedral, United Kingdom, begun 1093
The earliest rib vaults make this cathedral an important forerunner of Gothic style. A thin line of blue marble crosses the nave near the front of the church, marking the point beyond which women were forbidden to enter in the Middle Ages.

Aided by an abundance of limestone, granite, and sandstone, the Normans embarked on an ambitious building program that produced a series of magnificent cathedrals and abbeys at Canterbury, Lincoln, Rochester, Winchester, Durham, Norwich, and Ely. Strongly cruciform in character, these churches had long, narrow naves, often twin towers at the entrance, a tower over the crossing, large triforiums (an upper gallery over side aisles, above the tribune), and clerestories. Massive cylindrical or clustered piers supported the roof and featured incised geometric ornaments on their columns and capitals.

Some of the most enormous churches in Europe are the Romanesque cathedrals of England. Among them, Durham Cathedral is a supreme masterpiece. Built to house the remains of St. Cuthbert and the Venerable Bede (a historian who died in 735), Durham was part of a Benedictine monastery and castle complex.

Down the length of the 470-foot-long nave, huge composite piers with engaged colonnettes alternate with massive cylindrical piers. The columns, carved in zigzag and lozenge patterns, fairly writhe in a visual wave of movement. Originally highlighted with red, blue, and gold paint (before whitewashed by purists in the Reformation), they must have endowed the interior with an impressive zip.

The breakthrough achieved at Durham was not just decorative but structural. To allow more light into the interior (through side galleries and clerestory windows), rib vaults were used for the first time. These stone ribs strengthened the lines of the groin vaults and, coupled with pointed arches in the vaults, more efficiently carried the weight of the roof than could thick walls alone. In aesthetic terms, the stone rib vaults bind the interior together in a web of linear patterns and give it a strong vertical thrust—qualities characteristic of later Gothic architecture.

Angkor Wat, Cambodia, begun 1113 C.E.
The temple complex of Angkor Wat is an example of another religious structure rich in sculpture, as were Romanesque churches. A virtuoso version of monumental stone carving, its walls and towers, covered with writhing relief figures, achieve a complete integration of sculpture and architecture.

Carcassonne, France, thirteenth century, restored by Viollet-le-Duc
This walled city was built on sixth-century foundations by the Visigoths. Massive defensive walls encircle the castle, houses, and streets. Built on the edge of a plateau, the two concentric walls include fifty-two towers and two miles of battlements.

CASTLES: ALL ALONG THE WATCHTOWER.

After a hiatus of five centuries, the building of stone castles resumed in Europe around 1000. Between 1066 and 1189, the Normans alone built 1200 castles. Most European stone castles sprang up as by-products of feudalism and the eight Crusades that lasted two centuries. As European Crusaders trekked to Palestine to wrest the Holy Land from Saracenic Turks, they left along the route fortified strongholds, like Krak des Chevaliers Castle (1142–1220) in Syria, called "the bone in the Saracen's throat." Returning Crusaders brought back advanced knowledge of fortifications, which they used to improve Western designs. (They also learned how to communicate via carrier pigeon when besieged.)

Castles were essentially fortified villages that replaced Roman cities, which had all but disappeared in the Dark Ages. (The population of Rome plummeted from one million at the end of the empire to less than 50,000 after the barbarians attacked.) Surrounded by exterior walls up to 20 feet thick, the twelfth-century walled castle was a center of government, home for the feudal lord and his dependents, and military base.

The keep (or *donjon* in French) was the most fortified and doubled as a private dwelling for the lord's family. Its walls could be 15 feet thick, as in the 90-foot-tall White Tower, begun at the Tower of London by William the Conqueror.

DEFENSE! Walls were generally splayed or battered, sloping outward at the base, to make the footing more resistant to undermining. Loopholes and arrow-slits for defense were incorporated into lower levels of the tower keep. At the top, stone walls were crenellated, with crenels (openings in the battlements) alternating with solid upright sections called merlons. Machicolations—projecting battlements cantilevered out from the top of the wall—had holes in the floor for dropping stones or boiling pitch on invaders. Towers were arranged at bow-shot intervals to repel attackers.

OOPS: ARCHITECTS' MAJOR GOOFS

Architecture—a blend of fine and applied arts—has suffered some public mishaps. Frank Lloyd Wright's famous flat roofs on his prairie houses were notorious for leaks. The United Nations Secretariat Building's disastrous north-south siting made it broiling hot when the glass-wall eastern exposure absorbed morning heat. The Tacoma Narrows Bridge, a 2,800-foot-long suspension bridge in Washington, was known as "galloping Gertie" because of its tendency to twist in the wind. (A 42-mile-per-hour wind shredded it in 1940.) Wind oscillation caused one wooden bridge to collapse when a German infantry unit goose-stepped across (in unfortunate rhythm with the oscillations). Other structures have become celebrated monuments despite—or because of—their defects.

TUMBLING DOWN
Cathedral of St. Pierre, Beauvais, France, 1225–72
Its bishop supposedly suffered from the sin of pride. He wished to construct the highest nave in Christendom, to top the celebrated Amiens Cathedral, a nearby rival. At 157 feet tall, Beauvais's choir vaults are the highest of all Gothic cathedrals. Unfortunately, the exterior buttresses were too skimpy to resist wind forces. Without warning, they buckled, and in 1284 the roof came tumbling down. Fifty years later the vaults were repaired, with extra piers and cross ribs for support. After the transepts were added, a 502-foot stone spire was placed over the crossing in 1569. Big mistake—they should have used lighter wood, covered with lead. The piers supporting this enormous load were inches out of plumb. Four years later, the tower collapsed.

FALL-OUT
John Hancock Tower, Boston, by Henry Cobb of Pei, Cobb, Freed, 1972–76
When nearly complete, the 60-story glass-curtain-wall skyscraper developed a problem: its windows fell out. At one point, almost one half of the building was covered with plywood panels. Local wags joked it should be called the U.S. Plywood Building. Besides structural problems that caused the Hancock to pop its panels, the Hancock was accused of disdain for context. The tall, slender parallelogram stands in historic Copley Square near two important nineteenth-century masonry buildings—H. H. Richardson's Trinity Church and McKim, Mead & White's Boston Public Library. The Hancock's abstract, high-tech look is jarringly different. The architect sheathed the structure in reflective glass to mirror the sky and adjoining buildings.

Leaning Tower, Pisa, Italy, 1174–1271
Lean Times: Planted in soft soil, the area of base is too small in relation to the tower's height, producing excessive load on the foundation. The freestanding bell tower—an alarming 14 feet out of plumb—started to lean almost immediately during construction. To counterbalance the tilt, builders incorporated a wedge-shaped section in the top two stories—all in vain. Until a new foundation was laid recently to arrest subsidence, the 179-foot-tall tower increased its angle of incline by almost one-half inch a year.

The principal gate was the most vulnerable point, and it generally had twin flanking towers, to provide multiple angles for raining missiles down on assailants. Some castles had an exterior gatehouse called a barbican to question potential visitors. A room above had "murder holes" in the floor, through which arrows could be fired or stones dropped. Entrances incorporated right-angle turns to force intruders to expose their unshielded side to fire from above and preclude use of a large battering ram. Castles were always built with spiral stairs that wound around clockwise, so right-handed defenders could swing their swords freely while the center post blocked an attacker's sword hand.

With these design advantages, a small garrison of perhaps thirty could defend a castle against thousands of foes. (Crafty defenders sometimes propped dummies on the battlements to give an impression of numerous sentries.) At Château Gaillard (1196–98), built by England's Richard I (the Lion Heart) on a chalk cliff in Normandy, defenders resisted a siege for one year in 1204. The enemy got inside only when an intrepid French soldier crawled up the privy shaft and opened chapel windows—the only openings large enough to admit soldiers.

Not until the fourteenth century, with the use of gunpowder and cannons that could shatter the sturdiest wall, did these strongholds became obsolete. By the end of the fifteenth century, castles had lost their military role. Nobles built manors in the style of modified castles into the eighteenth century, and the Romantic movement catalyzed a widespread taste for medieval architecture in the eighteenth and nineteenth centuries.

How to Besiege a Castle

The armored tanks of their day, castles were supposed to be impregnable. Refusing to be deterred, invaders devised various strategies to circumvent the so-called invincible walls. The basic methods were to climb over the walls, knock them down, or tunnel underneath.

(1) Use a ladder to scale walls. This practice was most hazardous to attackers, who were exposed to fire from archers. (The crossbow bolt was delivered with such deadly force, it could penetrate armor.)

(2) Use a siege tower (a large wooden tower on wheels, covered with hides to protect from crossfire). When rolled into place, streams of attackers climbed the tower and lowered a drawbridge across the wall. Drawback: only works on level ground.

(3) Batter down the walls with catapults that fire stones, iron bolts, or javelins. Richard the Lion Heart used one, which killed twelve men in one shot. Not to be outdone, King Louis of France had a catapult nicknamed "Bad Neighbor" that could demolish long sections of wall. Attackers even hurled dead horses and corpses to land inside castle walls and spread disease.

(4) Dig a tunnel under the wall. This method was most effective, until castle-builders caught on and built round towers instead of square ones. (A rounded base was more resistant to undermining and offered more angles for shooting the enemy.)

CHARLEMAGNE'S CHAPEL: PRE-ROMANESQUE

Palatine Chapel, by Odo of Metz, Aachen (Aix-la-Chapelle), Germany, 796–804

Considered the Father of Europe, Charlemagne was the first world-class leader to emerge after Rome's collapse. A burly man more than six feet tall, with eyes the color of the sky, he took it upon himself to reincarnate the Roman Empire in the West. Not only did he order buildings to rival those of ancient Rome, he gathered a cadre of intellectuals to revive classical arts and letters. His empire extended from Denmark to the Adriatic.

The first public architecture to briefly illuminate the Dark Ages was known as Carolingian (c. 768–845), after Carolus Magnus (Charles the Great, or Charlemagne). His two-storied, octagonal chapel, part of a huge palace at Aachen, was a conscious imitation of San Vitale in Ravenna, which Charlemagne admired. Its central space is covered by stone vaulting, a technology that had nearly been lost during 300 years of chaos. When Charlemagne died in 814 at age 72, he was buried in the chapel sitting bolt upright on a throne.

GOTHIC: BUILDING LITE

Abbot Suger had a problem. On feast days, his church was packed to the brim. Among "the crowded multitude...who strove to flock in to worship and kiss the holy relics," he wrote, "no one among the countless thousands of people because of their very density could move a foot."

Enlarging the church was an obvious solution. But in remodeling, Suger had a vision. He wanted to tear down bulky walls, enlarge teensy windows, and disperse the general gloom of Romanesque abbeys. The French abbot imagined an interior where space would flow unimpeded by partitions, where walls would be thin and skeletal, where—above all—the light of God would figuratively and literally fill the church. When Suger reconstructed the choir of his church at St.-Denis (1135–44) along these lines, he invented the Gothic style. Within fifty years, officials who attended the consecration ceremony were building cathedrals of their own. From Scandinavia to Spain, edifices consciously imitated St.-Denis, growing progressively larger and lighter.

The Gothic style spread like measles across the face of Western Europe. From its origin near Paris in the twelfth century, for four hundred years it dominated construction of churches, town halls, hospitals, and universities. The desire and means to build on a monumental scale, over multiple generations, were new. This commitment reflected revived confidence in technology and human capacities. Aided by the growing wealth of cities and increasing power and patronage of the church and monarch, Gothic architecture became the quintessential urban mode.

The Gothic cathedral represented the Middle Ages' overriding concern: religious faith. A cathedral's magnificence symbolized the Heavenly Citadel, where virtuous souls would reside after death. Its very grandeur—especially the impossibly high vaults that served no utilitarian purpose—showed how immortality could transcend earthly limitations.

ENGINEERING: THE TRIUMPH OF LIGHT.

The mania for Gothic cathedrals started soon after the first Crusaders returned from Constantinople. Awed by the splendor of Hagia Sophia, knights spread the word about architectural wonders in the East. They brought back new technology, like winches to hoist heavy stones. The West learned the science of geometry in a new translation of Euclid's *Elements.*

What made the lightness of Gothic architecture feasible were both structural and aesthetic elements: the pointed arch and rib vault, flying buttresses, and thin walls pierced by expansive stained-glass windows. Other characteristics of Gothic style were an integration of structure and ornament, a sense of interior unity (replacing the compartmentalized Romanesque layout), elaborate entrances covered with sculpture, and a pronounced vertical emphasis.

POINTED ARCH, RIB VAULT, AND FLYING BUTTRESS.

To produce the Gothic miracle of height and light, master masons used ribbed, groined, four-sided (quadripartite) vaults. In each vault, two half-cylinders intersect at groins. The arched ribs along two diagonals give greater rigidity to the vault in the direction of the groins. The vault's weight is channeled toward the four corners, where it is supported by vertical piers. To resist the outward thrust of the arches, external supports called flying buttresses were devised. Wall-like pillars braced nave walls through curved half-arches supporting the groin vaults like giant fingers. The cathedral looked pure and uncluttered on the inside, while the outside bristled with a briar patch of bridges linked to pillars and pinnacles.

The pointed arch added greater flexibility to the modular system of construction, since pointed arches can span different distances while keeping their keys at the same height. By varying the angle of the arch, cross-vaults could be erected over bays of any shape or size. Visually, pointed arches look lighter than rounded arches. Their upward-pointing tip has a buoyancy to enhance the impression of lift.

Architect-engineers based their practice on trial and error, as well as on trade secrets passed down through the apprentice system. They chose to err on the side of conservatism, with masonry overbuilt and stressed only to a fraction of its capacity. Gradually, structures became leaner and more daring. In a century and a half, from Chartres (1194) to Palma de Majorca (1350), cathedral piers became three and a half times thinner. Before flying buttresses were invented at Notre-Dame in Paris, walls were 5 feet thick, but with the new technology used at Mantes, walls shrank to 16 inches.

The system of construction was audacious. Stability depended on interaction of all factors. If even a minor component failed, the whole frame was vulnerable. (See page 42, Beauvais Cathedral goes bust.) Architects pushed materials and methods to the limit to reach aesthetic goals: higher, lighter, grander, more ornate. The result was some of the most extravagant architecture ever created.

ST.-DENIS: THE FIRST GOTHIC CATHEDRAL.

In renovating his church, Abbot Suger used the essential elements of Gothic style—the pointed arch and rib vault —to further his theological beliefs. He wrote, "Man may rise to the contemplation of the divine through the senses." The visual experience of lavish beauty in architecture of color, light, line, and space would make the mind ascend from material glory to immaterial faith. Or, as Suger put it, the churchgoer would be "transported from this inferior to that higher world. . . ."

Equating God with "super-essential light," Suger replaced stone walls in radiating chapels with stained glass symbolizing divine light. He substituted thin columns for heavy piers in the ambulatory. He subordinated all parts to a holistic design to create a single spacious volume, where crowds and light flowed smoothly from chapels to altar. Increasing the size and number of windows and reducing the chapels' outward projection so they almost merged with the ambulatory made light flood the whole east end. Rebuilding the west facade, he installed the first rose window between two towers, other Gothic hallmarks.

The abbey church of St.-Denis set the pattern for Gothic cathedrals. Although ornament became more complex as the style evolved and each country contributed its individual fillip, the signature elements remained the same. A three-level elevation became standard inside, with an arcade of tall pointed arches, a narrow passage (the triforium), and huge clerestory windows with delicate stone tracery. Clustered colonnettes affixed to piers rose from floor to vaults, creating a continuous line of uplift. Cathedrals retained the Romanesque format of nave with side aisles, but transept arms became much shorter, reinforcing the sense of an inner spatial whole. Most striking was the virtual disappearance of walls, which became mullions for stained glass.

Profuse exterior sculpture, like the homilies in stained glass, illustrated Bible tales so the entire building became a teaching aid for illiterate masses. Not sure about the wages of sin? Check out the Last Judgment carving, generally in the tympanum above the main portal. A wavering varlet could see monstrous devils snatching sinners off to hell, while Jesus weighs souls and sends the virtuous wafting upward.

Nave, abbey church of St.-Denis, France, c. 1135–44
The flow of space and light through ambulatory, chapels, and choir was made possible by removing thick walls, enlarging windows, and thinning supports. The new style invented at this church was later termed Gothic.

The Architect

At the beginning of the Gothic period, architects were called master masons. (A tombstone inscription for architect Pierre de Montreuil calls him *doctor lathomorum,* master stonemason.) They learned their craft through long apprenticeships before rising to the rank of master. Although trained in carpentry or stonecutting, master builders also possessed intellectual, specialized knowledge (*scientia* in Latin). They were literate and skilled in the liberal arts. Architects occupied a privileged position as designer, contractor, and supervisor of enormous projects.

In some churches, architects are buried with signs of high honor. On tomb effigies, they are dressed like great lords, holding tools like a compass, measuring rod, or model of a building. The French King Charles V was godfather to the son of his architect, Raymond du Temple.

Things could be dicey in the building biz. One hazard was that the better the work, the riskier the reward. The countess of Bayonne had her architect beheaded after he erected a fine tower, to keep him from repeating the miracle for another. Since architectural principles were not founded on factual knowledge but empirical experience, hiring the right architect meant success or failure on a construction site. Tricks of the trade were so jealously guarded, one architect killed his own son for leaking secrets to a bishop.

By the second half of the eleventh century, the architect was a professional in the modern sense, and a quantum leap in the level of originality occurred. Buildings became increasingly sophisticated and daring, less reliant on tradition and more on an individual's powers of invention and intuition.

NOTRE-DAME OF PARIS: THE GOLD STANDARD. Victor Hugo called it "a vast symphony of stone." It must have seemed even vaster in the Middle Ages, for Notre-Dame (1163–1250) was the first cathedral of colossal scale and the prototype for all that followed. One French cathedral that preceded it, at Senlis (begun 1153), had "gigantic" 69-foot-high vaults. With its 115-foot-tall nave vault, imagine the awe that greeted Notre-Dame—the highest and longest edifice then attempted.

Its architect designed Notre-Dame in a compact plan, as one huge space with transept arms that do not project past the side aisles. He integrated large volumes by applying ornament to suggest lines of construction and stress the continuity of space. Shallow chapels hardly radiate; they sweep around the east end in a gentle curve.

With such enormous height and length, an aesthetic problem arose: how to blend great expanses of wall into the total conception. The solution: to balance horizontal and vertical lines so neither predominates, producing a harmonious whole. Nave walls are a series of recessions with little blank surface. The horizontal zones (arched arcade, tribune gallery, clerestory) lead the eye from entrance to the altar's crescendo. At the same time, vertical lines of triple colonnettes rise from floor to vaults to create an impression of dynamic upsurge. Thin moldings and exaggeratedly slender arches dematerialize walls, making them seem delicate and without depth. Wide clerestory windows further reduce the weight of masonry walls.

Flying buttresses were first used at Notre-Dame and span 50 feet on the outside of the church. Before, arches in the second-story gallery served as supports for vaults and nave walls. When windows in the tribune gallery increased in size (sacrificing solid walls to allow more light), nave vaults needed additional bracing. The taut buttresses transmit lateral thrust of roof and vaults to exterior pillars. Through this device, Notre-Dame achieves its grand scale without a massive shell.

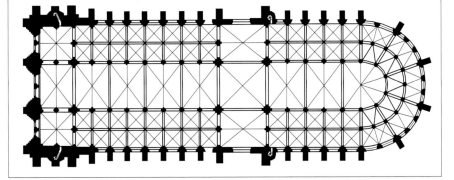

Plan, Notre-Dame, Paris
Its compact plan with a continuous ring of chapels and nonprojecting transepts reinforces the sense of one vast but coherent, unified space.

Notre-Dame, Paris, France, 1163–1250
With its flying buttresses to support walls and vaults, the Cathedral of Notre Dame became the prototype of subsequent Gothic architecture.

CHARTRES: THE QUINTESSENTIAL GOTHIC CATHEDRAL.

Looking at Notre Dame de Chartres, said the writer Henry James, "makes the act of vision seem for the moment almost all of life." As the most unaltered example of Gothic architecture, Chartres Cathedral (1194–1220) displays all the classic elements of early Gothic design in unparalleled purity.

Built to house one of the most sacred relics of Christendom, the tunic worn by the Virgin Mary when she gave birth to Christ, officials planned a suitably grand edifice after most of the original Norman structure burned down. Since cathedrals were also the heart of a medieval village and symbol of civic pride, funds to rebuild poured in from all classes of society. From lords and ladies to peasants, townspeople harnessed themselves to wagons to drag stones from quarry to construction site.

The main innovation of the design was elimination of the tribune level, with a low triforium (passageway over the slanted arcade roof) substituted. Because flying buttresses made a tribune structurally unnecessary, the designer was free to enlarge the arcade and clerestory to monumental size. With flying buttresses for external support, the clerestory windows became as tall as the main arcade of the first floor. This expansion transformed the upper story into a light show of supreme beauty. The chief glory of Chartres is its 26,000 square feet of stained-glass windows. "Flaming jewellery," the critic John Ruskin called the windows—90 percent original—because of their luminous blues and reds, which soften the cold stone of the interior.

Replacing the redundant tribune with a small-scale triforium also simplified nave walls and reduced the number of masonry elements, while maintaining a balance between horizontal (the three-tier elevation) and vertical (piers, vaults) elements. The triforium perforates the wall, making masonry less a dead zone than a pause between giant windows.

Chartres maximizes the vertical impulse of Gothic architecture with another contribution: *piliers cantonnés,* columns surrounded by four thin shafts, evenly spaced. These shafts rise uninterrupted to the springing of the vaults, like lines of energy spraying toward the sky.

Another reason to consider Chartres the epitome of Gothic design is its exterior sculpture. Around the portals, thin, columnar statues of Old Testament royalty, prophets, and apostles reinforce the structural lines of the building. Architectonic rather than superfluous, the statues are essential for the design's visual coherence. Sharply carved figures mold the facade into a play of light and shadow, animating the surface and banishing the monotony of flat planes.

Cathedral of Notre Dame, Chartres, France, 1194–1220
Chartres Cathedral exemplifies classic Gothic features with its central rose window, three sculpted portals, and paired towers. The south spire (on the right), constructed c. 1160, represents the simplicity of early Gothic, while the ornate northern tower (1507), capped with a Flamboyant spire, is High Gothic.

Chartres Cathedral, nave interior
Chartres brought together all the Gothic elements of exterior flying buttresses, pointed arches, rib vaults, three-part elevation, stained glass, and vertical accent.

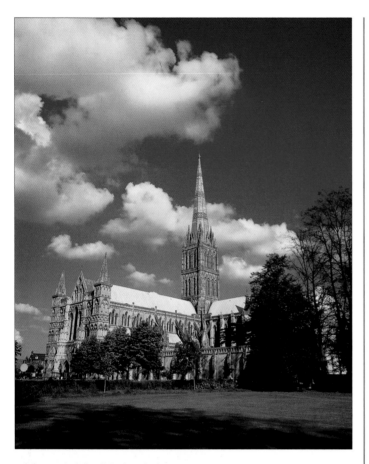

Salisbury Cathedral, Salisbury, England, 1220–66
Sitting on the church green not far from Stonehenge, Salisbury Cathedral's rambling plan is an example of Early English Gothic.

Ornament

Everybody recognizes gargoyles — those carved mythical beasts that serve as cathedral rainspouts. But not everybody looks for the green man hiding in most Gothic cathedrals. The green man is a holdover from pagan days, usually a human face with leaves and vines sprouting from his mouth, forehead, and cheeks. Rooted in pre-Christian fertility rites, these stone statues show how medieval craftsmen mixed divine and profane imagery without regard for consistency.

displayed an unprecedented degree of fantasy, with ribs twirling over vaults in nets, stars, or fan shapes. Finally, English cathedrals were not the cynosure of cities but were located on spacious greens in rural settings.

The purest example of the Early English style is Salisbury Cathedral (1220–66). Its foundations were laid only five years after citizens persuaded King John to acknowledge their rights in the Magna Carta. Although Cromwell's troops plundered its treasures in the seventeenth century, the cathedral remains a classic example of English Gothic. Its front is a screen to display sculpture, and its 404-foot-tall tower was the highest of the Middle Ages. Long and low inside (the nave is only twice as high as wide), Salisbury is fragmented into separate square-ended units, even though the nave is unified into one huge space. Horizontal moldings create a lateral emphasis, driving the eye down the length of the nave.

Featuring cloisters (1284) and that distinctive English contribution, the octagonal chapter house (1263), Salisbury reflects the compartmentalization typical of English style. At evensong, when choirboys in ruffed collars sing to ward off the perils of the night, one can almost imagine the Middle Ages still alive.

From 1250 to 1370, the sober Early English style gave way to the Decorated or Curvilinear style. Based on the ogee arch (a double-curved arch that slopes out, then in, on its way to a point), free-flowing forms proliferated. In Decorated interiors like the Lady Chapel at Ely Cathedral, all surfaces are enlivened by a fanciful screen of tracery. At Wells Cathedral (1330), ribs form an ornate net in choir vaults. The front of Wells is also extraordinary. Its 150-foot-wide expanse is a screen of 400 thirteenth-century carved statues, which were once gilded and painted.

From about 1330 to 1540, British architects reined in their curvaceous impulses, enshrining the Perpendicular style. Just as it sounds, this mode stressed rectilinear, vertical panels, as in the large mullioned windows and straight lines of Gloucester Cathedral (1337). This rigidity didn't stop ceilings, however, from transmuting into a decorative filigree. Ribs became less structural and more ornamental, multiplying into rich patterns incised on stone vaults.

The fan vault was a dazzling English invention. A cluster of nonstructural, thin ribs radiates from each column like an inverted semi-cone to create a whirlpool of lines. The trend was away from simplicity toward a more artful, decorative effect, so British carvers could demonstrate their virtuosity in wood and stone. Some ceilings are so extreme in their mesh of lines, they resemble a knight's chain-mail armor.

GERMANY: THE HALL CHURCH.

Regional variations occurred wherever Gothic took root. In Germany, from the mid-thirteenth to the sixteenth centuries, the need for a large space for preaching produced the hall church. Made of brick rather than stone, these churches had naves and side aisles that were the same height, separated only by rows of columns. Without a clerestory or triforium, the sense of one continuous interior space prevailed.

Simplifying the interior didn't prevent German architects from letting their powers of fantasy loose on the ceiling. Elaborate vaulting with ribs in net or faceted honeycomb formations splay across ceilings. Sometimes ribs (called "flying ribs") were completely independent of the vault surface, protruding into space like scaffolding. Piers took the form of bundles of shafts rising sinuously to become vault ribs.

Even in elaborate cathedrals like Cologne and Strasbourg, which slavishly imitated French designs, Germans added their own twists—in this case, the openwork spire. The spire on Strasbourg's tower is a cage of delicate tracery. The 630-foot spire at Ulm Cathedral (devised at the end of the fourteenth century but not built until 1890) is the highest in Europe.

ITALY: BARELY GOTHIC.

Italians were disdainful of architectural styles that originated north of the Alps. Nevertheless, they couldn't entirely resist adding an overlay of Gothic details like pointed arches or pinnacles to show they kept up with the latest fashion. Gothic in Italy was generally more highly colored and ornate.

The Doge's Palace (1309–1424) in Venice shows an Eastern influence in its Byzantine delicacy, but is superficially Gothic in its open stonework and stacks of pointed-arch arcades. The pink-and-white patterned marble veneer on the top level looks like a textile weave.

King's College Chapel, Cambridge, England, Reginald Ely and John Wastell, 1508–15
Fourteen ribbed panels from each springer and gilded bosses spin a decorative web of tracery. Although fan vaults are at their flashiest here, the severe lines of walls and windows reflect the rectilinear style of Perpendicular English Gothic.

Church of St. Anne, Annaberg, Germany, begun 1499
With ribs sprouting like tendrils to form flowers in the vaults, the decorative scheme of this hall church shows the trademark flowing lines of German Gothic.

Doge's Palace (Palazzo Ducale), Venice, Italy, by Pietro Baseggio, 1309–1424
Stone pointed-arch arcades and roof finials make this nominally a Gothic exterior, even though Italian builders never wholeheartedly embraced the style. With its frescoed, gilded, coffered, and carved ceiling, the Great Council Hall in the palace has been called "the sumptuousest room of all Christendome."

Milan Cathedral (1296–1485, with a nineteenth-century facade) is the most Gothic of any Italian building, with a riot of Gothic ornament applied over its basilica structure. The rosy marble exterior explodes in pinnacles, finials, and stone spikes.

Inexperienced in building on such a huge scale, more than fifty architects and sculptors debated the structure and supports at Milan. Although one consultant insisted, *"Ars sine scientia nihil est"* (practical craft without theoretical knowledge is nothing), none of the masons could agree on what size piers were necessary. Each mason proposed the form of the cathedral be determined by multiplying modules of a simple geometrical shape—either a triangle, square, or rectangle. Judging from the finished product, a master mason named Paul Mignot must have carried the day. He advocated a medieval system called triangulating.

In Spain, Gothic cathedrals were constructed with expansive proportions. The cathedral of Gerona contains the widest vaulted span in Europe—73-foot nave vaults. Seville boasts the world's largest medieval cathedral (begun 1402). Its creators planned a church "so great and of such a kind that those who see it finished shall think we were mad." It was to be so beautiful "that there shall be none its equal."

Grand scale, glorious beauty, with a touch of mad ambition pretty much sum up Gothic architecture.

Milan Cathedral, Milan, Italy, by Arnolfo di Cambio, Francesco Talenti, 1296–1485
Pointed arches and lavish ornament including pinnacles, flying buttresses, and profuse sculpture mark this cathedral as High Gothic. Builders based its architecture on geometric modules, as the triangular shape shows. The building was so huge and complex, construction continued for nearly 200 years. It was only finished when Napoleon ordered a speedup to crown himself king of Italy in the cathedral in 1805.

What's in a Name?

Gothic architecture wasn't called Gothic when it was invented. It was called *style ogival* (or ogive style) after its signature element, the pointed arch. Not until the sixteenth century did the first art historian, an Italian named Giorgio Vasari, dub it Gothic as a mark of disdain. During the Renaissance, the excesses of Gothic style so horrified Vasari that he was sure it must have been invented by barbaric Goths, whom he accused of sacking Rome and destroying classic structures. With an obvious shudder, Vasari criticized Gothic style for its "malediction of little niches one above the other, with no end of pinnacles and points and leaves." Gothic builders "filled all Europe with these abominations," he wrote, adding, "May God protect every country from such ideas and style of building."

THE ANNOTATED FLYING BUTTRESS

The critic John Ruskin said, "Architecture is the adaptation of form to resist force." Buttresses, or supporting structures to resist wind and gravity, have taken many forms in their indispensable role as props.

An aqueduct uses adjacent arches to counteract lateral thrusts that would otherwise cause the arch to spread and collapse. Each arch acts as a buttress to its neighbor, but at the end of an arcade of arches, definitive bracing is needed. In this Roman example,

the walls of a canyon spanned by the aqueduct serve as terminal buttresses.

Flying buttresses, or arched bridges projecting from the wall of a cathedral to external pillars, were invented at Notre-Dame. Transferring load and forces exerted by nave walls to the ground, these buttresses control downward forces generated by gravity and resist horizontal thrust. They spread the vertical load generated by vaults above the nave, distributing weight diagonally, like a person standing

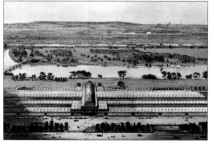

with feet far apart. Without buttresses, the open, high, lighted interiors and thin interior masonry supports that are the glory of Gothic churches would not be possible. They are supremely functional, decorative, and expressive.

The Crystal Palace is a whole building converted into a network of nearly invisible support. The glass-curtain wall was a skin more than a skeleton, so the lacy ironwork had to be stiffened by diagonal braces, making the structure a vast truss. Like skyscrapers, it achieves maximum structural performance from minimal materials. Made of prefabricated cast iron and standardized glass panes, the structure enclosed one million square feet—a space six times larger than St. Paul's Cathedral. Compared to a masonry building, its actual support was a frame of very little volume, its mass almost diminished to a vanishing point.

Similarly, modern skyscrapers use steel framing members linked by diagonal braces in the center of a building, forming a trussed spine to resist lateral wind pressure. Steel supports carry the weight of a building to the ground, while a skin of glass hides the actual physical frame. As a building grows in height, its need for resistance to lateral wind and earthquake forces increases dramatically. An interior stiff tower of wind-braced concrete often forms a core to support the outer, light steel frame. As in a Gothic cathedral, buttressing makes possible great height and light.

The Sydney Opera House uses steel cables for reinforcement inside precast concrete shells, allowing the building to be perceived as a total sculpture. Nested roof vaults, like leaping waves or puffed sails, rise 221 feet above the harbor. Such structural ingenuity does not come cheap. The original cost of $9 million soared to $400 million.

Counterclockwise from top left: flying buttresses, Notre-Dame, Paris, 1163–1250; Pont du Gard aqueduct, Nîmes, France, c. 25 B.C.E.; Crystal Palace, London, by Joseph Paxton, 1851; Sydney Opera House, Sydney, Australia, by Jorn Utzon, 1959–73; Seagram Building, New York, by Mies van der Rohe and Johnson, 1954–58

Renaissance and Baroque: All Roads Lead from Rome

We've seen it before. The simple, straight lines established in classical Greek architecture got pumped up to ornate Hellenistic frills. At the end of the Gothic era, pure linear forms became flamboyant spikes. Throughout history, architecture oscillates between mini and maxi.

The Renaissance and Baroque periods show the same pattern. Restrained Renaissance design stressed clarity, logic, and flat, straight lines. Exuberant Baroque went for emotion, sensation, and scalloped contours. Renaissance architects revered the rules followed by ancient Roman builders, while Baroque architects stretched the rules to the popping point.

The three Rs of Renaissance design may be Rome, Reason, and Regularity, but four Bs are essential for knowledge of both Renaissance and Baroque architecture: founding fathers Brunelleschi, Bramante, Bernini, and Borromini. It's no coincidence that they're all Italian. Both schools of architecture were invented in Italy, then became international styles practiced throughout Europe.

S. Ivo della Sapienza, Rome, interior of dome, by Borromini, c. 1660
Baroque architects took the smooth Renaissance dome and sculpted it into faceted forms full of visual excitement.

WORLD HISTORY		ARCHITECTURE
Renaissance begins in northern Italy	c. 1420	Brunelleschi begins construction of Florence Cathedral dome
Joan of Arc battles to drive English from France in 100 Years' War	1429	
	1446	Gothic King's College Chapel begun, Cambridge
Florence under Medici becomes center of Renaissance humanism	1450	
Gutenberg invents printing press with moveable type	1450	
Constantinople falls to Muslims; Byzantine Empire ceases to exist; 100 Years' War ends	1453	
Turks sack Acropolis	1458	
Dante's *Divine Comedy* printed	1472	
Spanish Inquisition begins	1481	
Botticelli paints *Birth of Venus*	1484	
Moors driven from Spain; Columbus discovers America	1492	
First Spanish settlement established in New World, at Hispaniola	1493	
Leonardo da Vinci paints *Last Supper*	1495	
	1496	Michelangelo goes to Rome to work
Vasco da Gama discovers sea route to India	1498	
Global modern age begins; Europe in contact with Africa, Asia, Americas	1500s	
	1502	Bramante's Tempietto signals High Renaissance
Slave trade begins	1509	
	1515	Raphael appointed architect-in-chief, St. Peter's
Sir Thomas More writes *Utopia*	1516	
Martin Luther launches Protestant Reformation	1517	
	1519	Mannerism begins to appear in Italy
Magellan's ship circumnavigates globe	1519–21	
Cortéz conquers Mexico, sacks Aztec kingdom	1519–21	
	1524	Michelangelo designs Laurentian Library
Castiglione writes *The Courtier* on courtly manners	1527	
Pizarro conquers Incas in Peru	1531–33	
Henry VIII breaks with pope, founds Church of England	1534	
Jesuit order founded to counter Reformation	1540	
Copernicus announces Sun (not Earth) is center of solar system	1543	
	1546	Lescot begins Square Court of Louvre, Paris
	1550	Palladio builds Villa Rotonda
Elizabeth I crowned in England (rules until 1603)	1559	
	1561	St. Basil's Basilica, Moscow, finished
	1563	Herrera begins Escorial for Philip II in Spain
	1570	Palladio publishes influential Four Books of Architecture
English found colony of Virginia	1585	
Philip II's Spanish Armada defeated by British	1588	
North America colonized; modern science emerges; religious wars continue	1600s	Baroque born
Shakespeare's *Hamlet* performed	1600	
Cervantes' *Don Quixote* published	1605	
	1615	Inigo Jones becomes England's chief architect
Harvey discovers circulatory system	1617	
Thirty Years' War begins	1618	
Mayflower lands in Massachusetts	1620	
	1628	Construction of Taj Mahal begun
	1629	Bernini takes over direction of work on St. Peter's
Galileo publishes theories on planetary motion	1632	
Opera developed as art form by Monteverdi	1639	
English Civil War begins	1642	
Descartes announces, "Cogito, ergo sum"	1644	
Charles I beheaded in England	1649	
	1656	Le Nôtre designs gardens at Vaux-le-Vicomte, France
	1661	Louis XIV begins renovation of Versailles
Royal Society (for advancement of science) founded in England	1662	
	1666	Academy of Architecture founded in France
	1675	Wren begins rebuilding St. Paul's, London
Dodo becomes extinct	1680	
Isaac Newton publishes mathematical theories	1687	
John Locke's essays launch Age of Enlightenment	1690	
Last of Mayan Civilization in Yucatàn destroyed by Spanish	1696	
Bach writes first cantata	1704	
	1715	Rococo begins

THE RENAISSANCE: AGE OF REDISCOVERY

Old and new collided around 1420. Out of the collision the Renaissance was born. It was a forward-looking era, with science and technology zooming from medieval to modern. It was also a backward-looking era, as artists imitated ancient Greek and Roman styles more than a thousand years old.

Most of all, it was an age of genius. The Renaissance architect Leon Battista Alberti wrote, "Men can do anything with themselves if they will." As evidence, writers like Shakespeare, Bacon, Marlowe, Jonson, and Donne transformed Elizabethan England into "a nest of singing birds." In Italy, artists like Leonardo, Botticelli, and Michelangelo and architects like Brunelleschi, Bramante, and Palladio reached a height of civilization. As Erasmus said at the outset of the age, "What a world I see dawning! Why can I not grow young again!"

New attitudes were rampant in Europe. In science, whole worlds opened up. On the map, literally, a New World was discovered and continents explored. Copernicus proclaimed the Sun center of the universe. Through his new microscope, Van Leeuwenhoek discovered in a drop of water worlds of "cavorting beasties." Mankind came to the fore, confident in the power of his intellect and will.

ANTIQUE CHIC. This explosion of discovery pointed forward, but humanist scholars looked to the past. Aided by the invention of the printing press that made ancient literature available, the rediscovery of classical techniques and texts consumed the best minds. In 1550, the artist-historian Giorgio Vasari described a *rinascità,* or renaissance, in art and architecture, based on antique styles.

Italians had always found Gothic architecture wild and woolly. Now pointed arches became anathema. Vasari denounced the style's "accursed little niches [and] array of pinnacles," which he considered "ugly and uncivilized." He accused the barbarian Goths of despoiling ancient Roman monuments, even of spitefully "killing all the architects in battle"—as if there were a special battalion of builders!

Retro-Rome was the new rage. Since Italy had a preponderance of ancient Roman ruins as models, it was on the Italian peninsula that the Renaissance erupted.

Although its principles did not spread to northern Europe until the seventeenth century, the Renaissance is generally dated from 1420 to 1600, the time of its flowering in Italy. The fifteenth century (called the Quattrocento) is termed the Early Renaissance, with most landmarks of the developing style located in Florence. The High Renaissance of the sixteenth century (the Cinquecento) saw a shift in scale, as Rome became the epicenter, and monuments grew imperial in size and grandeur.

FLORENCE: ATHENS ON THE ARNO. It wasn't something in the water that made Florence the birthplace of the Renaissance. It was, Vasari speculated, "the air of Florence making minds naturally free, and not content with mediocrity."

Culture was more advanced on the banks of the Arno. While the rest of Europe shoveled in food with their paws, refined Florentines ate with forks.

Of course, it helped that Florence possessed a family for whom *noblesse oblige* was mother's milk. The Medicis (especially Cosimo and his grandson Lorenzo) struck it rich in banking and spent freely to beautify Florence. Just when the city possessed such bountiful patrons of art, it also sheltered brilliant artists like the architect Brunelleschi, sculptors Ghiberti and Donatello, and painters Masaccio and Botticelli, all working in the *all'antica* (antique or classical) style.

Florence Cathedral dome and Baptistry by Brunelleschi, 1420–36
Brunelleschi's engineering genius, based on a study of Roman construction methods, allowed him to create the largest dome since antiquity.

BRUNELLESCHI: THE FIRST RENAISSANCE ARCHITECT.

Filippo Brunelleschi (1377–1446) is considered the father of Renaissance architecture. Although he began as a goldsmith and sculptor and was also a clockmaker, mathematician, and Latin scholar, Brunelleschi became most famous as the builder of the dome of Florence Cathedral. At 138 feet across, the space to be covered was the largest attempted since antiquity. By 1412, the church, begun in 1296, was finished except for capping the huge hole, a feat church officials despaired of achieving. Most domes were supported during construction by an armature of wood scaffolding, but the duomo opening was so wide, no trees were big enough to bridge the gap.

One scheme for supporting the dome proposed filling the space with dirt. Pennies would be mixed into the earth, and after the dome was finished, children would remove the dirt to find money—a sort of three-coins-in-a-mountain approach.

Skeptics called him a madman, but Brunelleschi was confident he could do the trick. He studied the Pantheon to fathom its structure. Then he announced his solution: to build circular courses of brick, tapering toward the top, in which each course supports the next. He also devised a double-shell covering of brick in a herringbone pattern, reinforced by ribs and metal bands. Construction began in 1420, with a lantern added after 1436. (The lantern acts as a capstone to hold the dome together and prevent spread.) Although the dome is Gothic in outline, its scale rivals that of imperial Rome and its engineering is an ingenious mix of old and new.

Brunelleschi's study of ruins contributed greatly to his triumph. He and Donatello were so fascinated by Roman antiquity that they were known as the "treasure men." (They were not only spending treasures to excavate half-buried structures so they could sketch them; they were also seeking architectural gold in their digs.) Brunelleschi's biographer said that analyzing Roman ruins was a revelation for the architect: "It was made clear to him almost as if God has illumined him."

Brunelleschi was more than an ivory-tower scholar; he was a hands-on supervisor at brick kilns. He designed scaffolds and invented hoists. Brunelleschi even installed a canteen on one scaffold so workers wouldn't have to waste time descending for lunch. He carved turnips to show masons the kind of joints he wanted. Such attention to detail paid off. Alberti called the dome "ample to cover

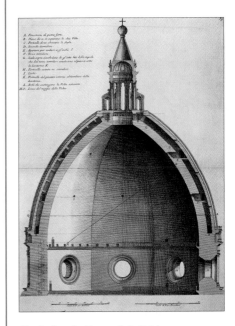

Sketch of cupola, Florence Cathedral dome

Foundling Hospital, Florence, by Brunelleschi, 1419–24
Brunelleschi's design is based on repeating modules (a cube outlined by two columns).

Santo Spirito, Florence, by Brunelleschi, 1434 or later
This church, in Brunelleschi's mature, classical style, is modeled on a Roman basilica, with simple geometric units and sculptural richness.

with its shadow all the people of Tuscany." One hundred years later, Michelangelo was asked to create a dome for St. Peter's to out-shine Florence's. "Larger, yes," Michelangelo replied, "but not more beautiful!"

Brunelleschi's first design that estab-lished a new Renaissance template was his Foundling Hospital. This first true Renais-sance building has a horizontal emphasis and clear, mathematical proportions. Columns of the loggia (or porch created by an arcade) are spaced as far apart as they are tall. Each arch is one-half the height of the columns, with pedimented windows centered above. Each domed bay, bordered by Corinthian columns, forms a cube. The scheme is rational, based on repetition of mathematical modules and classical motifs like columns, round arches, pilasters, and entablature. Yet the whole is not just a pastiche of Roman elements but an elegant, linear composition that looked both old and totally new. Brunelleschi's jaunty arcades seemed to be, it was said, "running races in their mirth."

Santo Spirito has a similar mathematical simplicity. The square under the crossing is the basic module, which is repeated in the choir and transept arms, augmented by four squares forming the nave and quarter-squares as aisles. With columns down the length of the nave and a coffered ceiling, the church format recalls a Roman basilica.

Brunelleschi revived the use of an entablature that was to define Renaissance style. Each column has a capital, then a segment of entablature before the springing of the arch. This line of entablature segments emphasizes the lin-ear grid that underpins the composition. A polymath, Brunelleschi invented the system of linear perspective used by Renaissance painters, and his use of dark pietra serena stone against light stucco walls outlines the architecture. These lines, like perspective, direct a viewer's gaze to selected focal points.

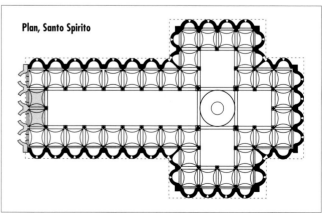

Plan, Santo Spirito

As much as his designs revel in rationality, Brunelleschi could wallow in emotion. He proposed a design for a Medici palace that Cosimo found too highfalutin, saying, "Envy is a plant one should never water." When rejected, the architect hurled his elaborate model to the ground, smashing it to smithereens.

ALBERTI: MR. EVERYTHING. Leon Battista Alberti (1404–1472) was more versatile than a triathlete. He could throw farther, jump higher, ride a horse faster, write a play better, compose a piece of music more sprightly, and design buildings more skillfully than 99.9 percent of the other near-geniuses who populated this era. A painter, mathematician, and scientist who was university educated, knew Greek and Latin, and studied law, he came as near to the ideal "Renaissance man" as possible.

A dilettante architect who designed buildings and left the construction to others, Alberti had a considerable influence through his ten-volume text, *De re aedificatoria* (1452). Based on Vitruvius, the ancient codifier of Roman architecture whose treatise was rediscovered in 1414, Alberti's theories equated beauty with pure geometry, enhanced by classical ornament. He defined architectural beauty as "that reasoned harmony of all the parts achieved in such a manner that nothing could be added, taken away, or altered except for the worse."

When Alberti refaced the exterior of S. Maria Novella (begun 1458), he based his design on an arrangement of geometric shapes like squares and circles, which he considered the most perfect forms. The whole facade fits inside a square of equal height and width, and the lower level is composed of two squares that are one-quarter the size of the large square. The upper story is the same size as the lower, and an upper central square is another quadrant of the whole. Volute-scrolls connect the upper nave to the lower side aisles, so the exterior of the church indicates interior form. Math and geometry determine everything.

With his design for the exterior and interior of San Andrea (1470), Alberti pushed Renaissance architecture away from the delicate lines of Brunelleschi's buildings into the strong, sculptural force of ancient Rome. In this church, Alberti created the first model for future Renaissance churches based on the triumphal arch and pagan temple. The facade has a large arch bordered by smaller arches (as in a tripartite triumphal arch). Its top is a temple portico consisting of pilasters and pediment. The interior, with its barrel-vaulted nave, has the heroic scale and flowing unity of the Basilica of Maxentius. Consciously imitating Roman models, Alberti replaced aisles with chapels similar to the side rooms in Roman baths.

Santa Maria Novella, Florence, facade by Alberti, begun 1458
Alberti's design for the facade was based on his conception of the most perfect forms—squares and circles. The lower level recalls a triumphal arch and the upper level a pedimented temple.

S. Andrea, nave, Mantua, by Alberti, designed 1470
The prototypes for Alberti's design were Roman buildings like the Basilica of Constantine and Baths of Diocletian. The barrel vault spanned 56 feet—the largest and heaviest since ancient Rome. This Latin cross plan was widely imitated in the sixteenth century. Side chapels opening off the nave recall how Roman baths combined areas of different scales.

HOW TO JUDGE ARCHITECTURE: CLUMSY VS. ELEGANT DESIGN

Palazzo Medici, by Michelozzo Michelozzi, Florence, c. 1430

Palazzo Ducale, by Luciano Laurana, Urbino, designed before 1468

When Cosimo de' Medici chose Brunelleschi's rival, Michelozzo Michelozzi (1396–1472), to design his palace, he got a journeyman architect instead of a genius. Although the exterior sets the standard of symmetry and mathematical proportion for a typical Renaissance palazzo, the interior courtyard is awkwardly designed. The problem occurs at the right-angle corners. Two arches meet on a single column, which creates a weak anchor to terminate two sides of the arcade. Over the arches, Michelozzi used rounded windows, following the Renaissance style of stacking voids over voids (and solid over solid). A resultant flaw is that windows at each corner are spaced more closely together than in the middle of the walls, upsetting symmetrical distribution. The roundels below the window centers are also crammed together too closely. The courtyard at Urbino offers a solution. An L-shaped pier at each corner holds engaged columns to carry the arcade arches. The pier is faced with pilasters meeting at the angle to close the end of the wall with a visually strong element. Windows on the second level are centered over arches without crowding at the angles, separated by pilasters over the ground floor columns.

Palazzo Rucellai, Florence, by Alberti, c. 1452–60
Alberti planned this facade as an exercise in regularity, with windows on a single level placed in the center of each bay defined by pilasters. Another feature that became standard in urban, multistory dwellings was an enormous classical cornice, in proportion to the bulk of the building, which hides the roof. As in Roman architecture, classical elements like pilasters provide no support for the entablature but are strictly aesthetic adornment.

PALATIAL HOMES. Federigo da Montefeltro, the Duke of Urbino, embodied Renaissance humanism. When he transformed his home from a medieval fortress to a Renaissance palace—the Palazzo Ducale (1460s)—Italy cast off its Middle Ages mentality for reborn gracious living. The switch from ecclesiastical architecture sponsored by the church to domestic buildings for private individuals marked another profound shift. Striving for happiness in the hereafter took a back seat to pleasure here and now.

Not to be left out, Alberti was Gianni-on-the-spot with the trend toward palazzo design. His early Palazzo Rucellai (1452–60), for a rich Florentine merchant family, derives from the Colosseum, with three superimposed orders of pilasters on successive floors. A Tuscan version of the substantial Doric order establishes a strong base, rising to Alberti's reinvention of Ionic in the middle and Corinthian at the top.

As formidable as palaces appeared from the outside (this was, after all, still an age of violence), they were sumptuous and relaxed on the interior. Built around a central inner court surrounded by arched arcades, rooms were open to breezes and light. Service areas or shops were on the ground floor, the family living area on the next level (called the *piano nobile*), and servants' quarters in the attic. Generally, the exterior of the ground floor was made of rusticated stone (blocks worked to resemble rough stones straight from the quarry). The rugged texture on the basement, contrasted to the smooth stonework of the *piano nobile,* reinforced the impression of impregnable solidity. This palazzo mode became the basic form of urban blocks throughout Europe.

HIGH RENAISSANCE: ROME

BRAMANTE. After 1500, Rome edged out Florence as the center of innovation in architecture. After successive invasions, the city had grown shabby. Cowherds and goats roamed the streets, and one writer compared it to a moldering corpse. Rome's revival was due mainly to the impetus of Julius II, the warrior-pope who restored the city's glory. To spruce up the Vatican, Julius hired three stars of the High Renaissance—Bramante, Raphael, and Michelangelo.

Like most Renaissance architects, Bramante had been trained as an artist. He studied painting with Piero della Francesca and Mantegna and was a friend of Leonardo. In his earliest building, S. Satiro in Milan, Bramante's skills as a painter came in handy. Because of site restrictions, the church lacked an east end choir. Undeterred, Bramante created a trompe l'oeil version of a choir at the back of the church. His low-relief painted "choir" includes convincing coffered vaulting, pilasters, and entablature.

Bramante came to Rome in 1499 and spent the rest of his career there. He hit the ground running with the Tempietto (the name means "little temple"), which is hailed as the epitome of the High Renaissance. This tiny (15 feet in diameter) circular monument marks the site of St. Peter's crucifixion (hanging upside down, as he requested, so as not to be compared to Christ) and was commissioned by Ferdinand and Isabella of Spain. Constructed in concentric circles, the Tempietto is modeled on the Roman temple of Vesta at Tivoli. Its peristyle of Doric columns surrounding a cylindrical cella has the simplicity and strict symmetry of Greek prototypes. The height of the temple to the base of its dome equals its width, showing the Renaissance love of simple mathematical ratios to create harmonious proportions.

Bramante had spent many an hour swarming over Roman ruins, yet he used antiquity not as a stencil but a point of departure. In the early Renaissance, borrowing from Roman models sometimes produced buildings of more archeological interest than coherence. Bramante's individual interpretation shows how the High Renaissance melded rules into personal style. The Tempietto's mini-dome became the model for celebrated domes from St. Peter's to St. Paul's and the Capitol in Washington, D.C.

Bramante's House of Raphael in Rome (designed by Bramante about 1512, but lived in by Raphael) had a similar widespread influence. A masterpiece of symmetry, the building had the first residential facade with paired Doric engaged columns to create rhythm, ornament, and sculptural interest. It became the ideal form for urban palazzos for two centuries.

Tempietto, San Pietro in Montorio, Rome, by Bramante, 1502
Bramante's High Renaissance masterpiece echoes classical temples with its Doric peristyle and steps surrounding a cylinder.

The Renaissance Artiste

In the Middle Ages, the architect was a master mason with callused hands. In the Renaissance he was an artist-scholar, unlikely to heft anything heavier than a quill. Alberti promoted the idea of architecture as a noble profession for a humanist and emphasized intellectual endeavor, like geometry, math, philosophy, theory, and classical culture. The architect, as Alberti wrote, "ought to be a man of a fine genius . . . of the best education." For the first time, in addition to wooden scale models, builders produced intricate drawings of plan, elevation, and section so they did not have to be on site to supervise construction. Most were trained in painting or sculpture rather than the building trade.

As the architect's pretensions rose, so did his status. A French mason told the story in 1585 of how Latin terms were bandied about with more ostentation than comprehension. On one building site, the visiting mason was "dumbfounded" when craftsmen talked of pedestals, obelisks, columns, capitals, friezes, "none of which he had ever heard of in his life." When it was his turn to speak, the unlettered artisan recommended building with "an adequate palison," and with "the equipolation of his heteroclites." His listeners "were amazed by him (they had no idea what he was talking about)" and "all those present deemed him a great man [who] must know a thing or two."

Villa Madama, Rome, by Raphael, begun 1517
Raphael embraced the inflated scale that marks the High Renaissance. He attempted to recapture the grandeur of Roman baths and based the bold decoration on Nero's Golden House.

Palazzo del Tè: Mannerist Manifesto

Giulio Romano (1492–1546) pushed Mannerism to extremes. In the country villa, Pallazo del Tè (begun 1524), he deliberately violated all rules. Each facade is different, marked by eccentric use of classical motifs. The design is intentionally asymmetrical, with columns and arches in an irregular rhythm. Inside, the feeling of insecurity is reinforced by a ceiling fresco showing a battle between giants and gods. Blocks of stone, rocks, and collapsing columns seem to crash down on spectators' heads. On touring the room, Vasari noted, a visitor "cannot but fear that everything will fall upon him."

RAPHAEL: THE SUBURBAN VILLA.

In the last six years of his life, the painter who embodied the High Renaissance took up architecture. Raphael designed three palaces, a chapel, and a villa. From the letters of Pliny, modern Romans got the idea that their forbears enjoyed escaping urban congestion for the simple country life. Although they had no idea what ancient Roman villas looked like, a stampede started among gentry to build a *villa suburbana.* Raphael's Villa Madama (begun about 1517) outside Rome was one of the most striking.

Modeled on the Golden House of Nero and the Baths of Titus, which had recently been uncovered, the design includes a wealth of niches, pilasters, and swags. Its rich decor is most evident in the ornate painted stucco in the vaults of the loggia. Various half-domed apses recall the layout of thermal baths.

These country villas were far from rustic. Raphael's design encompassed terraced gardens, a theater for *spettacoli,* a circular courtyard, and a monumental triple-bayed loggia. The groin-vaulted spaces and soaring domed vault have the epic scale of imperial architecture.

RENAISSANCE ARCHITECTURE

WHEN: 1420–1600

WHERE: Florence, Rome, Venice, western Europe

BIG NAMES: Brunelleschi, Alberti, Bramante, Raphael, Michelangelo, Romano, Palladio, Jones

INSPIRATION: Roman antiquity

MOOD: Calm, harmony, equilibrium

TRAITS: Round arch, columns, barrel vaults

PREFERRED PLAN: Portico with columns supporting pediment, rotunda covered by dome

ESSENTIAL ATTRIBUTES: Regularity, symmetry, proportion

BUILDING TYPES: Churches, urban palaces, châteaux, country villas, public squares

LATE RENAISSANCE

MICHELANGELO AND MANNERISM. In the Early Renaissance, architects rediscovered the rules of Roman design. In the High Renaissance, they achieved heroic scale, as in the rebuilt Basilica of St. Peter's in Rome. Then a reaction set in against official correctness. Michelangelo (1475–1564) was one of the first to play with the antique style, giving his designs a twist of subversion.

Mannerism was a protest against what was perceived as the sterile rationalism and fuddy-duddy propriety of classicism. Mannerist rebels bent, cracked, and almost broke the rule-driven mentality. Their designs were whimsical, complex, full of surprises and contradictions. To classicists, regular rhythm was God. To a mannerist, the off-beat was divine.

Michelangelo, who always insisted he was a sculptor, proved equally adept at architecture. He treated a building or an ensemble of buildings as a mass of sculptural solids and voids to be shaped. This feel for volume and space vitalizes his architecture. Michelangelo seemed to squeeze blood from stone by bringing marble to life. His architecture transformed buildings into a network of interlocking force fields.

In the Medici Chapel in San Lorenzo, Florence, Michelangelo quoted the classical vocabulary only to blaspheme it. He rejected the usual orders, designed blank windows that taper rather than inscribe perfect rectangles, omitted capitals from pilasters, and generally flouted all sacred prescriptions.

Walls were not flat planes for Michelangelo but part of a vital organism. The Laurentian Library (designed 1524) throws the Renaissance ideals of balanced proportion and stability out the window, setting the interior in disquieting motion. Michelangelo tucked columns, like statues, into niches, but—against all visual and intuitive evidence—they carry the weight of the roof.

His huge triple staircase perversely occupies most of the space in the room. At the bottom, it fans out like a cascade. Such defiance of tradition made Vasari describe Michelangelo as having "made such bizarre breaks in the outlines of the steps, and departed so much from the common use of others, that everyone was amazed." His

Vestibule, Laurentian Library, Florence, by Michelangelo, designed 1524
Michelangelo treated the entire interior as a piece of sculpture, energizing walls and stairs into a dynamic composition. His distortion of classical motifs inspired Mannerism.

Campidoglio (Capitoline Hill), Rome, by Michelangelo, designed c. 1537
Michelangelo was commissioned to restructure this area as a symbol of the New Rome. He sculpted voids and solids into a total environment, unified by an oval pattern in the center of the square.

Villa Rotonda (Villa Capra), Vicenza, by Palladio, begun c. 1560
Inspired by the Pantheon (which was then called Rotonda), this villa is a study in symmetry. Eighteen villas by Palladio survive in northern Italy.

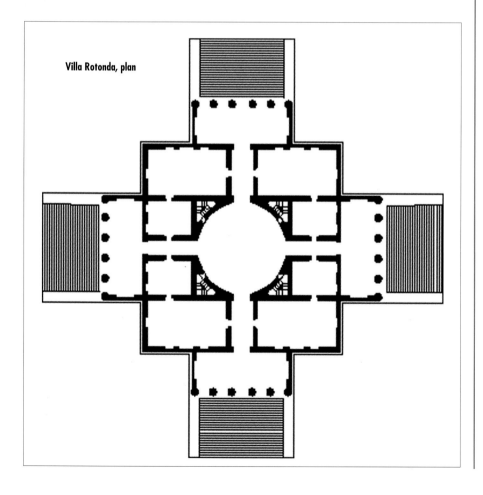

Villa Rotonda, plan

compositions were dynamic, utterly idiosyncratic.

Michelangelo's redesign of the Campidoglio Piazza in Rome is a triumph of organic composition. This square on the Capitoline Hill near the Roman forum, where Romulus allegedly founded the city, was down-at-the-heels and dowdy. Michelangelo created an imposing public center, in which every element interacts. He inscribed the central space surrounding an ancient statue of Emperor Marcus Aurelius with an oval design on the pavement, which looks from above like a dome. He designed imposing staircases and new facades for two extant buildings and added another building to create a trapezoidal space. On the facing buildings, he first used the giant order (45-foot-high Corinthian pilasters that spread over two stories) to imply a single, monumental unity.

Michelangelo took up architecture when past the age of seventy, proving it's not just a young person's sport. Perhaps because he was a mature artist, he "broke the bonds and chains of usage," as Vasari wrote. Michelangelo's shaping of a total environment, with sight lines and processional paths energized by imaginative design, reconceived the idea of a public square, around which cities were to be organized. His powerful architecture was a forerunner of Baroque drama.

PALLADIO: SUPREME SYMMETRY. The most widely copied architect ever, Andrea Palladio (1508–1580) was one of the rare Renaissance architects who actually trained in the building trade, as a stonemason. Yet at the first opportunity, he trekked off to Rome to measure ruins and study math, music, and Latin.

The means for obtaining a classical education were provided by his mentor, the poet-philosopher Trissino, who dubbed Palladio his protégé and molded the bricklayer into a humanist scholar. A quick learner, Palladio became the most rabid Roman of them all. His *Four Books of Architecture* (1570), which even Thomas Jefferson and George Washington owned, established his designs as universal prototypes throughout Europe and the Americas.

Palladio is best known for the country villas he designed, almost all near the northern Italian city of Vicenza. Here he practiced his theory that buildings should extend symmetrically around a central axis and that each room should relate to others in simple mathematical ratios. Under the mistaken impression that ancient temples derived from domestic dwellings, Palladio tacked Roman temple fronts on his villas, thinking he was duplicating antique villa designs.

His masterpiece is the Villa Rotonda. Identical temple porticos face all four sides of the building. The principal room is in the center, lit by an overhead dome (the first Renaissance dome as a dominant visual feature on a private residence). Located at the top of a hill with views from all rooms, the villa shows the new Renaissance concern for landscape as a valuable amenity. With his passion for symmetry and clarity, Palladio designed each room in proportion to the next, with the two halves exact mirror duplicates.

Palladian style was influential for two centuries. Throughout Georgian England, Palladian villas popped up, with at least four copies of the Villa Rotonda built in the eighteenth century. The poet Alexander Pope decried this Italian fashion, so unsuitable to the harsher British climate. English aristocrats, he wrote, were "proud to catch cold at a Venetian door." Jefferson's Monticello is an adaptation of a Palladian villa.

Meanwhile, Venice was hardly exempt from the wholesale Roman-cizing going on throughout Italy. *La Serenissima Repubblica* (the most serene republic) entered whole hog into the classic orgy, erecting new buildings and refacing existing buildings on Saint Mark's Square with antique trappings. So sumptuous had the city become, Henry III said wistfully in 1574, "If I were not king of France, I would choose to be a citizen of Venice."

Il Redentore (the Redeemer), Venice, by Palladio, begun 1577
Palladio faced the problem plaguing all Renaissance architects of basilica-style churches: how to create an impressive facade covering the juncture of two levels: high nave and lower side aisles. His original solution? Nesting porticos. Palladio wanted the dignity of a classical temple front, but he also wanted the facade to reflect the interior, so he interlaced separate pediments. The central pediment matches the height of the nave and builds up the composition toward the climactic dome. Another lateral pediment, stretched across the width of the church, actually braces the nave walls and covers side aisles.

Château de Chambord, France, by Domenico da Cortona, 1519–47
Located amid a vast forest, the château is a masterpiece of the French Renaissance, fusing medieval forms with classical Italian style.

Galerie François I, Fontainebleau, France, decorated by Rosso and Primaticcio, exterior facade by Gilles le Breton, 1530s
From the twelfth century, Fontainebleau was a hunting lodge for French kings. François I enlarged and embellished it in the sixteenth century to make his château a "new Rome."

THE RENAISSANCE IN FRANCE

Outside Italy, Renaissance style consisted of pasting classical references on medieval structures. Columns, pilasters, and niches were overlaid like a veneer of sophistication on native forms. Architects got their ideas on classicism from widely circulating pattern books, like the popular book of designs by Wendel Dietterlin published in 1593. Dietterlin, a German who was said to be demented, drew writhing fantasies that rival the phantasmagoric paintings of Hieronymus Bosch. When his motifs were plastered on a castle exterior, the result was a riot of intricate ornament (known generically in seventeenth- and eighteenth-century England as "ditterling" ornament).

In France the Renaissance was ushered in by a remarkable king, François I, who was enamored of *la mode italienne* and determined to adopt it. He imported Italian architects and artists like Leonardo and Benvenuto Cellini to gussy up his kingdom. The king's hunting lodge, Chambord (1519–47), was built by Domenico da Cortona in a strictly symmetrical layout. Basically a square inside a rectangular enclosure, the château's ground floor arcade echoes Renaissance rhythms. Its fanciful double-helix staircase, in which two ramps intertwine without meeting, may have been inspired by Leonardo's design.

Chambord, one of many extravagant châteaux in the Loire Valley, is medieval in its steeply pitched roof, towers, and turrets. More than 1,000 projecting chimneys, finials, and pinnacles on the roof are the antithesis of Renaissance serenity. With 440 rooms, its palatial scale rivals anything constructed by ancient Romans.

François, who became king at twenty-one, was a typical Renaissance prince in his lusty pursuit of living, loving, and learning. His cultivated court was awash with beautiful women to please his eye. "A court without beautiful women is like a year without spring and a spring without roses," the king was wont to proclaim. These châteaux, or *demeures de plaisance* (abodes of joy), reflect the French Renaissance stress on sensual delight.

The king's château near Paris, Fontainebleau, was his favorite—where he was, as he said, "chez moi" (at home). Baths fit for an emperor were a primary feature. A half dozen chambers with hot-water pools or hot-air rooms were hung with paintings by Leonardo, Raphael, or Andrea del Sarto. The king imported two Italian painters, Giovanni Rosso and Francesco Primaticcio, to decorate a dazzling gallery hall (1528–40) with elaborately carved stucco and paintings, thereby inventing the stylized Fontainebleau style.

Classicism was purer in the square court of the Louvre (begun 1546) that François ordered Pierre Lescot to design as his city palace. While most ambitious French buildings were still a pastiche of medieval and classical elements, the Louvre's understated simplicity established unalloyed classicism in France.

Escorial: The Reign in Spain

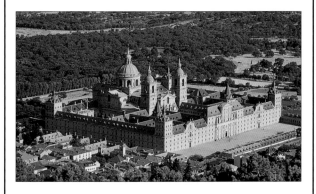

Renaissance austerity did not mesh well with ornate Spanish tradition. But when the monkish Philip II built a palace outside Madrid, he demanded "simplicity of form, severity in the whole, nobility without arrogance, majesty without ostentation."

The word *Escorial* (1563–84) means "slag heap." Its site was once a dumping ground for iron slag, and its appearance is just as forbidding as the name. The king who wanted to reestablish Catholicism through the Inquisition chose cold, gray granite and an *estilo desornamentado* (unornamented style) for his residence. And since he was hyperreligious, he made sure his compound included a monastery, seminary, mausoleum, and church. Four thousand rooms and 100 miles of corridors make the Escorial the largest building in the world. Its collection of 7,000 encased martyrs' bones is the largest anywhere.

The Escorial is dedicated to St. Lawrence, a martyr roasted alive on an open grill. Its plan is in the shape of a grill—an enormous retangle with a projecting central rectangle on one facade to resemble a gridiron. An iron grill, carved in stone or worked in metal, is a grisly design motif repeated throughout the complex.

From the outside, the royal residence looks like a prison. With his ascetic tastes, Philip wanted no frills. Unadorned except for Doric details, the ensemble includes 15 cloisters, 300 monks' cells, 88 fountains, and 43 altars. Philip, who preferred his hermit's cell to the pomp of court, described the Escorial as "un palacio para Dios, y una choza para mi" (a palace for God and a shanty for me).

ENGLAND AND INIGO JONES

The man who introduced Renaissance architecture to England began in show business. Inigo Jones (1573–1652) designed costumes and stage sets for masques, the forerunner of musical theater so beloved by Elizabethan aristocrats. He achieved even more prominence when he turned to architecture.

Half-timbered Tudor architecture, which preceded Jones's introduction of classical style, was mostly a matter of "sticks and dirt," as one foreign visitor described the houses of London. "No war, no waste, no Rome" was the motto of Reformation England, but Jones's elegant designs as Surveyor of the King's Works won the country over to the glories of Roman architecture (if not the Roman church).

Jones gained his faith through travels in Italy, the architectural Holy Land. He studied Roman antiquities, inhaled Vitruvius and—above all—Palladio to develop his own doctrine of geometry, proportion, and correct classical ornament. Although not many of his buildings remain, several novel structures reveal the extent to which he departed from embroidered Jacobean style.

The Banqueting House, an addition to the royal palace at Whitehall, London (1619–22), is the extreme of simplicity. Although the exterior indicates a two-level elevation, the interior is one giant room, arresting in its volume. Built for state banquets and revelry, the single room is a double cube 110 x 55 x 55 feet. Engaged Ionic and Corinthian columns on the exterior, topped by a garland of foliage and masks, meet Jones's criteria that "outward ornaments ought to be solid, proportionable according to the rules, masculine and unaffected."

Palladio was Jones's idol—Jones even practiced writing his signature like Palladio's. Jones's buildings have the bright interiors and horizontal, elegant lines of the master. The Banqueting House is not an undigested imitation but a thorough assimilation of classicism—almost more Palladian than Palladio. James I, the king whom Jones served, proclaimed, "We have found our cities and suburbs of London of sticks, and left them of brick"—a transformation due in some measure to Jones's influence.

Another structure by Jones is the Queen's House in Greenwich (begun 1616), notable for its stark symmetry. Jones and his disciple, John Webb, were responsible for a double-cube room at Wilton House (about 1649). Walls decorated in white and gold, a pedimented mantel, and portraits by Anthony Van Dyck establish a mood of luxury. With the eighteenth-century Palladian revival and rage for Neoclassic architecture, Jones became a dominant force in English domestic architecture for a century. Although England got off to a slow start, it kept the neo-Roman style going long after other countries had dropped it for dynamic Baroque architecture.

Banqueting House, Whitehall, London, by Inigo Jones, 1619–22
Jones introduced Palladian classicism to England. His original interpretation of a town palace has a balanced, well-proportioned two-story facade of exceptional breadth. Alternating segmental (rounded) and triangular pediments, carved swags at the capital level, balustraded roof, and a finely rusticated stone base show Jones's attention to detail.

Double-cube Room, Wilton House, Wiltshire, by Inigo Jones, c. 1635-53
A richly decorated interior contrasting with a simple exterior characterizes Jones's work. The room features a cove ceiling, a mantel like a miniature temple portico, Van Dyck paintings, and elaborate plaster moldings.

BAROQUE ARCHITECTURE: TWIRLS AND SWIRLS

If cool was king in the Renaissance, the Baroque era was hot to trot. It's the difference between a calm game of chess and juggling daggers and torches while riding a unicycle playing a kazoo. Renaissance architecture was intellectual, based on geometry, logic, symmetry, and simplicity. Baroque style was populist, appealing to a wide audience through hyped-up emotion and multimedia special effects.

Both styles commandeered the columns, entablature, arches, and domes of Roman antiquity. Renaissance architects used them to emphasize stability and stasis, while Baroque masters like Bernini and Borromini twisted columns into corkscrews. They set classical elements in motion, breaking pediments to make lines swoop. While Renaissance facades tend to look flat, with shallow surface planes, Baroque exteriors seem fluid, weaving in and out like a broken-field runner. It's the difference between an ice cube and a waterfall.

GOING FOR BAROQUE. Baroque extravagance came about when Renaissance restraint started looking boringly mechanical. Another factor was that, after the Reformation, Protestant churches were stripped of furbelows, pared down to Calvinist purity. When the Catholic church made a comeback and launched an ambitious building program, it promoted the opposite of minimalism. Church officials enlisted all the drama of music, painting, sculpture, and over-the-top architecture to create a mystical atmosphere and enhance devotion. Deprivation was out; ostentation was in.

The word *Baroque* derives from the Portuguese *barocco*, an irregular pearl. Rather than a perfect sphere, the premier Baroque form was an oval—elliptical like the orbit of the planets that had just been sketched by astronomer Johann Kepler. Other scientific advances popping up at warp speed may have influenced the style. When Isaac Newton formulated his laws of motion, architects devised buildings with revved-up spaces that seemed to move. Curved walls undulate; contours recede and project. And just as Galileo scanned the heavens with his telescope from the bell tower at Saint Mark's Square, frescoed ceiling vaults dissolved all earthly boundaries, seeming to stretch to infinity.

The vast scale, rich materials, dramatic lighting, and heavy ornamentation of Baroque buildings had a propagandistic goal. Seventeenth-century architecture gave visual form to the power of church and monarch, who ruled by divine right. "Un roi, une foi, une loi" (one king, one faith, one law) was the rule. In no uncertain terms, royal palaces and equally splendid churches proclaimed, "We're number one."

Baldacchino, St. Peter's, Rome, by Bernini, 1624–33
A colossal canopy (nearly ten stories tall) made of bronze and marble, the baldachin marks the burial site of St. Peter. Bernini planned it to be illuminated by golden light from the Cathedra Petri to heighten its emotional impact.

BERNINI: ARCHITECTURE AS THEATER.

Although Baroque architecture was to spread all over Europe, it was born in Rome and its founding father was Gianlorenzo Bernini (1598–1680). This precocious sculptor was selling his work at age sixteen to the Borghese family. By twenty, Bernini was so famous, the pope commissioned him to sculpt a papal portrait. Not content to excel in the plastic arts, Bernini was the greatest scene designer of the age. When he created a stage set, the illusion was so convincing, people in the front row fled in terror, convinced they would be drenched by flood or scorched by fire.

Bursting with talent doesn't begin to describe Bernini's abilities, for he was also an esteemed painter, poet, and composer. An English visitor recalled attending an opera in 1644 where Bernini "painted the scenes, cut the statues, invented the engines, composed the music, wrote the comedy and built the theater." If they had had popcorn, Bernini would have popped and buttered it.

In 1623, Bernini began his career as an architect. For the next fifty years, his fingerprints were all over Rome. His vision, skill, personality, and art shaped the grandeur, flamboyance, and emotionalism of Counter-Reformation Vatican City, and of the Baroque era in general.

PIAZZA SAN PIETRO: ARMS AND THE MAN.

The best example of Bernini's larger-than-life work is the piazza outside St. Peter's Basilica. Bernini conceived the piazza (1656–67) as an enormous oval framed by two colonnades of 284 columns and 88 pillars in four rows. Topped by an entablature with 140 statues of saints, the curved colonnades embrace a 650-foot-long oval like "the motherly arms of the church," as Bernini said.

Although composed of miscellaneous elements, the composition coalesces around a central obelisk originally brought to Rome by Caligula (it served as a turning point in Nero's Circus Maximus). Paving stones between two fountains and the obelisk indicate viewing points from which each wing of the colonnade seems to have only one row of columns rather than four abreast. Out of the vast scale and variety of elements, Bernini created a unified effect for visitors' first glimpse of St. Peter's.

Palazzo Carignano, Turin, by Guarino Guarini, 1679–92
The active, high-relief surface, play of light and shadow, and dynamic curves make this palace a masterpiece of true Baroque style.

Piazza San Pietro, Rome, by Bernini, 1656–67
Bernini's curving colonnades, which set the stage for St. Peter's, symbolically embrace pilgrims like maternal arms. The obelisk provides a central exclamation point and links the post-Reformation church to past glories.

San Carlo alle Quattro Fontane, Rome, by Borromini, 1665–67
Borromini eliminated the corner in architecture. He scooped gouges out of stone, as in the upper story with its concave bay and sectioned entablature. In the central oval medallion that swings forward, he made lines seem to bulge. On the lower level, a convex central bay with a continuous entablature swings back into two concave bays.

BALDACCHINO. Inside the basilica, Bernini's influence is pervasive. In its splendor, size, and exuberant form, Bernini's baldacchino (1624–33) over the high altar is the quintessence of Baroque spirit. A 95-foot-tall canopy of gilt-bronze and multicolored marble, with twisted columns writhing toward the towering dome, the structure is covered with carved vines and bees and crowned by angels. Its glitz and sense of movement have an overwhelming impact, while anchoring the visitor's eye in a dramatic focal point.

Bernini planned the visual vista through the church interior to culminate in the Cathedra Petri (1657–66), a sculptural and architectural tour-de-force intended to be viewed through the baldacchino's columns. The bronze throne encloses an ancient wooden chair used by St. Peter, and is an explosion of cherubs, gilded sunbeams, and billowing stucco clouds. An amber glass window irradiates both throne and baldacchino. This scenographic display of carefully calibrated, trompe l'oeil effects is typical of the Baroque style Bernini invented.

The most revered architect of his age, Bernini also designed famous fountains and buildings, like Sant'Andrea al Quirinale (1658–70) in Rome, an oval church of great dignity and originality. "It is our fortune," said Pope Urban VIII, "that master Bernini lives in our pontificate."

BORROMINI: ANIMATED ARCHITECTURE.

While Bernini's buildings have multiple voices like opera, the works of his rival Borromini have syncopated rhythms like ragtime. Francesco Borromini (1599–1667) was always out of step with the marching band. Compared to the suave, charming Bernini, Borromini was brooding, solitary, and gloomy, if not downright neurotic. An eccentric bachelor who committed suicide, Borromini was considered demented after his death. Bernini condemned his buildings as "chimerical," saying Borromini was "sent to destroy architecture."

Such an extreme reaction derives from the revolutionary nature of Borromini's work, which paid scant heed to convention. The son of a mason who worked in Rome first as a stone-carver at St. Peter's, then as Bernini's chief assistant, Borromini set off on his own path as soon as he won independent commissions.

A perfectionist whose personal style differed radically from any other, Borromini was nevertheless appreciated by church officials who hired him to design San Carlo in Rome. They praised its "caprice, excellence, and singularity," noting that the "spectator is stimulated to let his eye wander about ceaselessly."

Curtain Up

The most complete scene-stealer Bernini created was the Cornaro Chapel. At center stage is Bernini's marble sculpture of Saint Theresa, pierced by an angel's dart. The statue inhabits a miniature theater, or *aedicule,* with a broken pediment that curves forward. Saint Theresa is spotlighted by a hidden window behind the pediment, and this flood of light seems to extend heavenward on carved, gilded rays. A fresco in the vault includes high-relief, stuccoed clouds and angels. Bernini even carved marble relief figures of an audience in "box seats" on the chapel's side walls and set framing columns at oblique angles to improve sight lines. This *tableau vivant* epitomizes Bernini's mastery of scenic effect, optical illusions, concealed lighting, and manipulated perspectives. Its fusion of painting, sculpture, stagecraft, and architecture provided a prototype for sensational Baroque style.

Cornaro Chapel, Santa Maria della Vittoria, Rome, by Bernini, 1646–52

San Carlo, interior (1638–41), by Borromini
Borromini twisted wall planes to invent new forms. He is known for intricate geometry, fluid spaces, and radiant interiors.

Dome, San Carlo, by Borromini
Borromini's trademark plasticity is evident in the irregular contours of the dome. The various shapes of coffering decrease in size toward the lantern for an effect of increased height.

IT DON'T MEAN A THING IF IT AIN'T GOT THAT SWING. San Carlo alle Quattro Fontane is usually called San Carlino because of its small size. The design uses classical elements but handles them as if they were extruded clay. Individual members flow in a plastic whole based on a rough oval plan. An undulating cornice ripples under the dome, which is coffered like a honeycomb. The facade (1665–67) has a similarly sculpted effect. Concave and convex segments billow in and out.

At S. Ivo della Sapienza Borromini also molded mass and space as if carving solids and voids. Its complex plan is a six-pointed star around a hexagon. A curving cornice supports the base of the dome. The dome itself is a faceted, six-lobed, startlingly novel form—like no shape known to Renaissance eyes. (See page 54.) Borromini's fantasy style reached its peak in an eclectic lantern shaped like a spiraling ziggurat.

ELSEWHERE IN ITALY. Turin is a stronghold of Baroque monuments. Guarino Guarini (1624–1683) designed an intricate dome at the Church of San Lorenzo (1668–87), in which intersecting ribs form a network of volume and void. His Cappella della SS. Sindone (1667–90), built to house the Shroud of Turin, also has a dome with exciting spatial play. Stacked, flattened arches diminish in span, crisscrossing like an inverted nest. Also in Turin, Filippo Juvarra (1678–1736) designed both palaces and churches like the Superga (1715–31), in which he merged academic Classicism with Rococo flair.

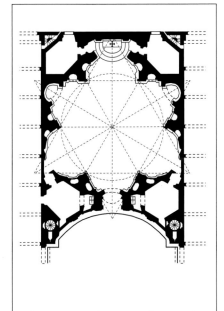

Plan, S. Ivo, Rome, by Borromini, begun 1642
This inventive plan shows the rhythmic Baroque plasticity pioneered by Borromini. (See page 54 for view of dome interior.)

BAROQUE CLASSICISM: FRANCE

Baroque architecture took two main forms: (1) the theatrical style of spatial flow pioneered in Italy, which later spread to Austria and Germany; and (2) the severe, Classical style, heroic in scale and opulence, found in France and England. While Baroque forms in Italy and its offshoots were complex, florid, highly decorated, and fraught with emotional appeal, French and English Baroque buildings were restrained in everything except spectacular size and effect.

The seventeenth century, known as *le grand siècle* (the great century), is France's century, since it was then France came to the fore in art, power, and wealth. It was a golden age of culture, during which academies for the arts of literature, painting, sculpture, and architecture were founded, based on rules to uphold the glories of *la belle France.* Arrogance and might were the qualities projected by French Baroque architecture. Borrowed Italian forms reinforced an absolutist political agenda. Buildings were more disciplined and two-dimensional than sculptural, very *comme il faut* in the grand manner.

The Louvre represents the ideal metropolitan palace. Its formality and dignity are unassailable, although some fault its facade with monotony and overweening grandeur. Its majestic dimensions, regular rhythm, and paucity of ornament give it an air of design-by-committee, lacking a strong sense of personality but expressive of authoritarian power. Claude Perrault (1613–1688) and

Garden front, Versailles, Seine-et-Oise, France, by Le Vau and Hardouin-Mansart, 1669–85
"The symmetry, always the symmetry," complained Louis XIV's mistress Madame de Maintenon. Over a quarter of a mile long, the facade of Versailles has imposing length and mass. Its straight lines and paired columns lend strength and stability.

Louis Le Vau (1612–1670) designed the eastern facade, with its unrelenting rectilinearity, tall base, and flat roof broken only by a central pediment.

With a population of twenty million, France was the largest nation in Europe, and architecture was state business, run by civil servants. The Academy of Architecture institutionalized taste, formulating conventions "which could be followed by all operators." The result was an official style, intended to convey permanence and incite envy.

VERSAILLES: THE SUN KING SHINES.

Louis XIII began construction of Versailles in 1623 as a *petit rendez-vous de chasse* (hunting lodge). His son, Louis XIV, made it into the grandest château of all. Its raw material was inauspicious. The duc de Saint-Simon called the property "the saddest and most barren of all places, with no view, no water, and no woods" before its embellishments from 1661 to 1710. The site was poorly drained, its mud "black and stinking with a stench so penetrating that you can smell it for several leagues around."

Shear Inspiration

Le Nôtre drained and leveled the land, designing vistas, groves, the canal, pools, and geometric flower beds. The formal gardens of the Petit Parc alone cover 185 acres, with the Grand Parc extending to the horizon. The rigorous scheme shows an absolute monarch's desire to regulate his realm absolutely.

Parterre du Midi, Versailles, by Le Nôtre, 1660s

Crème de la Crème

Baroque features of Versailles were its huge scale; rich materials; blending of painting, sculpture, and architecture; and monumental grandeur. The building impresses more by sheer size than refined details, but interiors were masterpieces. The Galerie des Glaces (Hall of Mirrors) includes a barrel-vaulted, painted ceiling arching over seventeen windows on the garden side. Opposite, seventeen mirrors are separated by marble pilasters with gilded bronze capitals. One visitor called it "an avenue of light." Lamps, planters, tables, and benches of solid silver, which Louis XIV melted down to finance one of many wars, originally furnished the 240-foot-long hall, one of the finest rooms in all Europe.

Galerie des Glaces, Versailles, by Hardouin-Mansart and Le Brun, c. 1678

Fortunately, Louis had the assistance of a brilliant team: the architect Le Vau, interior decorator Charles Le Brun, and the brilliant landscape designer André Le Nôtre. They transformed unpromising terrain into a marvel of order and proportion. In 1682, after successive enlargements, Louis made Versailles the hub of his court. In the palace's hundreds of rooms, 5,000 nobles lived, with thousands of others coming daily. (The entire court comprised 100,000.) The stables housed 12,000 horses and hundreds of carriages. The military staff and servants numbered 14,000, with an additional 30,000 townspeople in day jobs. Construction cost more than 100 million French pounds—so much that Louis ordered all official receipts burned.

As one English observer described Louis XIV, "If he was not the greatest king, he was the best actor of majesty that ever filled the throne." Versailles was his stage set. Renowned for its beauty and splendor and built on an unprecedented scale, the palace and gardens became the gold standard for royal residences. Its facade was a

quarter-mile long; paths in the five-square-mile park stretched farther than the eye could see. Gardens were preened to the max. All were a symbol of the king's total power over nation and nature.

GARDEN GALA. In his youth Louis danced in ballets, playing the role of the sun king, and everywhere at Versailles was his symbol: the sun god Apollo. Gardens radiate like sunbeams from the palace's midpoint. In the dead center of an axis that stretched for eight miles was the king's bedroom. The message of the iconography and layout of both château and gardens: the king is center of the world. And a rational world it was. Organized doesn't begin to describe Versailles.

André Le Nôtre was a supreme genius at landscape architecture. He leveled and drained the swampy land, constructing gardens *à la française,* laid out in rigidly geometric plots. The vast system of parterres (flower beds lined with clipped hedges), pools, canals, and radiating avenues extends

the symmetry of the building to nature. The precise design progresses in planned vistas to culminate in focal points like the Pool of Apollo. Diagonal axes diversify the scheme, leading to subunits like outdoor theaters. The ensemble was a backdrop for court ritual and spectacles like plays, concerts, and fireworks.

IT'S NOT EASY BEING GREEN. French gardens, in contrast to more natural-looking English landscapes, were called "gardens of intelligence," since they were strictly calculated. Just as sculptors chiseled marble statues to adorn the park, whole forests were pruned like topiary to frame outdoor hideaways. Tight formality near the building yielded to more informal sprawl at the edges, where the park merged with the countryside. The Grand Canal, more than one mile long, where a fleet of pleasure craft sailed, extended the eye to the horizon with no sense of closure. The scale of landscaping increased with distance so elements were perceptible from afar. Just as Louis's ambitions were

A Tale of One-upmanship

French finance minister Nicholas Fouquet spared no expense in building his country house, Vaux-le-Vicomte. He assembled the creative talent later responsible for Versailles: the decorator Le Brun, architect Le Vau, and landscape designer Le Nôtre. The unparalleled scale and unified design of house and gardens established the model for royal châteaux. Fountains continued the geometry of the ensemble, including one that spouted a dome of water, echoing the central dome of the château.

Fouquet made a big mistake. To show off his new abode, he invited Louis XIV to an opening gala. After dinner, a play by Molière was performed. A shell opened and a nymph emerged to deliver a prologue by La Fontaine, as music by Lully played. "Trees" came to life, "statues" walked. Lanterns on the cornice of the château made it seem on fire. Grottos were ablaze, and the walk toward the main canal gushed walls of water from one hundred jets. From the grass amphitheater, rockets launched fleur-de-lys. A whale steamed down the canal, spouting fireworks, as drums and trumpets simulated battle sounds. When the king turned toward the château, fireworks erupted from the dome, covering the whole garden with a canopy of flame.

Fouquet had his motto inscribed at Vaux: "How high will he not rise." Within three weeks, Louis cut him down, ordering a musketeer to arrest Fouquet for embezzlement. The king seized Vaux-le-Vicomte, transporting one thousand orange trees and countless statues to Versailles. While Fouquet spent the rest of his days in prison, Louis hired his design team to make Versailles the grandest showplace of all.

---

boundless, his state seemed infinite.

Built on a megalomaniacal scale, the château was huge enough to be prominent even in this gigantic setting. Unfortunately, its interior was subordinated to the impressive exterior, and rooms were said to be uncomfortable, dark, and cold as marble. The scent of countless orange trees in tubs could not mask the odor of sewage. Among the flower beds, the cloying smell of flowers was so overpowering, Saint-Simon recorded, "The gardens were admired and avoided."

A work force of 36,000 tended the gardens and renovations. Troops spent years erecting aqueducts to bring water from the Seine for Versailles's 1,400 fountains. The fountains served an aesthetic purpose. Their moving waters (shaped to simulate domes, obelisks, or pyramids) enlivened the taut symmetry of the composition. One drawback was that sufficient water could never be obtained. The *fontainier* (master of fountains) activated only fountains

within Louis's view as he approached. Even the king's power could not triumph totally over nature. His extravagance and isolation eventually brought about France's decline, and the sun set on Versailles with the French Revolution.

ROCOCO LIGHTENS UP. Dr. Samuel Johnson defined opera—the greatest art form of the Rococo period—as "an extravagant and irrational entertainment." Rococo interiors, too, were all about gaiety and smiles. In the last phase of French Baroque, a reaction set in against symmetrical interiors like Versailles's multicolored marble in stiff geometric patterns. After Louis XIV died in 1715, French nobility fled Versailles's stuffy formality. They reestablished themselves in Paris in townhouses of unsurpassed grace.

The word *Rococo* comes from a combination of *barocco* and *rocaille* (a term for the shell-encrusted grottos fashionable in gardens). It refers to the C and S curves, the shell and coral-like forms, and the organic, leafy

motifs of Rococo style. Beginning in Paris in the 1720s, by the mid-1700s Rococo had spread throughout Europe. It was characterized by white and pale pastel colors, lavishly accented with gilding. Light in color and light in feel, the wispy decor featured plaster flowers, shells, scrolls, clouds, and lacy tendrils. After sixty years of austere Classical clout, secular Rococo interiors were purely intended to delight. Discipline went to seed, and a jumble of seaweed, floral designs, and arabesques looped around walls and ceilings.

Germain Boffrand (1667–1754) was the greatest French Rococo architect. Although the exterior appearance of his buildings is simple, interiors are luxurious, with lines that dip and bob like minuet dancers. The Hôtel de Soubise (now Archives Nationales) with its Salon de la Princesse (1735–39) is the ultimate in Rococo revelry. Carved, gilded plaster work with large windows and mirrors create a blithe atmosphere.

Salon de la Princesse, Hôtel de Soubise, Paris, by Boffrand, 1735–39
All arts fuse in this oval room. A classical colonnade of windows and mirrors is overlaid with a cornice of fanciful designs.

ENGLISH BAROQUE: SOLID AND SEVERE

Lasting until the 1730s, the Baroque style in England was much less conspicuous than in France. Since England was on the path toward parliamentary democracy, it lacked an absolute monarch to glorify through bombastic architecture. Royal architects took pride in sober designs, shunning Versailles's pomposity. Kensington Palace, for instance—a modest country home more than a stately mansion—is more like Kensington House.

Grandeur was not completely alien to English soil. Sir John Vanbrugh (1664–1726) had a yen for display. A flamboyant swashbuckler, formerly an army captain, spy, and playwright of bawdy comedies, Vanbrugh had no formal training in architecture. Undeterred, he designed Blenheim Palace, one of the grandest piles in Britain. Built as a gift from the nation to the Duke of Marlborough after his victory over Louis XIV, Blenheim Palace was called by Voltaire "a great heap of stone, without charm or taste."

It consists of three huge parts —a kitchen court and stable court at either side of a main block—and a vast entrance court. Molded with copious ornament, the composition builds in scale with a pedimented portico at the center. Devising a theatrical approach, Vanbrugh narrowed the forecourt to funnel the eye toward the main entrance. Four corner towers boast fanciful lanterns, and the titanic scale of the whole is enlivened with picturesque details. Sculpted finials

Blenheim Palace, park facade, Oxfordshire, by Vanbrugh, 1705–24
Particularly English elements—weighty mass and spiky skyline—combine with Classical porticos and colonnades in this symmetrical design, a blend of Baroque and Renaissance styles. Blenheim's vast scale shows the theatrical flair of Vanbrugh, a wit who turned to architecture, without training, at age 35. (The writer Jonathan Swift mocked Vanbrugh's abrupt switch from playwright to architect: "Vanbrugh's genius without thought or lecture is widely turned to architecture.")

consist of the Duke's crown resting on a cannonball, which crushes the French fleur-de-lys. Vanbrugh bragged that he had a special feel for "the castle air."

Thomas Archer (1668–1743), James Gibbs (1662–1754), and Nicholas Hawksmoor (1661–1736) also mastered Baroque design, but the most prominent architect of the era was Sir Christopher Wren (1632–1723).

WREN: LONDON LEGACY. Just as Bernini did more than anyone to shape Rome, Wren left his mark on London during more than fifty years of building. A mathematician, professor of astronomy, scientist, and founder of the Royal Society, Wren was, according to Sir Isaac Newton, one of "the greatest Geometers of our times." Turning to architecture, Wren never forsook his love of numbers. "Mathematical Demonstrations," Wren wrote, "are the only Truths, that can sink into the mind of man, void of all uncertainty."

He used his knowledge of geometry to create balanced but inventive churches that are still the pride of the city.

Called "that miracle of a youth," at fifteen Wren was demonstrating anatomy at the College of Surgeons. As a young scientist, he invented a double telescope and a transparent beehive. At age thirty he took up architecture, traveling to France to soak up church and palace design and consulting books on building. He got the opportunity of a lifetime when the Great Fire of 1666 destroyed 80 percent of the old city of London, including eighty-seven churches and the Old St. Paul's Cathedral. Within six days, Wren had presented a plan for rebuilding the city. As Surveyor General, he designed fifty-two churches, including his masterpiece, St. Paul's, a synthesis of classical Renaissance forms and Baroque dynamism.

ST. PAUL'S: ENGINEERING MARVEL. Wren brought the dome to English architecture. The structural ingenuity

St. Paul's Cathedral, West facade, London, by Wren, 1675–1710
Wren's Classical dome dominates the exterior, framed by fluid Baroque towers. The interior is a mix of Classical restraint with Baroque spatial exuberance. Ever the mathematician, Wren stressed "the geometrical, which," he wrote, "is the most essential part of architecture." Wren is buried in St. Paul's. His inscription reads: "If you seek a monument, look around you."

HOW TO TELL THEM APART

RENAISSANCE	BAROQUE
Cool	Hot
Intellectual	Emotional
Simple, clear, uniform effect	Complex, mysterious, overwhelming
Flat, regular units repeated	Irregular surfaces zig and zag
Aim: to please eye, ennoble mind	Aim: to transport with sensual appeal

of St. Paul's huge dome required all his engineering genius. Its triple layers consist of a brick cone (to support the heavy lantern) between an inner, shallow cupola and a hemispherical, outer shell for maximum visibility. Around the drum under the dome, thirty-two buttress walls radiate to an elegant peristyle. (Wren detested the teeny balustrade that was added against his wishes to the dome, considering it mere frippery.)

Wren said his aim was to renovate St. Paul's nave "after a good Roman manner" and replace "the Gothick Rudeness of Ye old Design." A two-tier elevation runs all around St. Paul's, although the upper story is a false screen with blank windows, concealing buttresses to support the nave. From a distance, the church has a unified, massive appearance. The towers on the main facade are undeniably Baroque, reminiscent of Borromini's waving walls.

In designing churches to replace those lost in the blaze, Wren had to wedge new structures into confined sites. He had little scope for imagination in their exteriors, but his plans are varied and original. Wren's interiors are crystal clear, with huge windows to illuminate the main spaces, contrasting with dark wood pews. Determined to preserve the old skyline of London, he gave free rein to his invention in an extraordinary range of spires and steeples. Combining Gothic height with Classical elements, the designs add vitality to the cityscape even today. On St. Bride's steeple, tiers taper like stacked pagoda roofs.

In secular architecture, Wren specialized in an orderly layout and bright interiors. His Painted Hall (1698) of the Royal Naval College in Greenwich is one of the finest rooms in England. Its stunning ceiling fresco and heroic scale give it an impressive elegance.

AUSTRIA AND GERMANY: ROCOCO REIGNS

The confectionary style of French Rococo makes wedding cakes out of churches and palaces in Germany and Austria. Radiant interiors are frosted with gilded stucco ornament against a white background.

Most German Baroque buildings were erected in the Catholic south around 1710–50 after the devastating Thirty Years' War. Church builders in Bavaria were especially influenced by Rococo style, displaying the holistic blending of multiple arts, or *unisono,* that is Baroque's most salient trait. The Asam brothers, Cosmas Damian (1686–1739), a fresco painter, and sculptor Egid Quirin Asam (1692–1750), combined their talents in churches with melodramatic lighting, illusory spaces, and emotional pull. The altar of the Priory Church of the Assumption in Rohr includes a figure of the Virgin Mary actually hovering in air. Side-lit and supported by hidden iron bars, she levitates as if by a miracle.

The Zimmermann brothers, Dominikus and Johann, designed Rococo abbeys and pilgrimage churches like the famous Die Wies (1745–54) in Bavaria. A white and pink color scheme, delicate as porcelain, prevails in the jewel-box church.

The most Rococo of all was François Cuvilliés's Amalienburg Pavilion (1734–39) at Nymphenburg (see page 78). The former court dwarf and brilliant designer produced a circular room, 40 feet in diameter, that is lined with glass. Carved wood and silver filigree swoop around the walls with abandon. Stuccoed ornaments (carved by Johann Zimmermann) like harps, violins, butterflies, and birds lend a frothy appearance. With its cool blue background, the room has an airy delicacy that belies its purpose. The exterior of the pleasure pavilion's dome was a hunting stand for shooting pheasant.

FLUID AND FLORID. The greatest German Baroque master was Balthasar Neumann (1687–1753). An engineer by training, he designed the bishop's palace in Würzburg (c. 1735) that is Baroque to the hilt. Mounting the enormous staircase—going from dark, constricted space to radiant light—is almost an ascension. Flowing balustrades sweep up toward a ceiling fresco by Giambattista Tiepolo. Characters in the fresco, depicting "The Four Continents," spill out of the sky as if alive. Adding to the drama, the room's scale seems to increase in size and luminosity as one climbs. A curious achievement of Baroque design is that, although the structure of interiors was often concealed by sculptures, painting, stucco relief, and gilding, the viewer experiences open space and light, not mass.

Neumann's other masterpiece was a church known as Vierzehnheiligen.

Stair hall, Prince-Bishop's Residence, Würzburg, Germany, by Neumann, 1735
Crowned by Tiepolo's fresco, the ceremonial stairway is a progression from dark to light, constrained to unrestrained.

Hall of Mirrors (detail), Amalienburg Pavilion, near Munich, Germany, by Cuvilliés, 1734-39
Shall We Dance? Germany adopted the French aristocratic Rococo style, which changed Baroque from a manifesto of power to a declaration of pleasure. The Zimmermann brothers carved the stucco decoration, which dissolved the division between wall and ceiling. Stylized plant motifs replaced Classical detail.

The plan consists of contiguous ovals from floor to vault, with light pouring in through clear windows. Rococo decoration eddies through the space, creating a sense of movement.

From about 1690 to 1730, Austria produced its share of fantastic Baroque and Rococo edifices. Johann Fischer von Erlach (1656–1723) was a Classicist who combined restrained interior decoration with fantastic elements from antiquity. Outside the Pantheon-like portico of his Karlskirche (begun 1716) in Vienna stand twin towers, like nothing seen since Trajan's columns.

Lukas von Hildebrandt (1668–1745) was Baroque as Borromini. As court architect in Vienna, it was his job to match the glory of Versailles. With scenographic flair, he created a total environment of formal gardens, terraces, fountains, and lakes, clustered around the Lower (1714–15) and Upper (1720–24) Belvedere. A dramatic ceremonial staircase enhances the scenic effect. One can imagine Prince Eugene descending grandly to announce, "I'm ready for my closeup, Mr. De Mille."

Profusion, sensuality, and frolic are keynotes of German and Austrian Baroque. Baroque was complex and dynamic as the music of Bach or Haydn. Rococo was frothy as a comic opera by Mozart. Baroque gained verve in its transplantation to northern climes.

Baroque architecture stirred stone into curvaceous swirls. It took the utmost liberties possible with masonry construction. To push development further required new materials and the demand for new types of buildings that arose in the nineteenth century.

BAROQUE BASICS

WHEN: 1600–1750
WHERE: Italy, Spain, Germany, Austria, France, England
BIG NAMES: Bernini, Borromini, Wren, Vanbrugh, Le Vau, Neumann, Hildebrandt
STYLE: Massive, opulent, colorful
FEATURES: Broken contours, dramatic vistas, lavish ornament, dynamic effect
PATRONS: Absolute monarchs, Catholic church
DISTINGUISHING TRAIT: Plastic treatment of surfaces, fusion of architecture and sculpture
TRIUMPH: Creation of total environment for maximum emotional effect
ELEMENTS: Serpentine columns, irregular facades, oval plans
SUBUNIT: Rococo

Vive la différence!

A common element in Western Europe was the Classical language, but each country spoke with a different accent.

	RENAISSANCE	BAROQUE
ITALY	Florence: Early Renaissance, Static, orderly, harmonious, delicate, serene; Rome: High Renaissance, Epic scale, elaborate; Mannerism (tense, experimental)	Motion and emotion, synergy of arts, vast scale, dramatic lighting, rich materials
FRANCE	Classical overlay on châteaux	Severe Neoclassicism, stiff symmetry, then Rococo frivolity
ENGLAND	Palladian geometry in country homes	Large scale, orderly, decorative
SPAIN	Simple, severe, monumental	Excessive surface decoration
GERMANY, AUSTRIA	Gables, stubby columns inspired by Italy	Theatrical, pastel, gilded, Rococo churches and palaces with profuse ornament

Invented by Romans nearly 2,000 years ago, a dome is an amazing structure technologically. Made possible by the discovery of concrete, its structure is thin but stiff and strong, compared to the enormous girth spanned. A dome not only carries its own weight, it must also support the weight of wind and snow. These loads are channeled to the ground through curved vertical ribs, like a series of arches rotated in three dimensions around a common center. Horizontal courses prevent the spread of these ribs, like hoops of a barrel restraining the staves.

The precursor to modern sports domes that hold 80,000 people was the Pantheon. Its 143-foot internal span was not surpassed for 1,300 years, until the Duomo in Florence outstripped it by a yard in width. The Pantheon dome set the model for future structures that spread all over the Western world. Its dome varies from 2 feet thick at the top to 23 feet at its base. To lighten the load of the 5,000-ton dome, its composition changes from dense basalt at the bottom to lightweight pumice at the top. Coffers hollowed out of the surface further reduce its weight. A drum interlaced with arches and barrel vaults directs forces to the ground.

The Byzantine Hagia Sophia is another triumph of art and engineering. Pendentives provide the transition from a square plan to a circular support for the dome, which spans 107 feet.

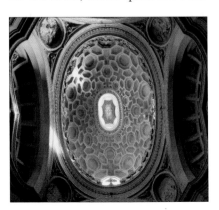

The Annotated Dome

Four great arches and corner piers support the dome, buttressed by barrel vaults and half domes. Forty ribs channel the weight of the dome, so that 40 windows can be set around its base, giving it the appearance of floating on a sea of light.

Francesco Borromini's Baroque masterpiece, the church of San Carlo, converted the round dome to an oval

Top to bottom: Pantheon, Rome, 120–27 C.E.; Hagia Sophia, Istanbul, by Anthemios of Tralles and Isidorus of Miletos, 532–37 C.E.; Inuit igloo; Left: S. Carlo alle Quattro Fontane, Rome, by Borromini, 1638–41; Right: Millennium Dome, Greenwich, U.K., by Rogers, 2000

plan. The dome is supported on four pendentives resting on pairs of columns. Coffers, niches, and moldings, lit by hidden windows in the base of the dome, activate the surface, creating a sense of dynamism.

As an example of vernacular architecture, the Inuit (or Eskimo) igloo uses the dome as an efficient structure for frigid climates. Built of blocks of packed snow arranged in a closing spiral, igloos can be constructed in a matter of hours out of endlessly available material. The half-sphere form is aerodynamically effective to reduce wind pressure and one of the strongest structural shapes possible. A campfire melts a thin layer of snow, which refreezes into ice, rendering the igloo impermeable to wind. The snow also acts as a thermal barrier, so that, while outside temperatures plunge from -10° to -30°F, temperatures inside may be a relatively balmy 35–39°.

Richard Rogers's Millennium Dome, at a cost of more than $1.25 billion, is a symbol of Cool Britannia at the opening of the new millennium. Intended as a contemporary version of the Eiffel Tower or Crystal Palace—an icon of technological supremacy—the dome is the world's largest, enclosing 20 acres. Even though maxi in size, its material is mini. The fabric-covered dome weighs less than the air it encloses, the lightest structure of its kind on earth.

The Eighteenth and Nineteenth Centuries: A Passion for the Past

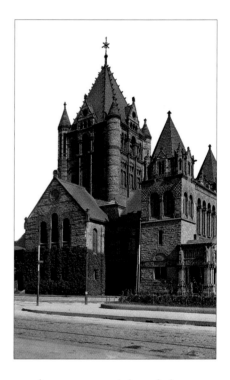

In the seventeenth century, architecture was almost monolithic. For a hundred years, buildings throughout Europe were recognizably Baroque or in the style of its extension, Rococo. In the eighteenth and nineteenth centuries, society became multilithic. The old absolutes—monarchy, church, and agrarian life—crumbled. Architecture turned volatile, prone to change.

It was an age of revolutions: American, French, and Industrial. For architecture, it was an age of revisions. In an era of uncertainty, with no unifying authority or standards of taste, architecture wrapped itself in revival modes.

The only signature style was a pastiche of the past. Neoclassic today, Gothic tomorrow. But always, derived from yesterday.

George Bernard Shaw said, "You use a glass mirror to see your face; you use works of art to see your soul." Judging by the architecture, the soul of the eighteenth and nineteenth centuries was not "a merry old soul," but just plain old. Builders recycled a bewildering variety of historic styles. The age revealed itself as a chaotic time, besotted with tradition while social and scientific innovation flourished.

WORLD HISTORY		ARCHITECTURE
	1700–80	Georgian style in America
	1715	Translation of Palladio appears in England
	1715–20	Concept of Picturesque landscape created
	1720–60	Palladian Revival in England
	1738	Herculaeum excavated
	1748	Pompeii discovered
Spinning frame invented, mass production begins	1770	
American colonies declare independence	1776	
	1779	First iron bridge erected
Industrial Revolution hits England	1780–1850	
	1785	Jefferson launches American Neoclassicism
French Revolution occurs	1789	
Napoleon seizes power in France	1799	
	1790–1830	Federal style in U.S.
Steam engine used to move rail cars 1804		
Fulton invents steamboat	1807	
Gas lighting available in London	1809	
Bolivar leads South American revolution	1811	
Napoleon defeated at Waterloo	1815	
	1800–30	Greek Revival popular in U.K.
	1819	Ecole des Beaux-Arts established
	1820–50	Neoclassicism sweeps America
First passenger railroad begun in England	1825	
Greece wins independence	1830	
	1833	First "balloon-frame" structure, Chicago
	1840s	Gothic Revival picks up speed
	1840–70	Stick Style in northeastern U.S.
Morse sends first telegraph message 1844		
Invention of sewing machine, refrigerator, telephone, film, automobile, phonograph	1845–95	
	1850–80	High Victorian Gothic gains
	1851	Crystal Palace built of iron and glass
Otis invents elevator	1852	
	1852–70	Paris transformed by Haussmann
	1857	American Institute of Architects founded; high-speed elevator installed, Haughwout Building, New York City
	1860–1920	Arts and Crafts movement popular
Civil War in U.S.	1861–65	
	1865	First U.S. architecture school, M.I.T.
U.S. rapidly industrialized	1870s	
	1875	Paris Opera launches Second Empire Style
Edison invents electric light	1879	
	1883	Brooklyn Bridge completed
Large-scale production of rolled steel 1880s		
	1885	First metal-frame skyscraper
	1880–90s	Gilded Age mansions built
	1889	Eiffel Tower opens
Reinforced concrete perfected	1892	
	1893	Columbian Exposition fans Neoclassic flame

THE EIGHTEENTH CENTURY: REASON AND ROMANCE

For 300 years prior to 1750, architecture in Western Europe was amazingly uniform. From North to South, styles flowed from the Renaissance, and ultimately from ancient Rome. The universal motto was not only when in Rome, but when at home, "do as the Romans do."

In the eighteenth century, this homogeneity crumbled. The social order shifted toward an urban society engaged in mass production. As the old preindustrial life ruled by church and monarch disintegrated, high-class Baroque and Rococo styles jarred with an increasingly secular, middle-class worldview.

The Enlightenment promoted a belief in rationality and progress. God was seen as a clockmaker, a hands-off technician who set the universe in motion, then withdrew to observe from afar. As the Catholic Church and absolute monarchs lost clout, the opulent architecture they favored became passé.

New forms were needed for a new age. History was a grab bag filled with Greek, Gothic, Chinese, Moorish, and Hindu styles, and eighteenth-century architects grabbed them all.

England was first to slough off seventeenth-century Baroque excess. It saw itself as opposed to the Catholic Church, monocratic rule, and overblown architecture. English tastemakers linked religious and political liberties to a purified, Neoclassic aesthetic. This austere style was thought to express the eighteenth-century reverence for reason.

At the same time, a contradictory impulse spread. As the old order rapidly mutated, nostalgia for an archaic past arose. Writers placed a high premium on sensibility and the beneficent effects of nature. These romantic moonings over bygone times and bucolic joys spurred a revival of medieval and exotic styles. Simultaneously, informal landscapes, designed to maximize opportunities for pensive or awe-inspiring views, became the rage, shoveling aside formal geometric gardens.

The result for eighteenth-century architecture meant no coherent trademark but a mishmash—call it a new pluralism—that has persisted to the present.

HEAD AND HEART

In its architecture, the eighteenth century schizophrenically celebrated both reason and romance. Two buildings on the grounds of Versailles show the extremes. The Petit Trianon, all straight lines and Spartan simplicity, is virtually a cube. Its stark symmetry conveys the Neoclassic love of reason and geometry. In contrast, the Hamlet, an artificial peasant village where Marie-Antoinette played milkmaid, displays Picturesque, "natural" forms. Romanticism, which coexisted with idolatry of reason, required irregular forms to evoke an unspoiled Arcadia.

Petit Trianon, Versailles, France, by A. J. Gabriel, 1762–68

Hameau (Hamlet), Versailles, by Richard Miqué, 1778–82

ENGLAND: BATTLE OF THE STYLES

NEO-PALLADIANISM. Except for a few seventeenth-century buildings designed for royalty by Inigo Jones, Renaissance style didn't make much of a dent in England. The situation changed drastically in 1715, when the first English translation of Palladio's book on style appeared. The volume, coupled with sentimental memories of the obligatory Grand Tour culminating in Italy, incited a fashion that seized England from 1720 to 1760. The vogue for the five orders of columns was so rampant, painter William Hogarth satirized the trend with an engraving, "The Five Orders of Perriwigs."

Palladian style meant refined, regular forms drawn from Classical architecture—the opposite of pompous Baroque structures like Blenheim Palace. Sedate Palladianism fit perfectly with the Age of Reason. It also fulfilled a desire to revel in historic forms, fleeing the upheavals of social change.

Since Palladian country houses were situated in informal English gardens, the ensemble also met needs inflamed by the Age of Sensibility. The retreat to the past through historic architecture and a mania for picturesque grounds killed two birds with one Palladian stone. The building itself was a four-square layout based on mathematical ratios, while the surroundings romantically evoked primeval bliss and historic glory.

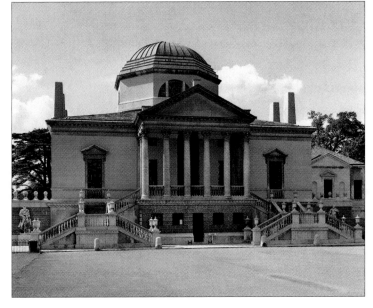

Chiswick House, outside London, by Burlington and Kent, c. 1723–29
This country house is England's most famous Palladian-style building. Although based on Palladio's Villa Rotonda, it differs substantially. There is no strict symmetry, identical temple porticoes are only on the sides, and a double-stair frames the front.

BURLINGTON AND KENT: PAIRED PALLADIANS.

Richard Boyle, the third Earl of Kent (1694–1753), was an amateur builder and connoisseur of architecture, obsessed with his mission to preach the gospel of Palladio. Until the mid-eighteenth century, Burlington and his protégé, William Kent, dominated the British architectural scene. Extremely influential, Burlington was so effective a style-setter, Palladian villas peppered the countryside, to "fill half the land with imitating fools," as the poet Alexander Pope wrote.

Burlington, with Kent's assistance, designed his own country house, Chiswick (pronounced Chis'ick), as a showplace of Palladian purity. Based on the Villa Rotonda, the rooms radiate from a central octagonal rotunda in measured proportions. Unfortunately, Chiswick is more a stage set of eccentric rooms than a livable domicile. Lord Chesterfield ridiculed its Palladian pretensions in verse:

> Possessed of one great house for state.
> Without one room to sleep or eat,
> How well you build, let flattery tell,
> And all mankind, how ill you dwell.

Around Chiswick, Kent created the first "natural," or English, garden—a conscious rejection of Versailles's formal layout. In their fervor for the antique, Kent and Burlington modeled the garden on Pliny's description of his Tuscan grounds. Landscape and house were conceived as an integrated whole.

Holkham Hall, sitting room, Norfolk, United Kingdom, by Kent and Burlington, from 1734
A severe exterior and ornate interior (combining elements from ancient Rome, Palladio, and Inigo Jones) are typical of eighteenth-century British style.

William Kent (1685–1748) created the English landscape garden in the 1730s and '40s. He was the first one, in Horace Walpole's words, who "leaped the fence and saw that all of nature was a garden." Kent's concept of the garden as an extension of the house revolutionized the relation of building to site. He created glades, grottoes, and copses of "wild" forests, littered with urns and obelisks along a winding path. The setting illustrated poems and popular sylvan paintings by Poussin or Claude Lorrain.

Kent also designed, with Burlington, one of the most sumptuous set pieces of British interior decor. The entry and staircase of Holkham Hall are richly carved and lavishly gilded. Based loosely on the interior of a Roman basilica, the room has an ornate coffered ceiling, carved and pedimented doorframes, niches, and heavy cornices. The restrained facade is very Palladian, very correct in its understated elegance and historical accuracy. Even the bricks were manufactured as in ancient Roman times.

ADAM: UNIQUE ANTIQUE. Around the 1750s, exact knowledge of Roman, Greek, and Hellenistic architecture increased, aided by archeological excavations at Herculaneum, Pompeii, and Paestum. Strict Palladianism began to seem too arid and bookish, and architects gained more arrows in their quiver, based on ruins at Palmyra, Sicily, and Baalbec. A new freedom and diversity in adapting ancient styles arose, brilliantly realized by Robert Adam (1728–1792) in his highly ornamented interiors for London townhouses.

Adam had traveled in Italy and along the Mediterranean. He had sketched, measured, and worshipped at the shrines of Classic architecture. In his own designs, he refused to follow slavishly the dictates of centuries-old stylebooks. "A latitude in this respect is often productive of great novelty, variety, and beauty," he affirmed, to justify his synthetic approach. Adam aimed at nothing less, he said, than "a revolution in the whole system of this useful and elegant art."

Syon House, Middlesex, by Adam, 1762–69
House of Mirth.
Adam synthesized many historic sources into an enchanting, individual style. "Dessert on plates" is how a colleague summed up Adam's circular designs on floor and ceiling. A brilliant decorator, he combined contrasting scales and shapes, as in Roman baths, to create lively floor plans. The plaster work of his exuberantly patterned moldings has a jewel-like polish. He was first to pay attention to every detail, designing everything—from carpets to keyholes—in a comprehensive scheme.

Adam's masterpiece is Syon House, in which he combined varied geometric shapes, like mixing a basilican hall with a rotunda. Although his exteriors are plain, red brick, the interior decor is spectacular. "We have adapted a beautiful variety of light moldings, gracefully formed, delicately enriched, and arranged with propriety and skill," he said.

No man ever spoke so true. Adam is known—above all—for his carved, low-relief stucco and painted wall patterns. (Walpole criticized the plethora of squiggles, calling them "snippets of embroidery.") Patterns on the ceiling repeat in carpets or floor tiles. Stylized motifs like swags, garlands, and rosettes form a frieze in gilded plaster or loop across mantels. White carvings on a pastel background give rooms the appearance of Wedgwood china. Other rooms use darker colors, based on Pompeiian frescoes or on Etruscan designs.

The anteroom of Syon House demonstrates the "movement" Adam desired. Created "in a style to afford a great variety of amusement," he said, the diverse moldings rise and fall, advance and recede, like dancers in a gavotte. Twelve blue marble columns—antique pillars dredged up from the bed of the Tiber River—form a screen. Their Ionic scrolls are based on the Erechtheion, but the capitals' necking derives from Roman baths. This fusion style broke the stranglehold of Palladian fussiness.

It also won Adam fabulously wealthy clients. His interiors formed the backdrop for their teas and social rituals, where aristocrats and *arrivistes* competed in sumptuous display. In 1767 one client wrote that Adam "has made me a ceiling and chimney-piece and doors, which are pretty enough to make me a thousand enemies; Envy turns livid at the first glimpsing of them."

Stourhead, Wiltshire, by Henry Hoare and Henry Flitcroft, 1741–81
Inspired by Vergil's *Aeneid* and paintings by Poussin and Claude, paths in this Picturesque garden provide views of temples, statuary, a grotto, and a rustic cottage. A replica of a Roman bridge spans the artificial lake. In the distance, a small-scale Pantheon spurs contemplation.

SIMPLY SUBLIME. England's most important aesthetic contribution, which was widely influential in Europe and America, was the eighteenth-century Picturesque landscape. In the English garden, called *jardin anglais* in France, landscape views were classified as Picturesque or Sublime. The concept of the Sublime, or thrills and chills, was based on awe- and terror-inspiring experiences of nature, as in craggy mountain peaks or thundering cascades. Picturesque landscapes were gentler and included irregularly shaped ponds, serpentine paths, rolling hills, and ruins to incite contemplation.

The Picturesque was easier to obtain than the Sublime in backyard plantings, but the ideal landscape included both. Constructing a Pike's Peak or Niagara Falls is hardly feasible on most estates, but one German prince built a 60-foot stone replica of a volcano, which could be induced to belch smoke and frighten visitors.

As Walpole said of England during the landscaping vogue, "Every journey is made through a succession of pictures." This scenic travelogue was the goal of the garden stroll—to glimpse vistas recalling ancient history, literature, and idyllic paintings. Stourhead garden was composed like episodes of a plot, tracing Aeneas's journey through the underworld as recounted by Virgil. The stroller encounters a mini Pantheon, pyramids, grottoes, straw-thatched cottages, and sham ruins as chapters in the story of life.

The Picturesque movement had an important impact on architecture. A new emphasis on architecture as just one element in a total environment arose. And architecture was devised to provoke imagination, emotion, and reverie.

"Follies"—or bizarre structures created for their sentimental associations or evocative power—were sprinkled profusely around the landscape. Where ruins did not conveniently exist already, mock ruins were built from scratch to induce rumination on times past. Some went so far as to create dwellings that were actual shambles. The broken pediment became not just a Hellenistic trick but an actual broken bit of masonry. A country house at Désert de Retz in France (1774–84) was literally in the form of a gigantic fluted column in decay. Its top was sheared off and crumbling, wrapped in vines. Presumably the wreck was both Picturesque in its asymmetry and Sublime in its imminent threat of collapse.

As Neoclassic gave way to Picturesque, irregularly composed buildings became the fashion. Italianate villas with asymmetric towers and castellated

'Tis Folly to Be Wise

In the eighteenth century, the gentry went gaga over follies. These whimsical structures were more like playhouses set amid landscape than actual buildings designed for use. They existed solely to spur Picturesque moments. Sir Francis Dashwood's estate, West Wycombe Park, between London and Oxford, was fairly peppered with tiny temples dedicated to Venus, Apollo, and sundry arts. One of his follies, the Music Temple, stands on an island at the center of a heart-shaped lake. Another lake on the property was dug in the shape of a swan.

After each addition was completed, Sir Francis threw a party. At the Temple of Bacchus ribbon-cutting, the proprietor and guests dressed like priests, priestesses, satyrs, and fawns. They made a sacrifice to Bacchus, then paraded to the lake, where a 60-ton frigate shot off cannons in a mock battle.

Sir Francis, with other aristocrats enamored of antique antics, formed the Dilettanti Society, which financed expeditions to ancient sites to record the ruins. The club also sponsored notorious toga parties, where members dressed in red velvet togas, recited Catullus, drank excessively, and engaged in various debaucheries. The Classical revival was far from staid.

Hallucinatory Architecture: From Decay to Deconstructivism

During the eighteenth-century mania for grunge, homeowners were dying to live in new buildings that looked like decrepit ruins. Barbier's circular building, shaped like a huge broken column, was surrounded by a Picturesque garden where one could meditate on the brevity of earthly joys.

In the twentieth century, members of a movement called De-Architecture designed new buildings resembling faux-demolition sites. Sculpture in the Environment, or SITE, led by James Wines, produced a series of showrooms for Best Products that were simple brick boxes. They looked completely ordinary, except for a disconcerting tendency to fall apart. In one showroom, a wall seems to be crumbling onto an awning over the front door. At "Notch Project" (1977) in Sacramento, California, one ragged corner is separated from the mass of the building, as if an earthquake wrenched it off its foundation. The detached fragment, on a mechanical track, can slide over to rejoin the bulk of the building. "Architecture is not just about form anymore," Wines said. "It's a matter of what it makes you think about."

In the 1980s, the philosophical theory of deconstruction—the idea that there is no fixed truth in a work, that an apparent order only camouflages chaos—found adherents in architecture. Peter Eisenman proposed buildings made up of parts that cannot be resolved into a unified whole. His Convention Center in Columbus, Ohio, illustrates this destabilized aesthetic. Off-axis walls and beams create an aura of discomfort. Discontinuity and distortion reign supreme.

(above) Désert de Retz, near Chambourcy, France, by François Barbier, 1774–84; (right) Greater Columbus Convention Center, Columbus, Ohio, by Eisenman, 1989–93

Nash was the leading exponent of Picturesque architecture, a movement that reached its peak in 1800–1830. The Royal Pavilion shows his wide range of styles, stirred together without regard for consistency. The main facade has Moorish arcades and a skyline of green domes, minarets, and pinnacles. The interior combines Gothic, Chinese, and Indian motifs. Its ceiling is like a deluxe tent for an Indian mogul. The huge kitchen has cast-iron pillars shaped like palm trees—complete with copper leaves.

Royal Pavilion, Brighton, by Nash, 1815–21

Gothic country houses appeared. City parks created in Europe and North America, like New York's Central Park, owe their origin to the English landscape movement. Nature was no longer something to be tamed and rigidly controlled, but an essential component of an interactive scheme.

During the 1750s to the 1780s, the English garden spread like thistledown across England. One of its most accomplished practitioners was William Kent's assistant, Lancelot "Capability" Brown (1716–1783). The nickname derived from his tendency to enthuse about the "capabilities" of a virgin site. In fact, one landowner professed he wanted to die before Brown, in order to see heaven before Capability "improved" it. When Brown was asked why he had not transformed any estates in Ireland, he answered, "I haven't yet finished with England."

Brown was known for merging house and grounds, sweeping away intervening elements like formal gardens, terraces, or balustrades. He brought the lawn right up to the house. For an unimpeded view, Brown installed what was known as a "ha-ha"—a hidden ditch that replaced fences around the perimeter of the property. Imperceptible from the house, the ha-ha prevented livestock from leaving their pasture to munch on shrubs, which Brown arranged in artful clumps. All visible barriers between nature and architecture were eliminated.

PICTURESQUE ARCHITECTURE.
The architect who epitomized Picturesque design was John Nash (1752–1835). Nash designed buildings in every possible style, no matter how exotic, from thatched cottages to Gothic castles, Neoclassic porticoes to Italianate villas, and Indian pavilions to Chinese pagodas. With their historic allusions and irregular plans and silhouettes, his structures were theatrical and eye-catching.

Nash translated Picturesque— which had been exclusively a style for country estates—into urban terms. Taking full advantage of stucco and cast iron, he sculpted buildings more than constructed them. In the process, he created lively urban scenery full of furbelows and statuary, as in Regent's Park, London, and the colorful Ionic Park Crescent he designed bordering the park. The Prince Regent was so smitten with Nash's proposals to revamp the park, he gushed, "It will quite eclipse Napoleon."

Sir John Soane's Museum, London, by Soane, 1808–9, 1812
Soane reduced Classical structure and ornament to rudimentary forms. He combined multiple levels, top-lighting, and hundreds of mirrors to blur divisions between areas, fragmenting and overlapping planes. The top-lit, tentlike ceiling seems to hover over simple corner supports. His work was both an eclectic synthesis of historical styles and a Picturesque departure into his personal optical agenda. "Architecture unshackled," as his mentor, George Dance, put it.

Old Colonial Office, Bank of England, London, by Soane, 1818 (now destroyed)
Soane overthrew the orthodox Classical canon, paring it down to sheer form. Each room in the bank flaunted a different style: a Greek Revival vestibule, Adamesque court, and a Stock Office like Imperial Roman baths. Superficially Neoclassic, the rooms exploit complicated spatial interplay and mysterious lighting. Soane used the elements of architecture as a means of expression, not an end in themselves.

Ledoux's Revolutionary Utopia

In 1774, Ledoux designed the first ideal city of the industrial age, La Saline de Chaux, near Besançon, France. Conceived as a "ville sociale," Ledoux's perfect community enshrined work at its symbolic heart. The central buildings for salt manufacture were encircled by workers' homes and gardens. An outer ring would contain various common buildings like a stock market, hospital, a building dedicated to the glory of women, and venues for recreation and education. Each structure's form reflected its function. The facade of a wheelwright's house, for example, would be circular. Whether grand or humble, Ledoux gave the same amount of attention to each. "The Great belongs to every kind of building," he said.

Large-scale, simple shapes, like the circle and square, define the outward appearance of each structure. The cohesive ensemble was intended as a new synthesis that would reconcile humanity and nature, the individual and the community, and overcome the alienation that followed the Industrial Revolution.

Never Built—Dream Architecture

Architects have sometimes proposed buildings so avant-garde, construction was impossible. They were essentially exercises in futuristic fantasy. In the eighteenth century, Étienne-Louis Boullée's grandiose funerary monuments were far beyond the technology of his age. His buildings were pure forms, like pyramids, cylinders, or cones stripped of decoration, on a vast scale. The shapes alone communicated their purpose. This giant hollow sphere—too strange and huge to realize—symbolized the universe. "The spherical body," Boullée wrote, "is the image of perfection."

In the 1960s, a radical British group called Archigram (short for architectural telegram, its newsletter) took up the challenge of envisioning wild designs too far-out to realize. Among the group's urban fantasies were sci-fi cartoon-designs like "Plug-In City." Part of the vibrant pop culture in the "Swinging Sixties" Beatles era, Archigram protested the grim look of postwar London, with its cheap row houses and drab concrete schools.

"Instant City" (1968) tried to drum up spontaneity and fun. Its designer, Peter Cook, imagined a tentlike roof held up by balloons that sheltered mobile modules of shops or nightclubs. Designs were flexible and temporary as a Lego construction. Ron Herron's "Walking City" (1964) proposed buildings that stalked around on giant legs. Although they never existed except on paper, Archigram's forms reflected the mobility and impermanence of modern life.

Project for Newton's Cenotaph, Bibliothèque Nationale, Paris, by Boullée, 1783

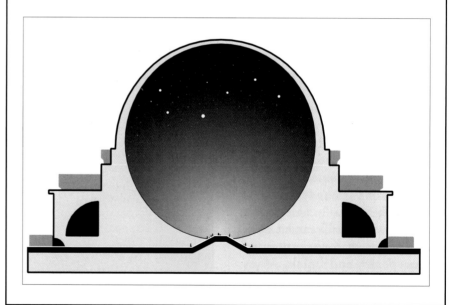

Galileo said, "Nature speaks algebra and geometry," and Soufflot's skeletal piers and straight lines were perceived as natural in their undisguised purity of form. From 1750 to 1800, French architecture was enamored of such crisp, austere composition—a daring union of Greek and Goth.

VISIONARY ARCHITECTURE. Simplicity reached an extreme in the hallucinatory designs of Étienne-Louis Boullée (1728–1799). Boullée considered himself a painter and gave up the practice of architecture around 1782. Although he built little (many of his designs were impractical), he was highly influential through his drawings and students. A believer in *l'architecture parlante* (expressive, or "speaking" architecture), Boullée proposed vast, overscaled projects, radically reduced to pure geometric forms. He invented, he said, an "architecture of shadows," not of substance.

From the 1780s to the 1790s, Boullée's designs grew to megalomaniac proportions. A 500-foot-tall sphere proposed as a monument to Isaac Newton sought to re-create the vault of heaven. "I have conceived the project of enveloping you with your discovery!" Boullée wrote of his gigantic hollow sphere, empty except for Newton's catafalque at the bottom and antlike human figures. Pierced by tiny holes at the top, the sphere simulated stars in the darkness of infinity.

Claude-Nicolas Ledoux (1736–1806) devised similarly bold compositions, but he actually built many of his radical designs. His buildings from the 1770s onward combine simple, consciously primitive components with great originality. Considering himself a prophet of revolutionary architecture, Ledoux broke with classical norms to produce radical compositions in the saltworks he designed for workers at Arc-et-Senans.

Director's House, La Saline, Arc-et-Senans, by Ledoux, 1779
An ardent experimentalist, Ledoux transformed the Classical vocabulary to express new functions and bold ideas. His surprising Director's House mingles square and cylindrical segments in robust columns. Ledoux advised, "If you wish to become an architect, start by being a painter." He exploited effects of light and shadow, geometry and texture. Behind the entrance is a grotto, with carved stone fluid "gushing" like saltwater through openings.

A RIVER RUNS THROUGH IT. Besides the housing and manufacturing buildings actually constructed at La Saline, Ledoux proposed an entire ideal city—never executed—for the nearby town of Chaux. He sketched buildings so intimately connected to their site, they make Frank Lloyd Wright's Fallingwater seem aloof. In a house for a river surveyor (1785–90), Ledoux conceived a cylinder set on its side like a huge sewer pipe. Water from the River Loue would gush through the center of the dwelling.

Ledoux's other proposals for his utopian city included a communal building to house sixteen families, a *Pacifière* where disputes could be settled amicably, and an *Oikema,* or Temple Dedicated to Love. Also known as the House of Sexual Instruction (a brothel), the ground plan of the latter was shaped like an erect phallus. His convictions that the right physical environment has a beneficial effect on inhabitants and that architecture could be a vehicle of social reform reflect the eighteenth century's high-minded idealism. Work and play were to be organized rationally, and progress would surely follow.

COLONIAL ARCHITECTURE: BUILDING THE NEW WORLD

For the first hundred years, colonists were too busy carving up the wilderness to care about niceties of design. A lean-to of poles daubed with mud and caulked with wattle was all the first settlers could manage. Beginning in the 1700s, with increasing wealth came a yen to emulate Old World style. A gradual improvement in sophistication brought imposing brick and timber houses. As Benjamin Franklin observed, "It appears that our people are not deficient in genius."

Two styles prevailed in the eighteenth century: Georgian (1700–76) and Federal (1776–c. 1830). Georgian homes were simple, two-story boxes with doors and windows symmetrically arranged. They frequently had a pediment over the door and a cupola on the roof. The roof was flattened at the top, edged with a wooden balustrade to form a terrace, or captain's walk.

Federal-style homes were also boxlike structures of brick or clapboard siding, but their interiors were based on the refined style of Robert Adam in England. An amalgam of Renaissance and Palladian motifs, with a dollop of delicate French Rococo, Federal homes reserved their flair for interiors, decorated with elegant moldings. Fanfare on the exterior was confined to the entrance, typically a door framed by columns or side windows, with a fanlight above.

Charles Bulfinch (1763–1844) of Boston was America's first native-born professional architect. Although educated at Harvard, he was self-taught in architecture. That didn't stop him from producing the distinguished

Westover, Charles City County, Virginia, 1730–34
William Byrd's elaborate house is an example of a colonist bragging in brick about his status and wealth. The scrolled pediment frontispiece was styled after a plate in a book on Palladio's designs. Typical Georgian features are the brick string course between floors, an embellished central entrance, auxiliary buildings on either side connected by low "hyphen" extensions, and external symmetry.

Vassall-Craigie-Longfellow House, Cambridge, Massachusetts, 1759
This Georgian house, where the poet Henry Wadsworth Longfellow once lived, has clapboard siding characteristic of New England. A projecting central pavilion with pediment, pilasters, and balustraded roof are Georgian features. Named for the period when the Georges ruled England (1714–75), the style differed from its Old World brick models because of the balloon frame developed in America and the plentiful supply of local hardwood.

Mexican Baroque

Metropolitan Cathedral, Mexico City, 1563–1800s

In Mexico, colonists took Spanish Baroque to an extreme of froufrou. Although the facade is Neoclassic, with its twin limestone towers, central portico, dome, and lantern, the church's interior reflects the motto of the Spanish conquistadors: "For God and Gold." An abundant supply of gold and silver allowed details like altars and panels, statues of angels and saints to be gilded and enriched with reflective surfaces. Drawing on local craftsmen skilled in carving, masonry, and metalwork, capitals and screens are adorned with a jungle of gilded, high-relief carving. The style bristles with broken pilasters (called *estípite*), almost a cascade of ornament.

Harrison Gray Otis House, Boston, Massachusetts, by Bulfinch, 1795–96
The plain exterior of red brick with white trim, ornamented by slender columns and a second-floor Palladian window, is typical of Federal architecture.

Massachusetts State House (1795–98). This important Federal building, derived from Palladio, won Bulfinch the job of Capitol architect in Washington, D.C.

Benjamin Henry Latrobe (1764–1820) was an even more ardent Classicist than Bulfinch. As he told Thomas Jefferson, "My principles of good taste are rigid in Grecian architecture." His Bank of Pennsylvania (1798–1800) was the first adaptation of a Greek temple in America, setting off a style that became pervasive in the early nineteenth century. (Latrobe also built the earliest Gothic Revival house in America—Sedgeley—in 1799, kicking off another fad that took flight in the next century.)

As the first fully trained architect in America, Latrobe knew how to apply historic motifs and when to strike out in a new direction. He built the House of Representatives (1811) for the United States Capitol, devising unique maize-leaf capitals to indicate America's new take on Classical style. Called the "corn-cob capitals" by Congressmen, the vegetal motifs were a populist hit. In the Senate anterooms, Latrobe used tobacco-leaf capitals, showing more of the country's agricultural roots.

Latrobe employed Classical elements synthetically, not slavishly, and in novel ways. His Supreme Court Chamber (1815–17) below the Senate in the U.S. Capitol has stubby columns and a half-dome ceiling. Ribs radiate overhead like an umbrella. Latrobe wanted to create architecture out of pure geometric units. His masterpiece, St. Mary's Roman Catholic Cathedral in Baltimore (1804–18), clarifies structure to serve expressive ends. "It is not the ornament, it is the use I want," Latrobe said. The cathedral's spacious, vaulted interior, containing America's first coffered dome, clearly displays how structural elements are put together.

THE NINETEENTH CENTURY: DÉJÀ VU ALL OVER AGAIN

"In what style shall we build?" asked the German architect Heinrich Hübsch in 1828. He called for "an architectural style of the nineteenth century," but Europe and America churned out a rerun of historical styles dating back 2300 years. Classical Revival, from Greek to Roman, was the choice for civic buildings, while Gothic ruled in church, university, and domestic architecture. Besides these major veins, architects mined the whole quarry of history, finding gold in Byzantine, Moorish, Chinese, and Egyptian styles.

Amid the major thrusts of historicism and eclecticism, what this copycat era lacked was originality. Most of the invention was funneled into engineering and scientific triumphs, where nonstop achievements changed the world. The Industrial Revolution hit England around 1780 and spread to the continent and America in the nineteenth century. Every aspect of life, including transportation, production, communication, and building technology, changed. Cities mushroomed. London grew from 1 million inhabitants in 1800 to 4.3 million in 1900, as New York increased from 63,000 to 2.8 million.

New functions required new building forms, like factories, railroad stations, department stores, and office buildings. New materials like cast and wrought iron, plate glass, rivets, steel, and reinforced concrete became available in unprecedented amounts. National economies boomed; faith in progress surged. Yet, amid this headlong rush toward the New, architects clung to the Old.

"Is this epoch, so fertile in discoveries, so abounding in vital force, to transmit to posterity nothing better in art than imitations?" asked the architect Eugène Viollet-le-Duc. In times of rapid change, conservatism flourishes. Instead of welcoming the possibilities of a new age and devising forms appropriate to the present, architects retreated to tradition. Only around the end of the century, in the upstart city of Chicago—where there was no tradition—did architects produce innovative structures, turning a brawny shoulder to the past.

Old and New Collide

The two faces of New York's Pennsylvania Station show extremes of style as architecture approached a turning point. The waiting room, an awe-inspiring public space, is modeled on the Roman baths, while the soaring concourse reinterprets ancient arches and columns in modern materials and engineering.

(above) Waiting Room, Pennsylvania Station, New York, by McKim, Mead & White, 1902–10

(left) Concourse, Pennsylvania Station

Crystal Palace, London, by Paxton, 1850–51 (burned 1936)
Paxton, a gardener, derived his inspiration for this Erector-set conservatory from observing the structure of a leaf. Just like the veins and infill of a leaf, standardized iron and glass modules provided skeleton and skin for the transparent building. The first prefabricated building on a giant scale, the Crystal Palace marked a huge leap in building size, use of new technology and media, and systematization of the building process.

THE CAST-IRON AGE

Yet all was not retro, especially in the industrial realm. Walt Whitman's paean to novelty in the 1860s hailed a new era of construction: "The shapes arise! / Shapes of factories, arsenals, foundries, markets, / Shapes of the two-threaded tracks of railroads, / Shapes of the sleepers of bridges, vast frameworks, girders, arches." It was in bridge and railway station design that new shapes and materials first appeared. Although these industrial structures were not considered "architecture," they heralded a future era of metal-frame, rather than masonry, support—the shape of things to come.

Throughout the nineteenth century, the most progressive buildings were for transport and industry, created by engineers in a simple, functional style out of iron and glass. If the challenge of the century was to develop a contemporary style, London's Crystal Palace (1850–51) showed the way. This vast exposition hall, created to display the wonders of Victorian technology, was an oversized greenhouse, devoid of historical ornament.

Its designer, Sir Joseph Paxton (1803–65), was not an architect but a horticulturist and builder of greenhouses. When Queen Victoria's consort, Prince Albert, decided to hold the first world's fair to show off England's industrial might, it was not possible to construct an ordinary building in the allotted time. Only a prefabricated shell would do, and that's what Paxton delivered. In six months, identical modular cast-iron columns and beams were manufactured, shipped to Hyde Park, and mounted with standardized panes. Covering 18 acres of ground, 18,000 four-foot panes of glass formed the roof and walls. Spaced 48 feet apart, 3,300 iron pillars marched the length of one-third mile (six football fields). For the first time ever, the volume enclosed surpassed the mass of a building—more a bubble than a box.

A contemporary critic called the Crystal Palace a "ferrovitreous triumph." Others were not so charitable. John Ruskin considered it "a cucumber frame." To a defender of Gothic style, A. W. N. Pugin, it was "a crystal humbug" and "a glass monster." Such a building of untraditional materials, without historical details or mass, was not—to them—a real building but a lattice sheathed in glass, more like a railroad shed or bridge. For this reason, its revolutionary construction did not influence orthodox buildings of the day. In fact, the Crystal Palace is more a forerunner of twentieth-century glass, curtain-wall skyscrapers than of Victorian structures.

National Icons

Some buildings transcend their specific time and purpose, becoming so identified with a culture that their images evoke a whole country. The contemporary architect Charles Gwathmey said architecture is about building "interesting ruins," but surely creating an icon for an entire society is the ultimate accolade. Among the structures to attain this stature are the Great Pyramid for Egypt, the Parthenon for Greece, and the Sydney Opera House in Australia.

The Eiffel Tower indisputably says "France." Its status was far from secure when first built. Cultural leaders called it "the horror." Critics denounced it as "monstrous." Yet this tower, visible all over Paris, became a beloved symbol of France. Hitler vowed to destroy it, and Algerian rebels plotted to dynamite it, as if by smashing the tower they could eradicate French pride. Serving no practical purpose, except as a viewing stand to survey the city, the tower provides a visual focus for Paris and is France's most famous landmark.

Opera House, Sydney, Australia, by Jorn Utzon and others, 1957–73

(below) Eiffel Tower, Paris, by Eiffel, 1887–89

(below, right) Taj Mahal, Agra, India, 1631–48

The Taj Mahal is a consummate blend of composition and setting that personifies India. Seventeen acres of gardens include rows of dark cypresses and a reflecting pool that lead the eye to the building's focal point. Four minaret towers at opposite corners frame the central domed structure, elevated on a marble platform.

INDUSTRIAL-AGE ARCHITECTURE. The structure that proved what a steel skeleton could accomplish was the Eiffel Tower (1887–89). At nearly 1,000 feet, it was for many years the world's highest structure, but its airy, lightweight frame was more void than volume. Designed by a bridge engineer, Gustave Eiffel (1832–1923), who also made the armature inside the Statue of Liberty, the tower marked the entrance to the 1889 Paris Exposition.

Like the Crystal Palace, the tower was an enormous jigsaw puzzle, composed of 15,000 wrought-iron sections and 2,500,000 rivet holes. Its 4-acre base supports 8,000 tons of metal trusses. Its silhouette is a direct expression of the tower's structure. Four wide-footed piers, stabilized by two platforms, gradually converge as the tower tapers toward the top. The only nonstructural elements are grillwork arches linking the bases, added by Eiffel to give the appearance of buttresses and reassure visitors that the novel structure was safe.

The Brooklyn Bridge (1883), which introduced a heroic new scale to the urban world, is another triumph of engineering. The first wire suspension bridge, its 1,596-foot span made it the longest—more than twice the length of the previous record—in the world when completed. Although the bridge is pure structure, its engineers designed the 300-foot-tall granite towers, with their pointed arches, in a nod to Gothic style—a fusion of old and new.

NUTS AND BOLTS. The first monumental public building in which iron was flaunted rather than hidden was the Bibliothèque Ste.-Geneviève (1838–50) in Paris. Its architect, Henri Labrouste (1801–1875), was a rebel. Although trained at the famed Ecole des Beaux-Arts, he broke with the dominant Neoclassic style. Labrouste believed the century should develop an architecture for contemporary needs and made of modern materials.

The radical novelty of Labrouste's design combines a traditional, arcuated, masonry exterior with an interior like none before it. The library's plan is simple—a two-story rectangle, where the entire upper floor is one vast reading room. Covering the reading room are 211 barrel vaults, supported by openwork, transverse arches of cast iron. In the center, dividing the room into two naves, is a row of slender cast-iron columns. Both functional arrangement and circulation are clearly expressed in the structure, using new materials without Classical overlay.

The Renaissance-style facade contains another innovation. In place of decorative stone columns, Labrouste had the names of 810 authors carved in rows of letters, almost like the columns of a newspaper. "Facade follows function" is not exactly a rallying cry for modern architects, but Labrouste anticipated Post-Modernism by adorning his building with text to declare its purpose.

Galleria Vittorio Emanuele II, Milan, Italy, by Giuseppe Mengoni, 1867–77

Although traditional buildings hid their metal supporting structure, shopping arcades roofed with glass and iron barrel vaults became common—a precursor to the modern mall. The Galleria takes the form of covered pedestrian streets, which intersect at right angles to form an octagon.

Reading Room, Bibliothèque Ste.-Geneviève, Paris, by Labrouste, 1838–50
This library was the first high-style public building to use iron in a visible, prominent fashion.

British Museum, London, by Smirke, 1824–47
Robert Smirke led the English Neoclassical movement. This Greek Revival building has two projecting wings flanking a central portico, unified by a screen of Ionic columns.

Taylorian Institution, Ashmolean Museum, Oxford, by Cockerell, 1839–45
Cockerell made important archeological discoveries during his Grand Tour of Greek ruins. He combined elements from classical proto-types of all periods, like a survey course in Classical inspiration. Here he joined giant Ionic columns from Greece with a Baroque broken entablature and Roman arches. The statues atop columns recall Adamesque design, while the rusticated base suggests Mannerist palazzos of the Renaissance.

ENGLAND'S NEO-CLASSIC REVIVAL: REMEMBRANCE OF THINGS PAST

Aside from a few harbingers of changing technology, most nineteenth-century structures still aped the past. In a time of social turmoil, war, and revolution, architects expressed continuity through antique designs. As the architect Viollet-le-Duc, who despised Classical affectation, wrote, "For although it is difficult for man to learn, it is much more difficult for him to forget." Apparently, it was equally difficult to invent new forms, since from 1800 to 1830, the Classical style reigned supreme in both Europe and America.

English buildings flaunted familiar elements: columns, rounded arches, temple fronts, domes, and flanking wings. Yet the combinations often weren't purely Greek or Roman but a generic mishmash called Neoclassic Revival.

Then Lord Elgin installed the Parthenon marbles in London in 1807, and a vogue for Greek simplicity displaced Roman imperial grandeur, associated with the detested Napoléon. Used in buildings like museums and post offices, Greek style had a virtual monopoly in England before Queen Victoria's ascension to the throne in 1837. Although the Gothic admirer Pugin inveighed against "the eternal sameness of a Grecian temple outraged in all its proportions and character" on every block, others felt Greek was the only way to go. Leading Neoclassic architect Sir Robert Smirke (designer of the

British Museum's Ionic colonnade) defended its staid simplicity: "When art chooses to frolic in masonry," he sniffed, "the effect is not only unnatural but indecorous."

The first London rail terminal, Euston Station (1837) by Philip Hardwick, clothed a brand-new building type in Doric columns, like an official stamp of approval to reassure a public uneasy about rail travel. In Scotland, Alexander "Greek" Thomson tried to make Glasgow "Athens of the North," but his Greek was polyglot. In the colorful eclecticism of Queen's Park Church (1867), Thomson pasted together an Egyptian portal with squat lotus-form columns and an astonishing Indian stupa tower.

Another leading Revivalist, William Wilkins, wouldn't use a single line or member "for which he could not find a precedent in some ancient Greek building." Like some King Midas of ancient style, everything he touched turned to old. Unfortunately, since nineteenth-century conditions of life were so far removed from antiquity, clinging to past styles became a musty, going-through-the-motions exercise. Revival buildings came to seem more smoke than substance, as dipping a tea bag for the umpteenth time yields pale water, not strong brew.

Others drew on the whole menu of antiquity, cooking up a potluck stew of basically Greek lines, enlivened by the rich surface texture of Italian Mannerism and the sculptural drama of Baroque. C. R. Cockerell's Ashmolean Museum, Oxford (1839–45), is as diverse as a duck-billed platypus. Neither Greek nor Roman, it seems to have been constructed by committee, with a dip of this and a dash of that.

Historicism and eclecticism made a confusing mix, and Neoclassicism fizzled fast. By the end of the 1830s, English taste shifted toward Gothic, leaving France and Germany to carry on the Olympian torch.

Arts and Crafts Movement

Red House, Bexley Heath, Kent, United Kingdom, by Philip Webb, 1859–60

The writer-designer William Morris (1834–1896) believed "production by machinery is altogether an evil." Emphasizing handicrafts, or art "by the people and for the people," Morris laid the groundwork for the Arts and Crafts Movement, which looked to medieval Gothic as the pinnacle of British culture. His own home, Red House, was intended to provide an informal, rustic alternative to overblown Victorian structures.

GOTHIC REVIVAL: FAITH AND FASHION. From 1830 to 1850, the major alternative to Greek Revival in England was Gothic. Neo-Gothic consisted of dark, craggy, irregular (in other words, Picturesque) forms, which were considered native to northern Europe. Some boosters of Gothic style, like A. W. N. Pugin and John Ruskin, equated Gothic architecture with an ethical society. It was, Pugin said, "not a style but a principle." Ruskin, who endorsed the vim and vigor of Gothic, hated Neoclassic, a "Square Style" he considered "pagan in its origin, proud and unholy in its revival, paralyzed in its old age." Others, like Viollet-le-Duc, a scholarly restorer of medieval buildings, pushed Gothic because of its rational structural principles, which could be adapted to industrial-age construction. By 1845, Gothic—"the organ after the harpsichord"—replaced Greek Revival.

When a new complex of the Houses of Parliament was built along the Thames River, Pugin clothed the plan by Charles Barry in Gothic detail. Although the facade along the river is symmetrical, the silhouette is completely asymmetrical. Pugin was aware of the contrast between Barry's clear layout and his veneer of medieval ornament. "All Grecian, sir; Tudor details on a classic body," he fumed. Nonetheless, he threw himself into designing the whole ensemble, from stone carvings, wallpaper, and umbrella stands to inkwells and hat racks.

HIGH VICTORIAN GOTHIC: STEEP AND STOUT.

HIGH VICTORIAN GOTHIC: STEEP AND STOUT. After 1850, Gothic architecture became increasingly bizarre. Buildings were chunky, bristling with brickwork and multicolored stones. Facades were striped with red and black brick in fussy patterns. Towers, sculptural detail, and boldly angular masses proliferated. As one critic put it, "anything striped, spiky, knobbly, notched, fungoid or wiry" was perfect to express England's new status, as colonial master of one quarter of the earth's territory.

Ruskin, who had an inordinate influence on architecture through his impassioned writings, decreed: "Ornamentation is the principal part of architecture." He was partial to profusely colored stones, in "every variety of hue, from pale yellow to purple, passing through orange, red, and brown" to green and gray. His taste ushered in an age of wild architecture: eclectic, dynamic, and flaming with intense tints like London's St. Pancras Station (1867–74) by George Gilbert Scott.

Houses of Parliament, London, by Barry and Pugin, 1839–52
The Gothic look of this building was so well received, it legitimized the style, which spread throughout England during the first 50 years of Victoria's reign (1837–87).

Sketch, Woolworth Building
This early twentieth-century skyscraper was inspired by the Houses of Parliament. The 58-story Woolworth Building by Cass Gilbert in New York was dubbed "the cathedral of commerce." It included flying buttresses, gargoyles, and other mock-medieval trappings.

House of Lords, interior, Houses of Parliament
Pugin designed this interior modeled on Perpendicular Gothic. Although roof trusses are framed in the new material of iron, medieval touches like murals, stained glass, mosaics, gilded panels, carved wood, and statuary lend a medieval air.

GERMANY: PRUSSIA EMBRACES THE PAST

A Prussian architect who began as a pure Greek Revivalist and gradually developed an intensely eclectic style was Karl Friedrich Schinkel (1781–1841). His Altes Museum (1822–28) has a facade like a Greek stoa with an impressive Ionic colonnade. Neoclassic expressed, for Schinkel and the Prussian state, the uplifting, educational aspirations connected to fine art, which the building housed.

Schinkel wanted, he said, "to emulate as far as possible Greek forms and construction." He succeeded faultlessly in the Greek-inspired Altes Museum. Schinkel's public buildings expressed the political ambitions of the Prussian state, whose architecture Schinkel dominated for thirty years.

After 1826, Schinkel's work became more Picturesque. In a villa at Charlottenhof (1826–27), he still used a Doric portico, but it was sited asymmetrically on a slope and combined with irregularly placed outbuildings and a water garden. A painter who produced dioramas and stage sets for operas, Schinkel was acutely conscious of the scenographic impact of his buildings. He blended architecture and the natural surroundings with a sure hand.

Schloss Charlottenhof, outside Potsdam, by Schinkel, 1826–27
Schinkel integrated buildings and setting. Here, the crown prince's house, garden, park, canals, and outbuildings are intimately linked in a Picturesque, asymmetrical plan. The ensemble demonstrates Schinkel's belief that "architecture is the continuation of nature in her constructive activity."

Mad King Ludwig: The Sound of Music

Ludwig II of Bavaria was an ardent patron of both architecture and music. Here he combined his two passions. The name Neuschwanstein means "new swan stone." The entire castle, built at incredible expense and effort atop a mountain peak, was a tribute to the myth of Lohengrin and the swan that inspired Richard Wagner's opera. The six-story, white fairy-tale castle (the model for the Magic Kingdom castle in Disneyland) is a mixture of Romanesque, Byzantine, and Gothic elements. Ludwig was so enamored of Teutonic myths, one performance of *Tannhäuser* had an "almost demoniacal effect" on him. As the music crescendoed, the king became convulsed, as if struck by a seizure. He built Singers' Hall (a near-replica of the site where a singers' contest occurred in *Tannhäuser*) to stage Wagner's operas. The fantasy environment was never completed, since Ludwig was declared mentally deranged in 1886 and removed from his duties.

Schloss Neuschwanstein, near Munich, Germany, by Georg von Dollman and Edvard Riedel, begun 1869

FRANCE: NAPOLEONIC SPLENDOR

Paris, like London, saw extraordinary changes in the nineteenth century. The population grew from one-half million in 1800 to 2.5 million in 1900. Unfortunately, the city's infrastructure was still that of a medieval town, woefully inadequate when it came to housing, circulation, and water supply. In 1852, Louis-Napoléon, or Napoléon III (nephew to the original Napoléon), decided to make Paris a "new Rome." *Voilà*—in less than two decades the city was transformed into a modern metropolis, festooned with Neoclassic trappings.

The metamorphosis was due to Baron Georges-Eugène Haussmann, also known as "Attila of the Straight Line." With ruthless efficiency, he cut 85 miles of straight avenues through the heart of old Paris, demolishing nearly 20,000 houses that blocked his ruled lines on the map. Haussmann provided 354 miles of underground sewers, enough aqueducts to double the water supply, gaslights, public fountains and parks, and hundreds of new buildings. From 1852 to 1870, he accomplished the most thorough reconfiguration of a city in history, a transformation that influenced scores of major cities, like Rome, Vienna, Brussels, and Washington, D.C. "The

old Paris is no more," lamented the poet Charles Baudelaire. "A city's form, alas, changes faster than the human heart."

The impetus behind this sweeping makeover was not only to improve circulation and eliminate annual cholera epidemics, but to prevent political uprisings. Insurgents routinely turned the old, narrow streets into barricades, so the emperor demanded broad boulevards, allowing good firing lines and easy access for troops. Haussmann aimed the boulevards toward vistas, with public monuments like the Arc de Triomphe or the new Opera House as focal points. The writer Gustave Flaubert complained to George Sand, "The whole trend in Paris is now toward the colossal." Henry James appreciated the results: "Paris is the greatest temple ever built to material joys and the lust of the eyes."

THE PALAIS GARNIER. The most successful of Haussmann's *points de vue* was the Opéra, called the Palais Garnier after its architect, Charles Garnier (1825–1898). This masterpiece of Beaux-Arts or Second Empire style has a Baroque exterior, which achieves maximum effect through sculpted mass, rhythm of solids and voids, and diverse but unified texture and forms. The facade was so impressive, Haussmann decided not to plant trees intended to line the avenue. He wanted nothing to block the building's noble silhouette.

Opéra, Paris, by Garnier, 1861–75
The grandeur and ostentation of the Opéra, with its smorgasbord of styles, forms, and motifs, changed the direction of French architecture. When Garnier won the design competition for the commission, the empress was furious and demanded, "What is this? This is not a style. It's neither Louis XIV nor Louis XV nor Louis XVI." Garnier replied, "Madame, it's Napoleon III and you're complaining." He gave the name of the emperor's reign to the new style, which perfectly captured the scale of the new Paris and the opulence of the Second Empire.

Massive, heavily decorated, with a symphony of colors in variegated marble and gilding, the Opéra achieves a crescendo at the terminus of one of Hausmann's boulevards. Garnier aimed at vivacity but not vulgarity in his design. "Although art can dance the gavotte or minuet," he said, "it must refrain from the can-can."

The interior is devoted to spectacle—a social stage for operagoers to see and be seen. Garnier enlarged lobbies and corridors to accommodate crowds eager to show off their finery. "The sparkling light, the resplendent clothes, the smiling, animated faces, the encounters which occur, the greetings exchanged," he said, were all part of the show. The main display case was the soaring flights of stairs, where patrons could regally ascend toward the auditorium. Garnier's greatest achievement is creating this setting for social ceremony.

Grand Stairway, interior, Opéra
Lined with painted ceilings, colorful marble columns, gilded statuary, and sumptuous chandeliers, the stairway drips with gilt and relief carving. One critic described it as "looking like an overloaded sideboard." To Garnier, the stairway was the climax of a total theatrical experience orchestrated by the building.

Plan, Opéra
The Ecole des Beaux-Arts, where Garnier studied architecture, stressed clear circulation patterns and the gradual unfolding of aesthetic experience of a building. Garnier accomplished the latter through a series of low-ceilinged paths approaching the grand stairs, giving way to the vast space of the stair hall, where the social pageant was at its most intense. His ingenious plan, on a diamond-shaped lot, includes different entrances for assorted operagoers, whether arriving on foot or by carriage, with facilities for season-ticket holders and those purchasing at the box office.

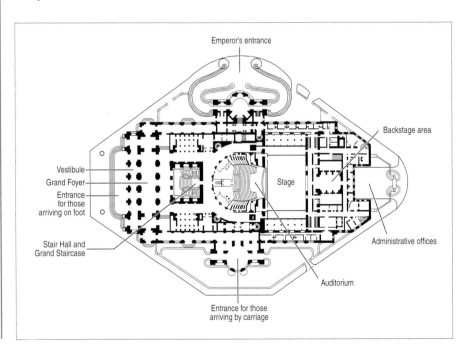

UNITED STATES:
NEW NATION, OLD STYLES

After the Revolution, America needed an alternative to the Georgian style associated with its colonial past. Seizing the democratic imagery of Periclean Athens and the Roman republic, they garbed the new capital in Washington, D.C., and much of the country in a Classical cloak. From 1800 to 1850, porticoed pseudo-temples were built not only for government buildings but for banks, schools, even homes. Commenting on the number of Greek Revival mansions along the Hudson River, James Fenimore Cooper said, "One such temple, well placed in a wood, might be a pleasant object enough, but to see a river lined with them, with children trundling hoops before their doors, beef carried into their kitchens, and smoke issuing, moreover, from those unclassical objects—chimneys—is too much even of a high taste."

Most Americans, suffering from cultural inferiority, were happy to borrow styles popular in European capitals. Latrobe's pupils, William Strickland (1788–1854) and Robert Mills (1781–1855), were among the chief practitioners of Greek Revival style. Strickland's Second Bank of the U.S. (1818–24), modeled on the Parthenon, marked the beginning of a strict Greek Revival. His Merchants' Exchange (1832–34) was less pure a copy but more imaginative. With its hemicycle of Corinthian columns topped by an Athenian circular lantern, the building brilliantly turns its corner plot into an asset.

Strickland's pupil, Thomas U. Walter, designed Founder's Hall of Girard College for Nicholas Biddle, whose motto was "There are but two truths in the world—the Bible and Greek architecture." The building is a Corinthian temple chopped up inside into classrooms.

Gothic was another popular choice for American builders. It evolved from the simple "carpenter Gothic" to colorful High Victorian. Frank Lloyd Wright detested the miscellany of Victorian Gothic mansions, with "gables, dormers, minarets, bays, porches, oodles of jiggered woodwork ruthlessly pointed, poking in or peeking out of piles of fancified stonework." American architects associated with Gothic Revival were Richard Upjohn, James Renwick, and Alexander Jackson Davis.

The immensely popular American writer Andrew Jackson Downing recommended Gothic residences to a legion of followers. Once Gothic surpassed its rival style, he wrote thankfully, "The Greek temple disease has passed its crisis. The people have survived it." A horticulturist by training, Downing advocated integrating house and landscape. Both should be picturesquely irregular. "A wooden castle, in a flat meadow," he wrote, "is as much out of place as a knight in armor would be running a tilt in the Jersey pine barrens."

Founder's Hall, Girard College, Philadelphia, by Walter, 1833–47
Walter's patron, Nicholas Biddle, insisted that the building design should be the most correct Greek temple in America. Walter wrapped marble columns around the whole building, making this not only the most expensive building of the era but a climax of Greek Revival.

Lyndhurst, Tarrytown, New York, by A. J. Davis, 1838–65
Inspired by Lowthar Castle, this Neo-Gothic mansion on the Hudson River is an asymmetrical mass of stone, covered with spiky ornament inside and out. Its architect, Alexander Jackson Davis, designed the interior with deep colors, dark wood, "vaulted ceilings," and stained glass. Davis raved about towers and turrets to his clients. He was abetted by the tastemaker Andrew Jackson Downing, who wrote, "There is something wonderfully captivating in the idea of a battlemented castle." Downing was so fond of Gothic mystery, he was wont to pop out of a hidden door behind his Gothic bookshelves to surprise his guests.

Washington Monument, Washington, D.C., by Mills, designed 1833
Egyptian Revival became popular following Napoleon's campaigns in Egypt. The style was used for memorials, tombs, banks, and jails (as in New York City's "Tombs" prison by John Haviland). Mills's 555-foot-tall obelisk was the world's tallest structure until its height was doubled in the Eiffel Tower. Critics denounced its Egyptian style, calling it an "architecture of embalmed cats and deified crocodiles." Mark Twain called the monument "a factory chimney with the top broken off," while others compared it to a "stalk of asparagus."

FEARLESS FRANK. The most flamboyant Victorian Gothic buildings in the United States were designed by Frank Furness (1839–1912). Dubbed "fearless Frank" for his heroism during the Civil War, Furness won the Congressional Medal for hauling a box of live ammunition under fire to beleaguered troops. His buildings were equally gutsy in their brawny power and bold shapes. Furness's Pennsylvania Academy of the Fine Arts is fanciful and forceful. Its richly carved exterior and contrasting textures create a lively but unified facade.

In the High Victorian period, architects became self-conscious artistic characters, considering themselves intellectual and creative leaders. This new role of tastemaker was reflected in their behavior and appearance. Louis Sullivan described his mentor, Frank Furness, as "a curious character. He affected the English in fashion. He wore loud plaids, and a scowl, and from his face depended fan-like a marvelous red beard, beautiful in tone, with each separate hair delicately wrinkled from beginning to end."

RICHARDSONIAN ROMANESQUE. Henry Hobson Richardson (1838–1886) introduced a new phase in American architecture. He was the first American to create a world-class, yet individual, style that was copied in America and Europe. Compared to the effete pseudo-classicism of his peers, Richardson's buildings were robust, massive, and compelling. Their trademark traits were use of heavy blocks of rough-cut granite or brownstone with bands of contrasting stone or brick, round arches, an accentuated entry, and horizontal strips of windows. Richardson's buildings reek of power and permanence.

Foyer, Pennsylvania Academy of the Fine Arts, by Furness
The interior of this extraordinary building almost luminesces with color. Gilt floral patterns adorn Venetian red walls. The cerulean blue ceiling glows with silver stars. Gallery walls are plum, ochre, sand, and olive green. The architect Louis Kahn called this Victorian masterpiece "a life-giving and inspired building."

Pennsylvania Academy of the Fine Arts, Philadelphia, by Furness and George Hewitt, 1872–76
Furness combined purple terra-cotta, red and black brick, textured brownstone, sandstone, and pink granite in this muscular building. He fused various historical styles derived from Gothic design (pointed arches), French sources (the mansard roof, projecting central pavilion), and Greek style (panels of incised tryglyphs).

Trinity Church, Boston, Massachusetts, by Richardson, 1872–77
Richardson's boldly simplified masonry construction relied on Romanesque motifs, like the round arch.

Stoughton House, Cambridge, Massachusetts, by Richardson, 1882–83
Shingle Style houses introduced an American contribution to architecture: the informal, open plan where spaces merge both inside and out. Wooden shingles wrap around walls in a fluid, horizontal flow.

Henry Hobson Richardson: First Great American Architect

"My God, how he looks like his own buildings!" an observer pointed out. Richardson was just as bulky as his massive structures. With his booming Falstaffian voice, dressed in a loose monk's robe to conceal his 350-pound girth, he had a gargantuan appetite for food and life. A *bon vivant*, the architect consumed a magnum of champagne and quantities of cheese at meals, even though forbidden by his doctor. "Ordinarily I lead a life of abstinence," Richardson would tell his guest, "but tonight I am going to break my rule to celebrate your visit." After suffering from nephritis for years, Richardson died at age 47. When a symposium was held in 1880 to name the ten greatest buildings in America, five were his.

Richardson's example brought order to the confusion of Victorian eclecticism. Instead of a back-to-the-past style, he synthesized and simplified diverse influences into a signature look. His Trinity Church is multicolored like High Victorian Gothic and composed of many parts. But its strong, earthy materials are unified into a large-scale, coherent form. The turreted tower, Richardson said, is the "main feature" that holds the church together from any angle.

SHINGLE STYLE. The French commentator Alexis de Tocqueville said American society was in such flux, it was almost classless. This social fluidity had its counterpart in a uniquely American form of architecture—the Shingle Style. The name derives from cedar shingles that sweep across exterior walls. No sharp corners halt the eye, as shingles curve around walls and over towers.

The Shingle Style is characterized by houses with flexible plans, minimum separation between rooms, and doors and windows that give easy access to the outdoors. Just as American society was much more informal than in Europe, the houses were not compartmentalized into small rooms, each closed off with forbidding doors. Appearing most frequently in northern seaside resorts, the houses often have wraparound porches, the kind made for Bentwood rockers and Edith Wharton novels. The architectural historian Vincent Scully described the summertime world where "old houses weathered silver, floating like dreams of forever in the cool fogs off the sea."

RETURN TO GRANDEUR. A French novelist who visited Newport was astonished at the marble palaces constructed for robber barons of the Gilded Age. Commenting on the mansions designed by Richard Morris Hunt (1827–1895), he said, "The best artist has been chosen, and he has had both freedom and money. Especially money!" In pre-income-tax days, money was no object in either building or furnishing these New World châteaux. As George Orwell described the

Stick Style

J. N. A. Griswold House, Newport, Rhode Island, by R.M. Hunt, 1862

The first original American style, the Stick Style was used for residences and featured wood crosspieces similar to those on half-timbered Tudor homes. Popular in New England from 1840 to 1870, the style featured irregular plans, lively outlines, and a facade articulated by thin wooden boards, or "sticks." The writer Horatio Greenough called for "the entire and immediate banishment of all make-believe," and this honest, straightforward look was close to a populist expression of structure, rather than a pastiche of historic ornament.

LIVING LARGE

Biltmore House, Asheville, North Carolina, by Hunt, 1888–95

The largest private residence in the United States, Biltmore House cost $4.1 million when built. This summer house for George W. Vanderbilt had 65 fireplaces, 34 master bedrooms, 43 baths, 3 kitchens, 255 rooms, and 11 million bricks. Its foundation covered five acres. The park, comprising 125,000 acres of woodland, with 11 million specimens in its arboretum, was designed by Frederick Law Olmsted, creator of New York's Central Park.

A thousand workers completed the mansion in six years, copying its spiral stair at left of the entrance from François I's famous staircase (c. 1525) at Blois in France. The interior is staggering in rich detail. The six-story banqueting hall has a barrel-vaulted ceiling. Furnished with thrones, Flemish tapestries, and a triple fireplace, the refectory seats sixty-four guests at the table.

A dinner invitation, once accepted, was such a sacred obligation, one aristocrat said, "If you die before the dinner takes place, your executors must attend in your place." At one baronial repast, six liveried servants (attired in Vanderbilt maroon) received guests in the hall. Seven courses were served on gold plates, with fifteen utensils per person and rare orchids decking the table. Fresh fish for fifty were shipped daily from New York, with lobster twice a week.

era, "There never was in the history of the world a time when the sheer vulgar fatness of wealth . . . was so obtrusive as in those years before 1914." Hunt used his clients' wealth to maximum advantage.

Hunt, the first American to attend the prestigious Ecole des Beaux-Arts in Paris, brought opulent French style (called Beaux-Arts style) to the United States. In an age of eclectic revivals, he restored order and correctness on a grand scale. His châteaux for Vanderbilts and Astors were historically accurate, vibrant with marble, red, and gold. The Breakers (1892–95), built for Cornelius Vanderbilt at Newport, resembles a sixteenth-century Italian palazzo. Hunt restored the universal principles of good architecture, like balance, expressive materials, rhythm, and—above all—proportion, which, as Edith Wharton said, "is the good breeding of architecture."

Fallen Arches

Many outstanding buildings that should be part of our architectural legacy have fallen to the wrecking ball. They were victims of shortsighted developers for whom new is always better. A number of buildings by the Philadelphia architect Frank Furness were considered dispensable when Victoriana went out of style but now are sorely missed in the urban landscape. The Provident Life & Trust Co. Bank was a masterpiece of Victorian Gothic. Massive in its explosive power, with squashed columns and narrow proportions, it looked as if it were squeezed in a vise. Furness's aggressive tone and exaggerated shapes emphasized the bearing members of a structure. Lavish ornament and complex color contrasts made his compact buildings forceful as a piledriver.

Henry Hobson Richardson's Marshall Field Wholesale Store was the wedge that shattered revivalism and set the stage for the Chicago commercial school of architecture. It ushered in the modern age. Occupying an entire city

William G. Low House, Bristol, Rhode Island, by McKim, Mead & White, 1886–87

block, the building showed how to unify a huge mass by sheathing the whole in quarry-faced granite with tiers of masonry arcades. Only the rough stones provided visual texture; Richardson stripped the facade of historical ornament. By building "lean and mean," Richardson expressed the large block as an authoritative, single unit. This seminal building was torn down for a parking lot in 1931.

The nearly abstract geometry of McKim, Mead & White's triangular William G. Low House was not matched for a half century. They sheltered a whole building under one sweeping gable (nearly 140 feet long). Inside, the plan was open, divided only by grilles, lattices, and sliding doors. Breezes wafted through the interior in summer, making this a quintessential Shingle Style house. It was demolished in 1952, replaced by a suburban ranch house.

SECOND EMPIRE IN THE UNITED STATES. In the public realm, government buildings aspired to the grandiosity of Parisian structures under Napoleon III. The style, known as Second Empire, featured a ubiquitous mansard roof, often with dormers; paired columns, Neo-Baroque plasticity of wall surfaces, and an emphasis on relief sculpture. The confectionary style of the Executive Office Building (1871–75) in Washington, D.C., relies on piles of ornament. Boston's City Hall (1862–65) and Philadelphia's City Hall (1871–1901) display the grand manner through dense decor and profuse sculpture. As cities experienced an economic boom, with railroads, steel mills, and mines proliferating, huge fortunes were amassed. Cities adopted a style of bulky clutter to flaunt their affluence.

Big Is Better

Not only factories and office buildings were built on an unprecedented scale at the outset of the twentieth century. Homes, too, burst the confines of neat little nineteenth-century cottages in this age of aspiration and expansion.

Theodore Roosevelt, archetypal image of the early 1900s' mania for size, planned his house, Sagamore Hill in Oyster Bay, New York, with scope to satisfy the song, "Oh, give me a home, where the buffalo roam." Sagamore Hill had ten bedrooms on the second floor and two on the third (in addition to maids' rooms)—an ambitious glimpse of the future for his young wife pregnant with her first baby. Roosevelt requested from his architects a big piazza and four huge fireplaces on each floor. The building's foundations are 20 feet thick, with joists and rafters sturdy enough to withstand an avalanche.

The architect Daniel Burnham summed up the spirit of this burgeoning period: "Make no little plans! They have no magic to stir men's blood. . . . Make big plans. Remember that our sons and grandsons are going to do things that would stagger us."

Stanford White: The Architect as Boulevardier

"One of these dynamic trumpeters" Stanford White was called. He was a man with the "same divine frenzy for making himself known that great politicians are born with." In his case, it wasn't hard to attract attention. Exceptionally tall and handsome, White had flaming red hair. His friend the sculptor Augustus St.-Gaudens sketched him as a sunburst. A born partygoer and partygiver, the architect "excited" and "buffaloed" his clients with his enthusiasm and *savoir faire*.

To furnish their Fifth Avenue mansion, White accompanied the Whitneys on a European shopping spree. They spent $350,000 in 1905 dollars on gewgaws like wood paneling from an Italian palazzo and a Louis XV ormulu and Meissen mantel clock. White once chartered an Italian sailing vessel to haul home frescoes, entire ceilings, and mantelpieces. Accumulating knick-nacks like stuffed mooseheads, he ran $100,000 over budget on one decorating project.

A gifted draftsman, White was indefatigable. He designed everything from an entire railway carriage to a yacht to party decorations and magazine covers. He had superhuman energy for architecture, travel, and love affairs. The husband of one of his former lovers shot him dead at a theater rehearsal.

Pennsylvania Station, New York, by McKim, Mead & White, 1902–10
McKim, Mead & White combined Neoclassicism with twentieth-century materials at Penn Station. Three porticos connected by wings were linked by repetitive columns. The waiting room roof can be seen in the background.

Columbian Exposition: Neoclassicism Triumphs

To commemorate the four hundredth anniversary of Columbus's discovery of America, the United States held a world's fair in Chicago in 1893. Although Chicago led the world in developing a new commercial style of oversized buildings, the organizers required uniform Neoclassic facades around a central lagoon. Hoping to impress foreign visitors with their sophistication, architects adopted imperial Roman style in an ensemble known as the "White City." When floodlit at night, the whole looked like a stage set of ancient Rome. Frank Baum was so inspired by the vision, he used it as a model for the Emerald City of Oz.

For the next fifty years, the influence of the exposition shaped American architecture. "It recalls the days of Greece, when men thought in marble," one commentator said. Yet a critic who disapproved of Beaux-Arts parodies scolded, "Men bring not back the mastodons nor we those times." The architect Louis Sullivan, a leader of the Chicago School, deplored the fair's pernicious effect, calling the architecture "an appalling calamity." Sullivan's highly personal Transportation Building was one of the few to express an indigenous style and win international acclaim.

RENAISSANCE REVIVAL: McKIM, MEAD & WHITE. After 1880, a reserved classicism reigned, epitomized by the genteel style of the most successful architectural firm, composed of Charles McKim, William R. Mead, and Stanford White. Their Pennsylvania Station (alas, felled by the wrecking ball in 1963) was a triumph of both engineering and Classical detail. The building was functionally superb, expressing its purpose through modern materials and clear forms. To convey the dignity of a major portal to New York City, its waiting room was modeled on Roman baths, increased 20 percent in size (see page 96). The exterior was pure Neoclassic, covering two city blocks on its eight-acre site (see page 113). At the concourse level, modern engineering reigned. Glazed groin vaults of exposed steel columns, steel arches, and glass were purely utilitarian to cover the tracks.

Edith Wharton deplored New York in the 1870s. Its flat grid of streets devoid of European amenities like fountains, towers, or porticos gave an impression of "deadly uniformity of mean ugliness." McKim, Mead, and White did their utmost to transform the city. From 1870 to 1920 the firm received one thousand commissions, clothing the Northeast in a mantle of tasteful Neoclassic style. In an era of flamboyance, their Villard Houses (1882–85) in New York were an understated interpretation of a Renaissance palazzo.

SKYSCRAPERS: NEW FORM FOR A NEW AGE. "City of the Big Shoulders," the poet Carl Sandburg called Chicago in 1914. Yet, raw and crude as this meat-packing town was, it gave the world the ultimate symbol of the twentieth century: the skyscraper. Sandburg's "tall bold slugger set vivid against the little soft cities," Chicago had no tradition, no height restrictions, and no highfalutin historical preferences. This "City of Speed" grew phenomenally, from fewer than sixty-three permanent residents in 1833 to more than one million in 1900 (the sixth largest city in the world). What tradition it did have was wiped out by a disastrous fire in 1871 that destroyed most of the city center. The way was clear for innovation.

With business booming in the 1880s, land values rose astronomically. The price for a quarter acre soared from $130,000 to $900,000. Thick bearing walls required for large buildings consumed valuable space in a building's lower levels—how to get more usable space per plot? The solution came almost by serendipity. When William Le Baron Jenney (1832–1907) was building the eleven-story Home Insurance Building (1884–85), a strike by bricklayers halted work. To finish, he used a skeletal frame of cast-iron, steel, and wrought-iron girders on both inside and outside walls. When the strikers returned, he hung masonry sheathing on the metal framework as a "curtain" (or non-load-bearing) wall. This was the first time a metal frame supported both walls and upper stories. It meant walls could be much thinner, pierced by ample windows. Buildings could be taller with more interior space. With the addition of the electric elevator in the 1880s, buildings grew from five to twenty stories.

The Chicago School of twentieth-century commercial architecture (1880–1910) launched a whole new building type: utilitarian, multistory buildings that express externally their skeletal frame and emphasize verticality. Henry James said, "All other things being equal, a building that sits is more pleasing than a building that stands." Chicago architects faced the challenge of designing "standing" buildings that were aesthetically pleasing.

Reliance Building, Chicago, Illinois, by Daniel Burnham and John Root, 1890–95
One of the pioneering firms in skyscraper design, Burnham and Root devised a scheme to unify the new tall structures. They divided a building's stories into three parts: a two-story base to provide a solid foundation, a tall central portion with alternating strips of projecting and flat windows and continuous vertical piers to express the steel frame and emphasize height, and a top treated as a separate unit with a prominent cornice. Many have compared the three-part structure's proportions to a classical column (base, fluted shaft, capital).

The firm of Burnham and Root showed the way. Their 14-story masterpiece, the Reliance Building (1890–95), has a pure curtain-wall facade supported by a steel frame. The gridlike exterior, almost more glass than terra-cotta, reflects inner structure. Aware that he had entered new architectural territory, John Root wrote, "All that has been done up to the present counts for nothing," and "Whatever is to be spoken in a commercial building must be strongly and directly said." He discarded Classical frills and let the building speak for itself, in the new language of modern engineering.

LOUIS SULLIVAN: FATHER OF MODERN ARCHITECTURE.
"It must be every inch a proud and soaring thing, rising in sheer exultation that from bottom to top it is a unit without a single dissenting line," wrote Louis Sullivan (1856–1924) in "The Tall Office Building Artistically Considered" (1896). Sullivan and his partner, Dankmar Adler, were preeminent among pioneers of the Chicago School. Their buildings were not only functional examples of metal-frame technology but successful artistically in unifying a skyscraper's repetitious components.

The Wainwright Building (1890) is a ten-story, steel-skeleton structure that emphasizes verticality with, for the first time, an aesthetically effective shell. Prominent corner columns and seven-story piers, like fluting between rows of windows, reinforce the "dominant chord," as Sullivan said, of "loftiness."

A major landmark in American architectural history, the Wainwright Building was hailed by Frank Lloyd Wright as the first structure with "height triumphant."

The Guaranty Building (1895–96), with its giant arches, even more gracefully meets the challenge of imposing coherent visual organization on a tall tower. If buildings by other Chicago architects were a frank expression of their frame, Sullivan's were a revelation of function and finesse.

Although he studied in Paris at the famed Ecole des Beaux-Arts, Sullivan was as much a trailblazer as Davy Crockett. Sullivan believed American achitecture should be *sui generis,* inventing its own forms and ornament without a nod to the past. As romantic an architect as Walt Whitman was a poet, Sullivan called for "a Democratic vista," incorporating "the undreamed of, a versatility, a virtuosity, a plasticity as yet unknown!"

To create this bold new architecture, Sullivan drew on both the beauty of nature and the verve of the new metropolis. Unlike his peers, he consciously shunned European influence. "American architecture will mean, if it ever succeeds in meaning anything," he wrote, "American life." He aspired to endow the tall commercial building, which he called a "sterile pile," with "sensibility and culture."

In Sullivan's treatment of the Guaranty Building, the whole seems to grow organically. He clad its strong, simple form in floral ornament, which he likened to "poetic imagery." With a deft touch, Sullivan transformed pure structure and function into an aesthetic statement.

After the 1893 Columbian Exposition cemented the mania for Neoclassicism, Sullivan found little work. He railed against the fad for a "fraudulent" pastiche of history. "However cleverly plagiarized, however neatly re-packed" Neoclassic buildings were, he considered them ersatz and irrelevant to the New World.

Eurocentric architects got all the commissions. They erected what Sullivan called "Little Lord Fauntleroy" buildings, paying fussy homage to the past. Sullivan kept his eyes straight ahead and paid the price. Forgotten by the public, he became an embittered, penniless recluse.

Sullivan broke the mold. American conservatism broke him.

Guaranty Building, Buffalo, New York, by Adler and Sullivan, 1895–96
Sullivan influenced a generation of architects by designing the modern skyscraper as an organic whole. "Form ever follows function" was his credo. "Whatever is beautiful rests on the foundation of the necessary." He delineated three major visible sections: a strong base with broad windows for shops, a middle section for offices with vertical elements to dramatize height, and a capping cornice housing mechanical equipment. The tripartite division corresponds to practical requirements. Here Sullivan doubled the number of vertical piers (every other pier is not load-bearing) to express not just function but as a design element forcing the eye to read the middle ten floors as one continuous, soaring unit.

THE ANNOTATED VAULT
UNDER THE BIG TOP: VAULTING THROUGH THE AGES

A vault is an arched ceiling or roof. Vaulting developed from its simplest form—the corbeled ceiling vault—to virtuoso Gothic fan vaults. Throughout its evolution, vaulting has been used to whip up a sense of grandeur that a ho-hum, flat ceiling lacks.

In a corbeled vault—the predecessor to the true arch—parallel layers of rock project progressively inward, with each course jutting beyond the row below to form a vaulted roof. The corbeled vault in the Treasury of Atreus, built during the heyday of the ancient Mycenaean culture, was made of 34 self-supporting courses of stone soaring over a circular tomb. The actual tomb was underground. Its beehive-shaped dome seems

designed mainly to impress. In perfectly proportioned geometry, the 45-foot diameter of the tomb matches the height of the ceiling.

Islamic, or Moorish, architecture is without equal in fantastic ornament, as vaulting in Spain's Alhambra demonstrates. Ceilings are gilded and plastered with stucco carved in stalactite and honeycomb patterns (called *muqarnas*). The profusion of scalloped swags has the paradoxical effect of dematerializing the surface, making it seem impalpable.

By the end of the fifteenth century, stonecutting

had advanced to the point where structure in late Gothic churches was secondary to audacious decoration. English architects excelled at the fan vault—an elaborate vault resembling a bouquet of ribs carved in stone. The fan vault begins with half-cones rising from side walls and splays curved struts across the ceiling like the spokes of an umbrella.

Nonstructural ribs, or "net vaulting," proliferated on the continent, too, especially in the hall churches of Germany. Bundles of molded shafts on piers seem to "grow" to become ceiling vaults. The freely curving ribs in the Church of St. Anne form a web of delicate floral forms that enrich the ceiling.

Henri Labrouste brought the vault into the Industrial Age, creating transverse barrel vaults out of cast iron, supported by slender cast-iron columns. His conspicuous exposure of structure and new building materials shocked conservative critics.

Hall of Justice, Alhambra, Granada, Spain, fourteenth century
King's College Chapel, Cambridge, United Kingdom, by Reginald Ely and John Wastell, 1508–15
Church of St. Anne, Annaberg, Germany, begun 1499
Bibliothèque Ste.-Geneviève, Paris, by Labrouste, 1838–50
Grand Staircase with Post-Modern Vaulting, Seattle Art Museum, by Venturi, Scott Brown & Associates

The Twentieth Century: From Hope to Irony

Throughout the history of architecture, styles have swung from plain to picturesque. The twentieth century saw radical shifts, from the straitlaced purism of Modernism to the florid pluralism of Post-Modernism.

During the first fifty years of the century, architects tried to change the world, remaking it in a stark image of abstract geometry. During Modernism's optimistic heyday (1930s to 1960s), the only accepted tradition was the idea of the New. Just as the machine was transforming production and consumption, architects thought a complete break with past styles would transform cities into utopia. The idea that new times demanded new forms prevailed. The industrial aesthetic triumphed. History and ornament were tossed out. But no utopia appeared.

In the late 1960s, the pendulum swung back. Disenchanted with Modernism's anonymous towers, architects embraced the past. Post-Modernists plastered a pastiche of historicisms on their buildings.

As the quest for novelty continued, a succession of movements, without any overall consensus, created diverse designs to reflect a global, multicultural society. New styles like High-Tech, Deconstructivism, even Neo-Modernism vied for attention.

As the century waned, a host of *isms* claimed to represent a fractured age. No longer was a style touted as a panacea to perfect society. The revolutionary phase of architectural aspiration has given way to an evolutionary strain. Today, nobody dares claim that style will save the world. Style is just that—style, not substance—and it's applied with a leavening dose of irony and ambiguity. Plain is gone. In a time of change and variety, plural is the only way to go.

The eminent architect Philip Johnson's long career has spanned two-thirds of the century. "I was a pupil of Mies van der Rohe's," he says. "To him, architecture was a serious business. Now architecture is a form where you can have fun. Modern architecture is more sexy than when columns and walls were straight. Dull is the enemy now."

WORLD HISTORY		ARCHITECTURE
	1902–3	Mackintosh builds Hill House
Wright Brothers fly first airplane; North Pole discovered	1903	
First well-known U.S. film, *Great Train Robbery*, made	1904	
	1906–10	Gaudí builds Casa Milá in Barcelona
Ford's model T goes on market	1908	
	1909	Wright invents Prairie House
World War I fought	1914–18	
Russian Revolution occurs	1917	
Prohibition, women's suffrage amendments adopted	1920	
Daily radio broadcasting begins	1921	
	1925	Gropius builds Bauhaus in Dessau
	1926	Buckminster Fuller designs Dymaxion House
Lindbergh flies solo across Atlantic	1927	
First "talking" motion picture, *The Jazz Singer,* made	1928	
Wall Street crashes	1929	
	1929–31	Le Corbusier's Villa Savoye sets style for Modernism
	1931	Empire State Building opens
Pearl Harbor attack brings U.S. into World War II	1941	
	1943	Pope's National Gallery is last major Classical building in U.S.
Atomic bombs end war	1945	
Supreme Court outlaws segregation	1954	
	1959	Wright's last work, Guggenheim Museum, opens
U.S.S.R. sends first man into space; Berlin Wall erected	1961	
Silent Spring launches environmental movement	1962	
President Kennedy assassinated	1963	
Civil Rights Act passed	1964	
	1966	Venturi's *Complexity and Contradiction* refutes Modernism
Neil Armstrong walks on Moon	1969	
President Nixon resigns	1974	
	1976	Pompidou Centre shows High-Tech style
	1978	Johnson's AT&T Building heralds Postmodern era
First woman Supreme Court Justice sworn in	1981	New Urbanism revives small scale and traditional design
AIDS epidemic ravages public health	1986	
World population hits 5 billion	1987	
Berlin Wall falls	1989	
China crushes democracy		
	1990s	Deconstructivism gets media attention
Apartheid laws abolished in South Africa	1991	
	1997	Cesar Pelli's Petronas Towers become world's tallest skyscrapers
		Gehry's Guggenheim Bilbao shows potential of computer-assisted design
President Clinton impeached; acquitted in Senate trial	1998–99	

1900–1965: MODERNISM, SPARE AND SQUARE

The twentieth-century architect Frank Lloyd Wright spoke of "shelter not only as a quality of space but of spirit." In the first fifty years of the century, architects built shelters to liberate the human spirit. Intoxicated with the potential of mass production, architects were convinced technology would make beauty and utility available to all. Buildings would not just keep out rain and cold; they would ensure health, happiness, and equality.

After turning out period pieces for so long, architects responded to the age of science with an outpouring of innovation. The Russian Revolution, the writings of Darwin, Marx, Freud, and Einstein, coupled with dazzling inventions like the automobile, airplane, electricity, radio, and cinema, spawned a gung ho zest for experimentation. "History," Henry Ford said, "is bunk," and architects threw the past on the trash heap, eager to use revolutionary techniques and materials to express the *zeitgeist*.

Movements like Art Nouveau, the Vienna Secession, and Expressionism showed this resolve to dump nineteenth-century historicism. Individual architects like Wright seemed to start from scratch. Freedom from the past meant, for architecture, free form, free plan, and free facade. Free form took the shape of abstracted, geometric shapes. Free plan dissolved boundaries for interior flow and a multipurpose floor plan. Free facade

Art Deco Delight

Chrysler Building, New York, by William Van Alen, 1926–30

Art Deco put the fun back in functional. The style, named for a 1925 fair in Paris, the *Exposition des Arts Décoratifs et Industriels Modernes*, had its heyday in the 1920s and '30s. Art Deco was a way to shed historical baggage without giving up ornament. It was sleek, flamboyant, colorful, and futuristic. Streamlined stripes in glass, tile, mosaic, and brass echoed the curves of ocean liners. The look is aerodynamic, jazzy.

The Chrysler Building's aluminum spire, with its zigzag accents and eagle-head gargoyles like hood ornaments, is pure Art Deco. The architect, Van Alen, was so flamboyant, he was called "the Ziegfeld of his profession." "No old stuff for me!" he proclaimed. "Me, I'm new! Avanti!"

The best place to see concentrated Art Deco is Miami's South Beach, where, as Lenny Bruce said, "neon comes to retire."

meant stripping away ornament and separating inner structure from visible skin.

These trends resulted in the Bauhaus or International Style, which swept across the globe from the 1930s to the 1970s. Unpainted, unmolded, unadorned modern buildings popped up like an army of robots from Slovenia to Peoria. Standardization, function, and structure reigned supreme. Tom Wolfe, in *From Bauhaus to Our House*, wrote of the "whiteness and lightness and leanness and cleanness and bareness and spareness of it all."

The first half of the twentieth century saw the avant-garde jettison the rear guard. A search for novelty, the siren call of abstraction, and a love affair with the machine led to unprecedented new forms for a new age.

ART NOUVEAU: CURVES AHEAD.

Gilbert and Sullivan's lyric "sentimental passion of a vegetable fashion" could have been written to describe Art Nouveau. Literally meaning "new art," the style born in Belgium and France was an attempt at radically novel design owing nothing to the past. For inspiration, its main practitioners—Horta, van de Velde, Guimard, and Gaudí—turned to the plant and animal kingdom. The Art Nouveau craze spread to Germany (*Jugendstil),* Italy (*Stile Liberty),* and Spain (*Modernismo).* It flowered fast, like buds in an early spring, but faded faster. Art Nouveau's heyday was 1890–1905, kicking off the twentieth century with a flourish of swirling lines and stylized plant forms.

Victor Horta (1861–1947) was the key Art Nouveau architect. His Tassel House (1892–93) in Brussels sums up the style. Its staircase twists in nonstop curlicues. Whiplash wrought-iron railings, wiry light fixtures, mosaics, murals, and tiles form an overall composition of creeping tendrils. Horta created a new idiom of ornamental motifs that rejected history and embraced the jungle.

Tassel House, Brussels, by Horta, 1892–93
One of the first Art Nouveau buildings, this villa shows the integrated decor and structure of swirling lines and plant motifs.

Art Nouveau interiors are all-or-nothing. The home of Henri van de Velde (1863–1957) near Brussels was a one-man show. He designed all the furniture, carpets, cutlery, and fittings in sinuous Art Nouveau curves. Allowing no jarring note, he even designed his wife's clothing (flowing kimonos embroidered with dragons) and selected the color composition of meals.

The most visible Art Nouveau relics are the entrances for the Paris Métro (1899–1904) by Hector Guimard (1867–1942). His glass canopies look like dragonfly wings and lampposts like praying mantises. Forms are billowy and serpentine, stressing the malleability rather than rigidity of iron.

GAUDÍ'S WARPED WAVES.

If anyone heeded the voice of the vegetable, it was Antoni Gaudí (1852–1926). The name is pronounced Gow-DEE, although "gaudy" seems pretty apt.

"Everything comes out of the great book of nature," the Catalan architect said. "Anything created by human beings is already there." But he took the natural look to an extreme of originality, with buildings so mind-boggling, they seem to come from another planet. His chimney pots are shaped like mushrooms, gables drip like stalactites, roof lines flow like a petrified wave, and barnacles of rough stone encrust columns.

Gaudí insisted there are no straight lines in nature, so his architecture is all curves. Lines cavort, leap, and writhe, embedded with brightly colored shards of ceramic to create texture with a capital *T.* His forms may be derived from nature but they are set in motion by Gaudí's powers of fantasy.

Casa Milá, Barcelona, by Gaudí, 1905–10
The curving walls of this apartment house fuse organic naturalism and surreal imagination.

Church of La Sagrada Familia, Barcelona, by Gaudí, begun 1884
One of the most original structures ever, this unfinished stone church looks like a drip sandcastle. It reflects Gaudí's interest in natural forms, as well as his Catalan and Moorish heritage.

Barcelona is a treasure trove of Gaudí masterpieces. Casa Batlló is called House of Bones for its bonelike columns that lean inward. (A structural genius, Gaudí tilted piers to counteract outward thrust and avoid the need for buttresses, which he called "crutches.") Walls pulsate with undulating movement. No flat surfaces or right angles impede the flux and flow.

The irregular walls of Gaudí's Casa Milá, known as La Pedrera (the quarry), resemble weathered sea cliffs. Its wrought-iron balconies are a jumble of lines like tangled kelp. The entire building is plastic as a giant, extruded clay sculpture.

When a young man, Gaudí was a dandy and gourmand who loved to dress and eat well. He later became deeply religious and in 1884 was chosen to build Barcelona's most striking monument, the Church of La Sagrada Familia. To prepare, Gaudí fasted to cleanse himself of youthful sins. In his ardor, he went overboard and had to be dragged out of bed and forced to eat.

Gaudí supervised all details of construction, even executing some of the carvings himself. He gave up everything, moving into the church crypt and living in monkish solitude while the building went up. Gaudí devoted himself to the church, which was unfinished when he died in a streetcar accident outside the church.

Gaudí believed that architecture—the image of organic forms—should grow naturally like a tree. He expected other architects to add their own rings of growth and to finish the huge church. Construction continues today as his huge, openwork spires—resembling surreal, perforated anthills—rise above the city and set a standard of originality likely never to be equalled.

MACKINTOSH: ARCHITECTURE SQUARED.

Another innovator who set the stage for modern design was the Scotsman Charles Rennie Mackintosh (1868–1928). A rabid individualist like Gaudí, Mackintosh jotted down lecture notes stating his credo of unorthodoxy: "Go alone: crawl—stumble—stagger—but go alone."

This resolve impelled Mackintosh to invent his own fusion-style architecture, which framed Art Nouveau curves in a rectilinear grid borrowed from Scottish baronial dwellings. Mackintosh's buildings, mostly in Glasgow, combine floral motifs with angular lattices of stone and wood.

His Glasgow School of Art has a Modernistic gridded facade, leavened with Art Nouveau curling ironwork. Its irregular window placement and turrets harken back to Scottish manors. The library interior is all height, light, and verticality. Windows rise 25 feet tall, and wooden beams and posts intersect in crisscrossing perpendicular lines. The effect is starkly modern—almost Mondrian—twenty years before Modernistic architecture existed.

Glasgow School of Art, by Mackintosh, 1907
This building pioneered the European modern style, breaking free of revivalist imitations with functionalist, abstract forms.

In contrast to the spare lines of Mackintosh's exteriors, he (and his wife-collaborator Margaret Macdonald) designed stunning white-on-white interiors that seem soft as his stone walls are hard. Hill House (1904) has stark, unornamented exterior walls but lush interiors full of pale panels, enamel, colored glass, and beaten metal. Although walls and woodwork are all-white, a green-and-mauve rosebud motif is stenciled on walls and installed in cabinets.

The architect Edwin Lutyens described Mackintosh's tearoom interiors as "gorgeous," but "a wee bit vulgar . . . all just a little outré." Entering the opalescent white-on-silver Ladies Luncheon Room (1901) is like being enveloped in a cloud. Mackintosh was not just a hands-on architect. His fingerprints are all over the tearooms. He and Macdonald designed every last visual effect, from chairs, murals, stained glass, and doors to metalwork and lamps. Ornament and structure were one. A chair with a stylized, squared-off willow tree motif for a back served as both seat and screen.

Mackintosh's contribution was to merge the organic curves of Art Nouveau with regional tradition. Although his imitators were called "Mockin-tosh," his buildings are inimitable. They fused architecture and decorative design into a new style distinctly his own.

Willow Tea Room, Glasgow, by Mackintosh and Margaret Macdonald, 1901
An example of total design, the tea room by Mackintosh and his wife unified structure and ornament. They distilled motifs from nature in stained glass, ceramics, and metalwork. Mackintosh's spare, cool interiors were transitional between Art Nouveau frills and a simplified, modern style soon to appear.

Secession House, Vienna, Austria, by Olbrich (1867–1908), 1898–99
Architects attempting to find an art that symbolized the *zeitgeist* launched the Vienna Secession movement. This gallery housed works by artists who seceded from the traditional art establishment.

Steiner House, Vienna, Austria, by Adolph Loos, 1910
Haus und Garten. The smooth, bare facade and cubic forms of this building predate Bauhaus Modernism by 15 years. Loos wanted extreme geometric purity. He took the Vienna Secession even further, eliminating ornament altogether.

Innovation has its price. Mackintosh was revered abroad, especially in Vienna, where his designs became the catalyst for Vienna Secession style, but he couldn't get jobs at home. He died penniless. In 1995, a magnificent desk he designed brought $1.2 million at auction, the highest price for a twentieth-century piece of furniture.

A modern French architect wrote the words "si j'étais Dieu" (if I were God) above his studio door. A friend asked, "What would you do?" The answer, without hesitation: "I should design like Mackintosh."

VIENNA SECESSION. An Austrian version of Art Nouveau, Vienna Secession architecture was characterized by stylized floral patterns repeated on glass, ceramic, textiles, metal, and stone. Growing out of the Viennese Arts and Crafts movement, the Secession included a group of architects who self-consciously seceded from the mainstream of convention.

Josef Olbrich's Secession House was built as a gallery for Secession artists. Bronze doors by Gustav Klimt open beneath the inscription "To the Age Its Art; to Art Its Freedom." The building's open metalwork dome (dubbed a "golden cabbage") is a ball of gilt laurel leaves. Despite this abundant leafiness, the rest of the building shows restraint in its simple contours.

Josef Hoffmann (1870–1956) is typical of these designers who took a more experimental approach to architecture, developing a stripped-down, antiperiod style. His cubiform buildings won him the nickname of Quadratl-Hoffmann. Stoclet Palace, in Brussels (1904–11), even with its flat lines and stark exterior geometry, manages to look impressively rich, due to lavish materials (marble framed in bronze and mosaics).

Fly Me to the Moon

Saarinen (1910–1961) really wanted to be a sculptor. Instead he became a sculpturally expressive architect, combining Modernist abstraction with romantic imagery. Each Saarinen building reflected not only the site but its purpose and structure. The TWA Terminal is a giant symbol of movement, celebrating the excitement of flight. In these winglike concrete shells, advances in technology finally caught up with an artist's imagination.

TWA Terminal, JFK Airport, New York, by Saarinen, 1956–62

EXPRESSIONISM: CULT OF PERSONALITY. Around World War I, some German and Italian architects tried to launch a new style of architecture defined by bold sculptural effects. Buildings of extravagant form were considered symbolic of communal values or expressive of a designer's artistic vision.

An example is Erich Mendelsohn's Einstein Tower (1919–21), an observatory in Potsdam, Germany. To some, the seven-story structure resembles a sphinx; to others, it's a shoe. Drawn from the realm of fantasy rather than rationality, the building has a cavelike entrance.

Caves and crystals were favored motifs of Expressionism. Hans Poelzig's Schauspielhaus auditorium in Berlin (1919) is so cavelike, tiers of spotlit stalactites hang from a domed red ceiling. Bruno Taut's Glass Pavilion (1914) is a three-level, glass-walled structure faceted like a jewel. Glass was considered a modern medium that could tame the savage beast and hasten utopia. "Glass destroys hatred," Expressionists believed. The see-through building advertises this mythology.

Although the voluptuous forms of Expressionism were soon eclipsed by the dominant, straight-as-an-arrow Bauhaus school, Expressionism reappeared later in the century. Neo-Expressionists like Jørn Utzon, designer of the Sydney Opera House, Eero Saarinen (TWA Terminal), Frank Lloyd Wright (Guggenheim Museum), and Le Corbusier (Ronchamp) revived the abstract sculptural style that was popular from 1905–25.

Einstein Tower, Potsdam, Germany, by Mendelsohn (1887–1953), 1919–21
Mendelsohn wanted to find a form for the future. His daring designs put intuition before logic, devising expressive shapes for his vision. He wished to create a new order that would be "simple and sure like the machine, clear and daring like the construction."

FRANK LLOYD WRIGHT: BREAKING THE BOX

They Don't Call It Fallingwater for Nothing

Genius though Wright was, there's a downside to going where no architect has gone before. Those dramatic cantilevers tended to sag with the years. And Wright's low-slung roofs may have been a perfect analogy for the prairie, but they inevitably accumulated snow and leaked. At the first dinner party in the last great Prairie House, Wingspread, the roof started to leak on the head of the owner, Herbert Johnson. The irate client called Wright to complain. The master's reply: "Why don't you move your chair?"

The most famous architect of the twentieth century—perhaps of all time—was the quintessential American individualist Frank Lloyd Wright (1867–1959). His great discovery was, he said, "the idea of eliminating the containment which is the box, reaching out and amplifying space, dragging things in from the outside." Wright invented the open plan in which space flows unobstructed from room to room and inside to out, "a new realm of architecture which," he noted, "has never existed in the world before."

Even before his birth, Wright was destined to be an architect. His mother was so set on his vocation, she hung engravings of great cathedrals in the nursery. She gave her son maple blocks to play with so he could learn the basic geometric shapes underlying natural and man-made structures. Thanks to this toy, he said, "I began to look into things, not at things. That was my gift from my mother."

ORGANIC ARCHITECTURE: THE PRAIRIE SCHOOL. Wright explained his design philosophy: "Nature builds a tree from the inside out. That's what organic architecture is. It's building the way nature builds." Wright started with the concept of free-flowing space, then designed a structure not only to blend with the natural site but to maximize interaction between indoors and out.

By 1909, his experimentation resulted in the first pure Prairie House, the Robie House. Its roof lines are long and low, like the flat prairies that stretch through the Midwest. Anchored by a central stone hearth and chimney, interior space flows from room to room without walls or doors. The space seems to extend visually through bands of windows and out to verandas and terraces. Cantilevered roofs parallel the ground, sometimes extending 20 feet, to further the impression of sweep and spread. To weave the sprawl together, interior trim (usu-

East Meets West

Japanese architecture was designed to harmonize with nature. Verandas under overhanging gables extend the axis of the indoors to the outside. Translucent sliding panels are the only partitions in the interior. Both Frank Lloyd Wright and Walter Gropius of the Bauhaus called Japanese pavilions the origin of modern modular architecture.

Wright admired the projecting eaves and sweeping roof lines of Japanese architecture when he saw a reproduction of a temple, the Ho-o-den, at the 1893 Chicago World's Fair. The floating roofs, absence of walls, and interior-exterior flow influenced his concept of the Prairie House.

Korakuen Villa, Okayama, portions c. 1700

ally bands of oak) links the radiating channels.

When Wright broke the box of Victorian architecture, with its tiny rooms closed off by walls and doors, he released new spatial possibilities. Space became a sculptural element that could be energized, interlocking horizontal and vertical voids. Wright commented that his Unity Temple taught him that "now architecture could be free." His revolutionary use of poured concrete (adopted for budgetary reasons) created a huge unit of flowing space, unified by ornamental banding. "I discovered something tremendously important," Wright recalled. "That the reality of the building did not consist in the walls and roof of that structure but in the space in here to be lived in."

Organic architecture also means site-specific. Wright's own home, Taliesin East (pronounced Tal-ee-EH-sin) in Wisconsin, sits not on the peak of a hill but on its brow (the name is Welsh for "shining brow"). "No house should ever be on any hill," Wright explained. "It should be of the hill, belonging to it, so hill and house should live together each the happier for the other." Wright sought to discover a landscape's underlying geometry, then to enhance it with a building that echoed, shaped, or unified the setting. The low-slung roofs, deep eaves, and horizontal massing of Prairie Houses reflected the endless flow of the prairies. At Taliesin East, the architect added a "birdwalk," a long projecting gangway hovering above the ground, so his wife could walk out at treetop level.

Yet Wright acknowledged that a home needs to offer not just a sense of liberation but also shelter. His projecting roofs embrace the whole structure to provide security. His huge chimneys imply rootedness. Although there were few internal barriers to flow, Wright incorporated "phantom"

Robie House, Chicago, by Wright, 1908–9
Wright invented the modern suburban "ranch" house, with carport, terraces, and horizontal rooflines to reflect the prairie.

The Wright Stuff

"Eliminate the decorator" was Wright's motto. He designed all elements of a building's interior, considering both architecture and furnishings his exclusive domain. In his own house, his first wife, Catherine, obligingly wore the dun-colored clothes he designed so she wouldn't upstage the decor.

Others were not so accommodating. Some clients insisted on installing their own cherished possessions. "Very few of the houses, therefore, were anything but painful to me after the clients moved in and, helplessly, dragged the horrors of the Old Order along after them," Wright lamented. Even he had to admit that the hard, upright chairs he favored were torture-racks for the human anatomy. "I have been black and blue in some spot, somewhere, almost all my life from too intimate contact with my own furniture," the architect admitted.

Francis W. Little House, Peoria, Illinois, by Wright, 1913

partitions through furnishings and level changes to create intimate spaces that functioned as rooms. In the Robie House, high-backed chairs (a counterpoint to the prevailing low, horizontal lines) outlined a dining area.

Wright had many fallow years in the United States. Traditional Beaux-Arts architects who designed in historical styles won most commissions from about 1909 to 1936. Influenced by his mentor, Louis Sullivan (whom he always called his *lieber Meister*, or beloved master), Wright refused to adopt revival styles, preferring to create his own authentic, democratic architecture native to America.

His career was jump-started in 1937, when at the age of nearly seventy he created his masterpiece, Fallingwater. No building better illustrates the idea of organic architecture. The home seems an extension and amplification of the cascade it straddles.

Its owner, E. J. Kaufmann, when he saw the plans, exclaimed to Wright, "I thought you'd place the home near the waterfall, not over it." Wright replied, "I want you to live with the waterfall, not just look at it, and for it to become an integral part of your lives." Architecture, the egotistic Wright explained, takes "guts. People will come to you and tell you what they want, and you will have to give them what they need."

Fallingwater is unquestionably a triumph of daring. A boulder in the stream bed, which the Kaufmann family used to picnic on, became the fulcrum of the design. Embedded in the floor in front of the hearth, the boulder is the still point from which all cantilevers radiate out. Perpendicular stacked shelves of concrete terraces hover over the waterfall. The buff color (Wright originally wanted gold leaf) of the terraces echoes the rock. Rusticated masonry forms the chimney and walls, looking like natural ledges. The balconies' horizontal sweep is balanced by the vertical uplift of the chimney core, which anchors the house to the ledge and reflects the falls.

A totally different, but no less innovative, design was the Johnson Wax Administration Building. Its magical interior creates a sense of a protected community, an ideal workplace where space is allotted according to egalitarian principles. All curves, the huge interior is one vast work area. A ceiling of glass tubing between circle-topped columns admits diffused light to give a submarine glow to the interior. The form of Wright's sixty columns (each 30

(above) Fallingwater, Bear Run, Pennsylvania, by Wright, 1937–39
Possibly the most famous work of modern architecture, Fallingwater is an example of Wright's organic architecture that seems to grow from its site.

Johnson Wax Administration Building, Racine, Wisconsin, by Wright, 1936–39
Wright became interested in curves as a means of generating a design. His commitment to democratic architecture produced this ideal communal working place. For Wright, decoration is integral, not applied. He designed all circular furnishings and fittings to harmonize with the structure.

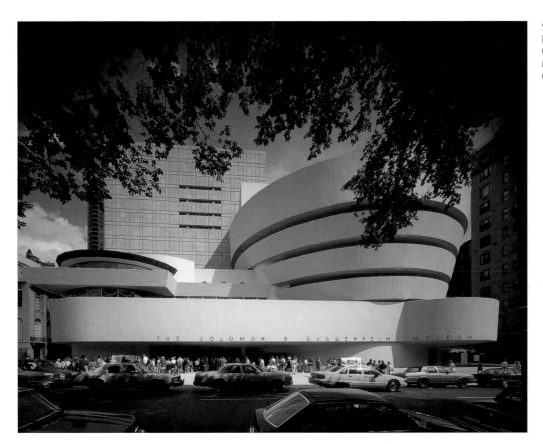

**Solomon R. Guggenheim Museum,
New York, by Wright, 1943–59**
One of Wright's last works, the Guggenheim
Museum achieves the architect's lifelong
dream of complete interior flow.

feet high) has been compared to lily
pads or golf tees. Although fanciful,
they serve a practical function. The
hollow tubes are storm drains.

Wright's tall research tower
(Price Tower, 1952), also for Johnson
Wax, achieved his goal of building
like nature. The floors of individual
laboratories are cantilevered out off a
central stalk like branches of a tree.
Wright called the skyscraper "the tree
that escaped the forest."

GUGGENHEIM: GO WITH THE FLOW.
Completed the year of his death
(1959), the Guggenheim Museum
reveals yet another incarnation of
Wright as a discoverer of form. In it,
he finally achieved a building of
continuously unrolling space. Its helix
gradually expands in a spreading
spiral ramp for ultimate flow. The
interior is an ocean of space capped
by a skylit dome.

David B. Gamble House, Pasadena, California, by Greene and Greene, 1908-9
Deep eaves and exposed post-and-beam structure make the house almost a pergola opening to the outdoors. In their new, native
style, the Greenes designed not only the stickwork with their legendary craftsmanship, but every inch of the interior furnishings.
Beautifully shaped wood, artfully joined into a flowing whole, was the essence of their art.

Byodo-in Temple: Phoenix Hall, Kyoto, Japan, 1053
Greene and Greene adopted the exposed timber construction, overhanging eaves, elaborate wooden brackets, and interaction with the landscape of Japanese architecture. In both, architecture derives from handcrafted construction.

Women's Club, La Jolla, California, by Gill, 1913
Gill adapted the classic simplicity of Spanish colonial missions, producing unornamented exteriors as early as seminal European Modernists. Gill made the new medium of concrete acceptable by the natural settings he designed around his stark buildings. Walls without cornices or trim of any kind were softened by vines creeping across their plain surface.

CALIFORNIA DREAMIN'

In the 1920s in the United States, only Frank Lloyd Wright and a few architects in California were designing buildings in a free, nonhistorical style. Although they were not united into a coherent movement, architects like Maybeck, Greene and Greene, Gill, Schindler, and Neutra were evolving a proto-modernist style that was not indebted to the European past.

GREENE AND GREENE: JAPANESE JOINERY. Charles Sumner Greene (1868–1957) and his brother Henry Mather (1870–1954) achieved an architecture of great complexity from elements of utmost simplicity. As Ralph Adams Cram wrote, "It is a wooden style built woodenly." Taking their cue from the consummate woodworking of Japanese pavilions and their philosophy of truth-to-materials from the Arts and Crafts movement, they built bungalows in the Los Angeles area that are as meticulously assembled as fine cabinetry.

In their Asian-inspired residences, beams are linked to beams with wooden pegs, then carved, oiled, and hand-rubbed until they glow like mahogany nests. Projecting eaves and balconies expose the building's structure in an unabashed display of workmanship. Out of simple, solid shapes and local materials, Greene and Greene developed a style that was both forthright and sophisticated.

The Gamble House (1908–9) consists of low roofs carried on elaborate brackets and a rustic timber frame, which is a major visual element. Surfaces of teak and mahogany, stained-glass windows and lighting fixtures, and hand-forged ironwork project a sense of warmth, texture, and articulated detail.

MAYBECK: AGELESS ECLECTIC. Bernard Maybeck (1862–1957), who worked around San Francisco and Berkeley, took the Stick Style and gave it a spin around the globe. He, too, emphasized exposed wooden structure as a primary visual feature, but he combined this Arts and Crafts technique with new materials and technology. His First Church of Christ Scientist (1910) has Japanese pagoda gables, Gothic tracery, Classical piers of reinforced concrete, and Byzantine drama.

GILL: MAN WITH A MISSION. Irving Gill (1870–1936) also rebelled against the European historical tradition, believing that California life and the local climate created unique architectural needs and opportunities. For Gill, the West was "the newest white page turned for registration," and he was determined to leave an indigenous mark. His architecture embraced the local heritage of Spanish colonial missions.

While his buildings were inspired by the simple geometry and symmetry of missions, with their round arches and plain surfaces, Gill was one of the first to use reinforced concrete and steel structural members. His concrete structures were innovative by their very simplicity, presenting unadorned facades at the same time as Adolph Loos, whose 1910 Steiner House in Austria is usually considered the first Modernistic, unornamented building.

Gill wanted houses to be "simple, plain, substantial as a boulder." He proclaimed, "We must not weaken the message of beauty and strength by the stutter and mumble of useless ornaments." For Gill, "the source of all architectural strength" was fundamental: "the straight line, the arch, the cube, and the circle."

Gill's buildings around San Diego, like the Scripps House and La Jolla Women's Club, are lean, pure compositions of his trademark arches and courtyards. With their flat roofs, they seem like sugar cubes, whose only adornment is the clean geometry of openings in the walls.

Lovell House, Hollywood, California, by Neutra, 1929
Progressive European-style architecture appeared in California before the mass migration of Bauhaus architects to the United States in the 1930s. The horizontal cantilevered spans echo Wright, while the flat roof and walls, ribbon windows, hovering planes, and white walls are pure International Style.

Keeping the Faith

High Museum of Art, Atlanta, by Meier, 1983
Richard Meier (b.1934) has remained a pure Modernist, continuing to build International Style, all-white buildings into the present.

SCHINDLER AND NEUTRA: WRIGHT DISCIPLES. Two other early Modernists, both transplants from Vienna, learned from Frank Lloyd Wright the concept of sprawling spaciousness. R. M. Schindler (1887–1953) combined the developing European abstraction with Wright's spatial complexity. From the mid-1920s, Schindler designed site-specific houses with open plans and intersecting outer and inner spaces. His California homes are more stark and simplified, more blocky, than Wright's. The Lovell Beach House (1925) consists of spare rectangles, with spaces that interlock vertically.

Richard Neutra (1892–1970) designed homes that epitomize not only the golden age of Modernism but also the California ideal of flowing open space, natural light, large expanses of glass, and connection to the outdoors. Neutra's Lovell House (1929) uses a prefabricated steel skeleton to support a structure of white-painted concrete, glass, and wood. Raised on stilts, the house projects out through space on cantilevered terraces, in a deliberate interplay of vertical and horizontal lines.

These progressive architects, while isolated from developments in Europe and cut off from academic East Coast style, were at the forefront of design. They realized the implications of new materials and how to use them for structural expression. Their houses for rich clients were sprawling showplaces of nonhistorical, modern design. Yet they kept a regional flavor and meshed with the California landscape.

THE BAUHAUS: INDUSTRIAL STRENGTH

Although Constructivists in Russia and Futurists in Italy were proposing radical designs around World War I, the style that came to dominate world architecture and define Modernism was born in Germany. The Bauhaus, a state school founded in 1919 to unite fine and applied arts in "a new architecture" was its epicenter.

Bauhaus Modernism was a movement or method, not a style. It proposed simple, streamlined houses for workers, which would be affordable, efficient, and well designed. Living in such an environment, it was thought, would improve the human condition and foster an egalitarian society. Mass production was key. Only standardized components were feasible to fill the urgent need for mass housing quickly and cheaply.

Architects considered themselves leaders of a social revolution. They would create a new society on the drafting board—social, not just aesthetic, reform. For the first time, great architects concentrated not on designing palaces for royalty or monuments for church and state but ordinary housing for the common man.

Traits of Bauhaus architecture that proliferated across the globe in high- and low-rise structures from 1930 to 1970 were free-plan interiors; use of concrete, glass, and steel; stark white cubes; unadorned wall surfaces, strip windows flush with the wall plane; and flat roofs. This "white architecture" was called factory or machine design. Order, regularity, and a sense of space rather than mass predominated.

Bauhaus Workshop Wing, Dessau, Germany, by Gropius, 1925–26
This building, with its famous glass-curtain facade, gave birth to Modernistic architecture. Built from standardized industrial parts, like prefabricated, reinforced concrete, metal, and glass, it illustrated the machine aesthetic that Gropius thought would transform the world.

The first recognizable Bauhaus building was the workshop wing (1925–26) at the school designed by Bauhaus founder Walter Gropius (1883–1969). Dubbed an "aquarium" by uncomprehending critics, the building had floating planes of glass that hid its interior structure. Its clarity—based on straight lines, right angles, and flat roof—set the pattern for countless knockoffs. To Gropius, his glass-and-steel cage represented "the new structures of the future [that would rise] from the hands of a million workers like the crystal symbol of a new faith."

When the Nazis closed the Bauhaus in 1933, its teachers scattered, spreading the concept of rectangular minimalism across Europe and the United States. Architects like Gropius and Marcel Breuer, who taught at Harvard's Graduate School of Design; Ludwig Mies van der Rohe, who led Illinois Institute of Technology; and Lázló Moholy-Nagy, founder of the Chicago Institute of Design, infused the gospel in a generation of architects.

"Make it new," the poet Ezra Pound proclaimed as a Modernist manifesto. In architecture, "new" was in; "old" was out. Gropius banished the study of architectural history at Harvard, fearful that knowledge of the past would stifle creativity. Two rallying cries were behind the wholesale rejection of the past. Adolph Loos had pronounced "ornament is crime" in 1908, and Gropius had dubbed the machine "our modern medium of design." A building's industrial production, function, and structure would determine its form, "unencumbered," Gropius said, "by lying facades and trickeries."

INTERNATIONAL STYLE: THE ART OF SUBTRACTION

The original Bauhaus philosophy was based on liberating humankind from a class system through a machine-age environment. When it hit the United States in the 1930s as the International Style, it was quickly co-opted into an aesthetic style stripped of utopian leanings.

The name came from a 1932 Museum of Modern Art exhibition of the new architecture, which displayed examples of Modernist homes for the wealthy rather than housing projects for workers. But this style, which was truly international, was Bauhaus in all but name and heart. The characteristics were the same: simple rectangular boxes, absence of applied ornament or historical reference, flat roofs, white walls, large windows, and the holy trinity of concrete, glass, and steel.

Gerrit Rietveld's Schröder House (1924) is a pure example of the style. It looks like a painting by De Stijl artist Piet Mondrian come to life. Flat rectangular planes intersect asymmetrically. Accents of yellow, blue, and red float in the pale linear composition. Inside, the abstract forms continue with railings, lamps, chairs, and tables all relentlessly rectilinear. The house is neither left-wing nor right-wing. It's right angle.

The first International Style skyscraper was the Philadelphia Saving Fund Society (PSFS) Building (1931) by Howe and Lescaze. While other skyscrapers of the time were festooned with historical furbelows or Art Deco chevrons and setbacks, this thirty-six-story tower was brazenly honest. Its design (divided into

Schröder House, Utrecht, The Netherlands, by Rietveld (1888–1964), 1924
A three-dimensional version of Piet Mondrian's abstract paintings, this house is plain geometry inside and out. De Stijl theorists believed "an ornament-free architecture demands the maximum purity of the architectural composition."

zones for a public bank, offices, and building services) reflects function. Each use is expressed on the exterior. The lower floors with large windows housed the bank, offices were behind the horizontal strips of tower windows, and elevators, stairs, and bathrooms were housed in the rear section. Intent only on expressing structure and purpose, the architects dumped traditional high-rise elements like cornices or columns. They eliminated moldings, niches, and embellishments for a ruthlessly pure, smooth surface.

MIES VAN DER ROHE: RADICAL COOL.

Mies's most famous statement, "Less is more," could be inscribed on his tombstone. This philosophy of *reductio ad minimum* permeates every building he designed. Mies (1886–1969) constantly subtracted, purified, and refined until he reached his goal, an architecture of "almost nothing."

"For me, novelty has no interest, none whatsoever," he said, adding, "I don't want to be interesting. I want to be good." His architecture is pure form reduced to its rectangular essence. Floor plans were open, undifferentiated space, ready to be adapted to new uses as they evolved. At Illinois Institute of Technology, the buildings he designed, with their undivided interiors, are almost indistinguishable from each other (or from warehouses) inside. He created an infinitely adaptable template. Even the IIT chapel is a clone of classrooms or research buildings. The box is the thing.

The Farnsworth House is the ultimate in glacial reductiveness. Its floor-to-ceiling glass walls and lack of interior division make it almost negative architecture—generic space that fit Mies's observation of "the trend of our times toward anonymity." The building is basically one huge room with a roof, four glass walls, a door,

Farnsworth House, near Plano, Illinois, by Mies van der Rohe, 1950
Mies reduced the components of a domestic dwelling to an absolute minimum: a rectangle of steel and glass floating on a concrete slab. Mies's structures visually reveal how a building is made.

Seagram Building, New York, by Mies van der Rohe and Johnson, 1954–58
This steel-framed building, wrapped in a curtain wall of bronze I-beams and tinted glass, became the most refined model for countless office towers built in the next two decades.

a floor, eight steel I-beams, and a terrace. A tour would take about two minutes. "It is a prototype for all glass buildings," Mies said.

Its owner, Dr. Edith Farnsworth, thought it a prototype for ruin. With the architect forbidding her to add tchotchkes to humanize the pure space and only two small, high windows that opened (and no air conditioning), she found it too costly, too public, and downright unlivable. The dissatisfied client huffed, "Something should be done about such architecture as this or there will be no future for architecture."

STEELY TRIUMPH.   Unable to go further in paring down a domestic dwelling, Mies turned to corporate commissions. His Seagram Building (1954–58) is the ultimate International Style skyscraper. Seagram's proves the point of Mies's oft-quoted epigram "God is in the details." His inspired idea was to apply scaled-down bronze I-beams to the exterior glass curtain wall. The non-load-bearing beams frame the amber-tinted window bays and stress verticality over the entire facade, adding texture and visual interest. The vertical lines also echo the invisible steel structural frame. The architect Louis Kahn called the building "a beautiful lady with hidden corsets."

The interior (designed with Philip Johnson) reflects the obsession with detail. The architects designed everything: lavatory, lettering on lobby mailboxes, light fixtures, door handles, and mail chutes. The extreme discipline of the design implies Mies's belief that "Reason," as he quoted St. Thomas Aquinas, "is the first principle of all human work." Mies never stopped believing that architecture could bring much-needed order to "the godforsaken confusion of our time."

What he didn't foresee was how trickle-down versions of his pristine glass boxes would become, in lesser architects' hands, a cliché. As Robert Venturi later put it, "Less is a bore." Mies reduced architecture to fundamentals, and his abstinence from flourishes produced concisely elegant forms. But without the rich materials he used or attention to details in his flexible modules—not to mention his alchemy with scale and proportion—the corporate office towers he spawned became faceless, monotonous, sterile boxes. Mies had a narrow range, which he honed to perfection. Rip-offs of his style are just so many radiator grids blighting the urban streetscape.

LE CORBUSIER.   Charles Edouard Jeanneret (1887–1966), who took the name Le Corbusier, was another giant of modern architecture. Like the Bauhaus architects, Le Corbusier wanted to overhaul the world. He believed in environmental determinism—that design could improve human nature. If a dwelling was logical, functional, and efficient as a machine, its inhabitants would be similarly rational, enlightened, and relieved of tedium.

"Soleil, espace, verdure" (sunlight, space, and greenery) was his motto. He achieved light from wraparound ribbon windows, space with double-height living rooms (the forerunner of today's "cathedral" ceilings), and greenery from the views, roof gardens, and area beneath his houses on stilts.

International Style

Steel, concrete, glass
Flat roof
Strip windows wrap around corners
Right angles
No applied ornament
Independent structural frame
Flexible interior space

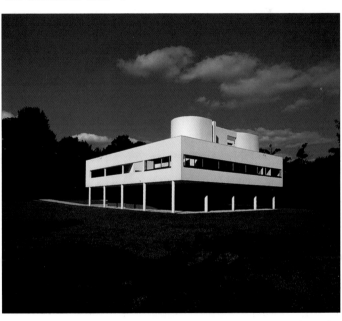

Villa Savoye, Poissy, France, by Le Corbusier, 1929–31
"Architecture," Le Corbusier said, "is the masterly, correct, and magnificent play of masses brought together in the light." This house has impeccable minimalist credentials (flat roof, ribbon windows, geometric shape, unornamented surface), but it maximizes light and space.

Unité d'Habitation, Marseilles, France, by Le Corbusier, 1945–52
This mass housing project illustrated Le Corbusier's belief in architecture as an instrument of moral and social reform. Spartan on the outside, it housed a complete village inside.

Corbu is known for calling a house "a machine for living in." He thought a house was, like a car, a "tool" for humanity, "serviceable as a typewriter." The machine aesthetic for him meant a stripped-down approach. "The straight line is the great achievement of modern architecture," he wrote. "We must clean the cobwebs of romanticism from our minds." Architecture should express its era. "We must start again from zero."

Le Corbusier's recommendations, published in an influential book translated as *Towards a New Architecture* (1923), were firm: a building raised on pillars (pilotis), its interior a free-flowing floor plan, long horizontal strips of windows, and a roof garden on a flat roof. He boasted that this universal prescription would work "for all nations and climates."

The villas Corbu designed express his machine aesthetic. The Villa Savoye (1929–31) is a square box on legs, a composition of thin planes, austere white walls, and simple geometry. Interior ramps link the different levels. Curved walls like steamboat smokestacks provide a windbreak for the roof garden. The shape of the first floor is determined by the turning radius of cars in the garage. The villa was called "Les Heures Claires," or bright hours.

Le Corbusier's most influential design was the huge eighteen-story housing block (with apartments for 1,600 people), L'Unité d'Habitation (1945–52). Inspired by socialist ideals, the complex included communal facilities for childcare, shopping, and recreation. The goal was a total environment, enhanced with all the amenities of civilization, so one would never need to leave. It is architecture as an instrument of social transformation *par excellence*.

Unité's high-rise, high-density format became the model for mass housing. A rectilinear block of reinforced concrete rests on massive legs. The main visual feature is the balconies with deep overhangs for sun protection (called *brise-soleils*). Surfaces are painted different colors to enliven the bleak mass of concrete. Le Corbusier diverged from his prior smooth surfaces by emphasizing surface texture. The concrete was left rough, marked with the knots and grain of its wood forms.

Le Corbusier, considered the "Picasso of architecture" for his inventive shifts in direction, developed a late style totally alien to his early pronouncements. "Burn what you loved," he advised his students. The pilgrimage church of Notre-Dame-du-Haut at Ronchamp (1950–55) exemplifies a

Bad Architecture Is Bad for People

International Style advocates promised the factory aesthetic would enhance residents' lives, a sort of "if we build it, they will bloom" assurance. Designed as a model of efficient housing, this low-income project became a death trap. Anonymous tower blocks, with their large-scale repetition of uniform elements, not only failed to improve the human condition, they exerted a detrimental influence. Uniform mass housing—prey to vandalism, high crime, and defacement—was belatedly judged socially undesirable. These towers were deemed so hazardous to residents' spirit and character, they were dynamited seventeen years after construction.

Pruitt-Igoe housing project, St. Louis, built 1955 by Minoru Yamasaki, demolished 1972

Church of Notre-Dame-du-Haut, Ronchamp, France, by Le Corbusier, 1950–55
Le Corbusier turned to sculptural expressionism in this church with rounded walls and an uplifting prow.

Interior, Notre-Dame-du-Haut, by Le Corbusier
Thick walls and irregular stained-glass windows create an intimate atmosphere of great mystery.

bold, new sculptural approach. The swelling roof has been compared to a nun's wimple or a mushroom, although Corbu said he was inspired by a crab shell he picked up on Long Island. The thick walls create a grottolike interior. Deep window slits of different sizes admit colored light to create a mysterious, subterranean effect. The shafts of light seem almost palpable.

Corbu called the modern movement "an Homeric cleansing of architecture." With Ronchamp he shoveled out everything done before and started anew. "Courage alone can define the quality of an existence," Corbu wrote. His courage in following his convictions was not always appreciated. When he built a house for his parents in Switzerland, the local council called it a "crime against nature" and prohibited copies.

Le Corbusier believed modern architecture required no interior gussying-up. "Modern decorative art is not decorated," he insisted, recommending replacing wallpaper, hangings, or stencils with a coat of white paint in every room. "Cleanse your home . . . then cleanse yourself," he admonished.

Corbu collaborated with an interior designer, Charlotte Perriand (1903–1999), who enlivened his homes with clean, fresh furnishings and built-in cabinetry. A Modernist pioneer, Perriand agreed with Le Corbusier that furniture was "equipment for living." She invented a style to express the possibilities of industrial design. "I don't see why I should do what has been done before. I express my era, period," Perriand said in an interview, adding, "We made our century sing."

"Architecture is stifled by custom," Le Corbusier wrote in 1923. "There exists a new spirit." It's a spirit he did more than anyone to invoke.

The Winner Is . . .

According to a 1982 vote conducted by the American Institute of Architects, "the best six American buildings" of the past 125 years were:

Fallingwater by Frank Lloyd Wright

Seagram Building by Mies van der Rohe and Philip Johnson

Robie House by Frank Lloyd Wright

Wainwright Building by Louis Sullivan and Dankmar Adler

Trinity Church by Henry Hobson Richardson

Dulles Airport by Eero Saarinen

MODERN REBELS

Phillips Exeter Academy Library, Exeter, New Hampshire, by Kahn, 1969–72
The strong geometry of Kahn's composition gives the building an almost mystical power. Four exposed concrete circles frame the stacks, flooded by light from above.

Salk Institute, La Jolla, California, by Kahn, 1959–65
A travertine central plaza opens to the sea, flanked by angled laboratory buildings with concrete walls and teak insets. The oceanic space, bisected by a slim channel of water, leads the eye to the horizon, creating a sense of infinite scope.

KAHN: SENSUOUS GEOMETRY. The Philadelphian Louis Kahn (1901–1974) was America's foremost Modernist. A late bloomer, Kahn didn't win his first major commission until the age of 52. His Yale University Art Gallery captured international attention with its structural exhibitionism, rational order, and abstraction. The ceiling tells it all. It consists of a tetrahedron grid of exposed concrete. For Kahn, raw structure had decorative potential. The stairs are a concrete cylinder, the elevator a bare rectangle.

Kahn was something of a guru, a teacher who mesmerized students and clients with aphorisms like "What does the brick say?" His basic concern was to discover what a building "wants to be." At the stunning Phillips Exeter Library he decided the essence of a library was "picking up a book and going to the light." The library is a celebration of that act.

The library's outer walls are a brick box surrounding a huge interior atrium. The four-story well of space is bordered by gargantuan concrete circles that reveal the stacks encircling the atrium. A huge concrete brace in the shape of an X crosses the skylit central court. The geometry is rigid but the soul of the building is humane and functional. It feeds the eyes and mind.

Kahn believed each component activity deserved its own space. In the Richards Medical Research Building (1957–65) at the University of Pennsylvania, he allotted separate structures to the "servant" areas (blind shafts that house utilities) and the "served" (windowed towers for laboratories and offices). The entire composition of vertical towers recalls the many *campanili* in the village of San Gimignano, Italy.

The Jonas Salk Institute for Biological Studies (1959–65) creates a monastic setting for research. Two rows of studies in four-story towers line a masonry court. As in a minimalist painting, a slim strip of water cuts across the court, falling toward the Pacific. This understated structural drama animates the mute space and links it to the limitless sea. Reaching "the sublime through the rational" is how architect Richard Rogers describes Kahn's design.

The Kimbell Art Museum (1966–72) shows Kahn's wizardry with light. A barrel-vaulted gallery is lit by slits of daylight peeking over the top of the vaults. Metal reflectors bounce the light upward, bathing the curved concrete ceiling in radiance like polished silver.

AALTO: FORM FOLLOWS FOREST.

The Finn Alvar Aalto (1898–1976) was a soft Modernist who humanized the machine aesthetic. Although he began in a crisply functional style, as in his early Viipuri Library (1927–35), even then the cool exterior form was warmed by abundant use of wood inside. Wavy wood strips ripple across the ceiling of the auditorium.

Aalto combined International Style geometry with local color. Since Finland is all birch and pine, he brought this regional flavor to his designs. At first glance, the Villa Mairea (1938–39) looks like a mutant in its forested site. Aalto softened the Modernist flat roof, white walls, and right angles with a free-form entrance canopy. The interior is alive with lumber. Stairs are lined with wood poles like a bamboo grove. Aalto mixed inorganic, machine ingredients with organic elements. He fused technology with tradition and craft, going beyond high-tech to high-touch.

Aalto captured international acclaim with his Finnish Pavilion for the New York World's Fair (1938–39). The architect took an ordinary warehouse and converted it to a visual vacation. A three-tiered wavering wall of wooden poles leans forward, seeming to flicker like the aurora borealis. It was evident this was no pure rationalist. When Frank Lloyd Wright saw the installation, he said, "Aalto is a genius."

Staircase, Villa Mairea, Noormarkku, Finland, by Aalto, 1938–39
Slatted ceilings, columns bound by willow withes, and a staircase that metaphorically represents the forest show how Aalto emphasized the psychic dimensions of architecture.

Green Architecture: Designs for a Sustainable World

Glass office towers became a generic corporate logo after World War II. In terms of thermal load and heat loss, they were outrageously impractical. When the energy crisis struck in the 1970s, architects sought more efficient construction. In Foster & Partners' Business Promotion Center in Duisburg, Germany, computers analyze weather conditions constantly to moderate the building's microclimate.

In home design, passive solar heating caught on. New materials like recycled newspaper and straw bales were used for insulation. Self-composting toilets were installed, and buildings were designed to minimize energy consumption or generate their own energy.

The essence of eco-architecture is to use only renewable resources, employ recycled materials, preserve old buildings, and take maximum advantage of climate, site, natural light, and ventilation.

Auburn University students are premier recyclers. Building houses for the poor in rural Alabama with their own hands, they scavenge materials and turn junk into architecture. In 1995, they built a chapel in Alabama out of 1,000 discarded tires. They filled the tires with dirt, stacked them like bricks, and coated the walls with cement-based stucco.

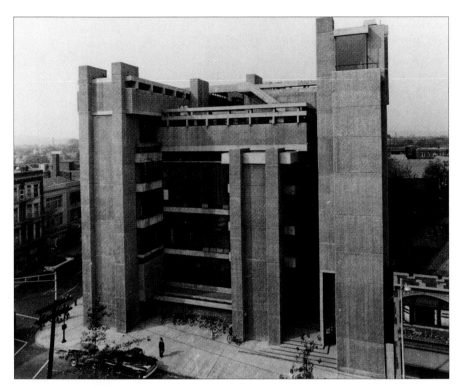

Art and Architecture Building, Yale University, New Haven, Connecticut, by Rudolph (1918–1997), 1959–63
This building introduced Brutalism, a style that juxtaposed massive planes of rough, exposed concrete.

Aalto believed the concept of rational design should be expanded to "include psychological requirements." He considered wood "a deeply human material" and used a palette of cheerful colors to enliven abstract forms. In the Baker House Dormitory (1947–49) at Massachusetts Institute of Technology, human considerations dictated the shape. Aalto created a long, S-shaped building with an undulating facade, so each student's room offers an oblique view of the Charles River. Architecure, as Aalto proved, could be aesthetically daring and socially responsive. "It is still the architect's duty to attempt to humanize the age of machines," he said.

"One must achieve a simultaneous solution of opposites," Aalto believed. He synthesized reductivist, Modernist form with additive, expressive elements. A transitional figure between Modernism and Expressionism, Aalto combined the opposites of standardized machine technology with organic materials of sensual, tactile appeal. He balanced regional and international influence, modern with vernacular styles, nature and industry.

BRUTALISM: ABRASIVE ARCHITECTURE. Inspired by the *béton brut* (raw concrete) used by Le Corbusier in his late style, Brutalism was in vogue during the 1960s and early '70s. Its identifiable feature is a rough concrete exterior showing the textured imprint of formwork on the surface. It's a chunky, aggressive look. Masses without polish or finish seem to crash together. Surfaces are scored and corroded; construction is coarsely exposed—the visual equivalent of grunge.

Paul Rudolph's School of Art and Architecture Building (1959–63) at Yale University is an archetypal Brutalist building. It's a collage of colliding parts. Nearly forty different floor levels intersect in the seven-story building. The rough texture, inside and out, was due to hammering the corrugated concrete surface to expose aggregate. It's so hard-edge, you could literally bleed from bumping into a wall. Rugged, aggressive, heroic—the building has attitude. Form routs function.

A bevy of British architects used the abstract vocabulary and aggressive exteriors of Brutalism. Willfully avoiding elegance and comfort, the buildings of Peter and Alison Smithson (born 1923 and 1928) expose structural materials with unabashed gusto. Plaster and paint are banished. Plumbing and electrical conduits hang out—technology as decor.

James Stirling (1926–1992) and Colin Wilson practiced a high-tech form of Brutalism. Stirling's Engineering Building at the University of Leicester (1959–63), built with James Gowan, has the sharp juxtapositions and raw energy of this factory aesthetic.

Needless to say, such buildings are not very popular with their inhabitants. "I want a building to move people," Rudolph said. His Yale building did. Students considered it so hostile, they tried to burn it to the ground.

100 Years of Skyscrapers: A Tall Order

A quintessentially American invention, skyscrapers were born in the 1880s when the electric elevator met the steel skeleton. In Chicago, skyscraper form emphasized height, structure, and function, clothed in the three-part format of a Classical column. New York skyscrapers celebrated height and added period details. Their decorated, sculpted masses soared into flamboyant spires. The International Style discarded the past for the austere glass box. Recent towers have rediscovered history, casting aside a purely rational stance for more lively silhouettes.

Guaranty Building, Buffalo, New York, by Adler and Sullivan, 1895–96

The first "modern" skyscraper with aesthetic merit was invented by Louis Sullivan. His office towers were analogues of a classical column. Zones corresponding to base, shaft, and capital expressed different interior uses. Chicago School skyscrapers frankly stated their steel frame, terminating with heavy cornices on top.

Woolworth Building, New York, by Cass Gilbert, 1911–13

This Neo-Gothic "cathedral of commerce" shows how the profile of a skyscraper changed from a tall column to a tapering ziggurat. Instead of basing form on frame, as Sullivan did, Gilbert added medieval trappings to please his client, who admired the Houses of Parliament. New York skyscrapers emphasized height with their elaborate crowns and pasted contemporary or historical motifs on the tall form.

Empire State Building, New York, by Shreve, Lamb & Harmon, 1929–31

In 1916, zoning regulations required setbacks to prevent Manhattan's tall towers from turning the city into sunless canyons. Skyscrapers adopted a rakish profile. The mass tapered at stages, climaxing in a graduated spire. At 102 stories, the Art Deco Empire State Building was the world's tallest structure from 1931 to 1971. It made a new point: The sky is not the limit anymore.

Seagram Building, New York, by Mies van der Rohe and Johnson, 1954–58

This building epitomizes the revolutionary glass curtain-wall construction that defined corporate headquarters. This oblong glass box set the pattern for impersonal commercial architecture worldwide. Unfortunately, a good building can be a bad model. When replicated in cheap imitations, the towers became anonymous and alienating.

Sony Building (formerly AT&T Building), New York, by Philip Johnson and John Burgee, 1984

Philip Johnson, one of the first to embrace the International Style, was one of the first to abandon it fifty years later. By putting a broken pediment (to look like a Chippendale highboy) on top of this thirty-six-story corporate headquarters, the architects declared the dull glass box dead. International Style buildings had scorned history and tried to create structures that owed nothing to the past. Post-Modern buildings raid history, using past decorative motifs while commenting on them. The 65-foot arcaded entry is an inflated Renaissance Pazzi Chapel. The lobby gleams with gold groin vaults.

Piazza d'Italia, New Orleans Louisiana, by Moore, 1975–78
Moore combined Classical and commercial, local and exotic styles in his theatrical structures.

Po-Mo architecture connects directly with the public, a major aim. Instead of faceless, bland Modernism (considered prissy "either/or" absolutism, according to Venturi), Post-Modernism embraces the multiplicity of "both/and." It's an inclusive, accessible style communicating readily with a public turned off by sterile Modernism.

Probably because it proved popular and easily commercialized, Po-Mo elicited huffy putdowns from critics. Hilton Kramer termed it "ersatz contrivance," a style of "architectural one-liners" without subtlety or depth. It's been called "bimbo" architecture, obsessed with gimmicks of surface decoration, a packaged version of history that appeals to a sensation-hungry public.

MOORE AND MORE. For Charles Moore (1925–1993), an archetypal Post-Modernist who heaped on multiple allusions, more was never enough. An outspoken opponent of anonymous bedroom suburbs and interchangeable cities, Moore wanted architecture to recapture a lost "sense of place." Each commission was an opportunity to highlight what the ancients called "genius loci," or special attributes of a site. Moore's Sea Ranch housing (1965–72) on the California coast was an early example of ecological architecture. The houses, modeled on local barns, are nestled into the site, sheltered from prevailing winds. Slanted roofs both deflect wind and collect sunlight.

Most of Moore's buildings have a theatrical flair. They're whimsical, playful—impish as Moore himself. The structure that best shows this flamboyance is the Piazza d'Italia (1975–78) in New Orleans. Brightly colored, superficial as a Hollywood stage set, the composition of arcades, fountains, and mosaics has all the exuberance of this carnival city, where *"Laissez les bons temps rouler"* (let the good times roll) is the motto.

With its startling colors of rust, yellow, and orange, the Piazza is brassy as a trumpet. Its scenographic design recalls diverse monuments like Hadrian's Maritime Theater at Tivoli and the Trevi Fountain in Rome. The neon-outlined blue and orange pergolas and pseudo-triumphal arches are pop Classicism at its gaudiest.

Moore alluded to historical motifs only to spoof them. His capitals consist of water jets shaping Corinthian "leaves." Stainless-steel Ionic volutes and streams of water flowing down columns to suggest fluting are a mischievous takeoff on Classical style. In a high-camp parody, medallions shaped like Moore's head spout water.

Moore stressed the need for "joy" in architecture. An omnivorous usurper of historical forms, he considered himself somewhere between "litmus paper and a piranha fish" in his relation to high and low culture. His own house had at its hub a pavilion with Classical columns over a sunken tub.

Moore's structures were often made of ephemeral materials—plywood or stucco—because they were cheaper and lighter. Some, like the Piazza d'Italia, have suffered from the passage of time. For Moore, permanence was not attainable. He lamented the "presence of the absence"—the loss of identity in our increasingly homogenized culture, which he tried to rectify. At his memorial service, a New Orleans jazz band played to honor the architect who brought humor and humanism to design.

GRAVES: METAPHOR MAN.
Michael Graves (b. 1934) designed the first major Post-Modern building, the Portland Public Services Building (1979–82). He has said he designs as if he were a child, and the building looks like a toy block colored with crayon. Classical elements are vastly overscaled, like seven-story pilasters topped by huge brackets and a three-story keystone. In a Post-Modern touch, the fluting in the pilasters and "joints" of the keystone are really bands of ribbon windows. Applied ornament consists of abstracted swags and garlands, also inflated enormously.

Graves, who originally wished to be a painter, color-codes his buildings to create what he calls "metaphorical landscapes." Shades derive from nature, with blue as an analogy for sky, green and earthtones for landscape. It's as if he's carving his own butte, albeit adorned with his personal interpretation of Classical motifs. He wants his architecture to be "capable of being read by anybody."

The Denver Public Library shows Graves as a master collagist. The ensemble looks like a heap of children's building blocks. Different shapes like cylinder, pyramid, and rectangle are piled up and painted with watercolor tones.

Portland Public Services Building, Portland, Oregon, by Graves, 1979–82
Color and pseudo-Classical elements, like inflated keystone and pilasters, are typical of Post-Modernism. Graves decorated a basic cube with attention-getting decor. "The nature of architecture is that it changes," Graves says. "In designing a building, one shouldn't preclude that a building will change its stripes." The excitement is on the outside, while the inside is flexible.

IN THEIR OWN WORDS

Axline Court, Museum of Contemporary Art, La Jolla, California, by Venturi, Scott Brown, & Associates, 1994–96

"Architecture should look at and acknowledge the context of a setting and the ethos of a place and relate a new building to it," Venturi says. "You can achieve harmony from contrast as well as analogy. . . . We're trying to create continuing harmony that involves evolution. We don't explicitly strive for originality. If architecture is really good, it's original and 'whammo' in incidental ways. At second glance, you realize the subtle variations. . . . The main words are 'context' rather than 'original signature' and an emphasis on generic architecture that allows for spaces that can be modified over time."

As Denise Scott Brown puts it, "We like to think of movement systems and how they relate to buildings. The main circulation system—a street that goes through the building—must be clear."

@ Home

Microsoft mogul Bill Gates's home near Seattle is made of the usual stone, wood, glass, and concrete. It's also made of the not-so-usual software and silicon. The world's richest man is the most plugged-in, making his $53-million home a prototype for the Information Age. Occupants wear an electronic pin programmed with their preferences. This chip makes the house respond instantly, providing a micro-environment of personalized amenities. As you walk down a corridor, lights dim behind and illuminate before you. Screens display your favorite images or films, and speakers emit music or news, according to your whim. The temperature adjusts as you enter a room; a phone rings only in your presence. For a techie, there's no place like cyber-home.

VENTURI AND SCOTT BROWN: LEARNING FROM LIFE.

Robert Venturi (b. 1925) and his wife and partner, Denise Scott Brown (b. 1931), are realists and theorists. With Steven Izenour, they produced an influential book, *Learning from Las Vegas* (1972), that demanded respect for the actual landscape of our lives.

Analyzing the Las Vegas strip for its vitality rather than its vulgarity, the architects praised the honky-tonk energy of pop culture. Venturi had already reopened the door to the past with his first book, and now he welcomed the commonplace qualities of vernacular (everyday, nondesigned buildings) and commercial structures. One result was that buildings learned to be "contextual." Unlike aloof, Modernist boxes, they attempt to blend with their surroundings. The authors jettisoned elitism for populist "people's architecture."

Venturi's Guild House (1960–63) in Philadelphia is a textbook example. With Quaker self-effacement, the building is consciously banal, so understated as to look indistinguishable, at first glance, from its unremarkable neighbors. "Main Street is almost all right," Venturi wrote. Guild House is almost straight Main Street. Subtly exaggerated elements and dissonant touches infuse a zip of Mannerist humor.

The Vanna Venturi (or Chestnut Hill) House (see page 143), which the architect designed for his mother, shows this tendency toward sly double-entendre. The house is similar to a typical suburban tract house, but Venturi parodies the format with wit and irony. He distorts the scale of elements, like the too-thin lintel, which is not tectonic but merely applied as decoration. The gabled facade is split, and the broken arch is nothing more substantial than molding. These allusions to history are like pasted-on icons to decorate a basic "shed," but the whole is a carefully calculated composition. When critics called his work "ugly and ordinary," Venturi accepted the term as high praise.

The firm's Sainsbury Wing addition (1991) to London's National Gallery shows their philosophy of simultaneous analogy and contrast. To balance old and new, Venturi and Brown maintained the same scale and materials as the original 1838 building. But instead of spacing out their pilasters in regular rhythm, they adopted a syncopated beat, with pilasters that overlap or recur at unpredictable intervals. Windows are "blind" and entries resemble squarish garage-door openings. Paying homage with one hand to the Classical vocabulary, they undermine its solemnity with the other.

Some criticize Post-Modernist buildings for excessive concern with packaging space rather than manipulating or shaping it. The lobby interior of Venturi and Brown's addition to the Museum of Contemporary Art, San Diego, shows they can create spectacular spaces. The court is topped by an oval lantern and high, clerestory windows on each side of a seven-pointed star. Dramatic vistas and processional paths radiate from the court in multiple directions, directing the gaze toward the ocean, the art collection, or the surrounding city.

The exterior of the museum, with its simplified, arched openings and plump-columned pergola, is all deference and decorum. The architects pay homage to the architect of the original 1915 building, proto-Modernist Irving Gill. Gill believed "an artist is known rather by what he omits." In counterpoint to Gill's reductivist sensibility on the outside, Venturi and Brown pumped up the volume inside. The fanfare of their lobby includes neon-lined perforated-metal fins that recall both the Benday dots of Roy Lichtenstein's Pop Art paintings and an octopus. "We needed a dash of contrast," said Venturi, an admirer of "messy vitality."

JOHNSON: TWENTIETH-CENTURY CHAMELEON.

It's no wonder Philip Johnson's favorite quote comes from Heraclitus: "Everything flows and nothing abides; everything gives way and nothing stays fixed." His own identity as an architect has been protean for sixty-five years. At the center of every major movement in architecture since he burst on the scene championing the International Style in 1932, Philip Johnson (b. 1906) morphed from a Modernist to a Post-Modernist to a Decon dilettante and, most recently, a member of the architecture-as-sculpture school.

Glass House, New Canaan, Connecticut, by Johnson, 1949

Glass House, interior
Johnson described this house as "Modernism taken as far as it could go."

Centre Pompidou, Paris, by Piano & Rogers, 1971–77
High-Tech architecture fetishizes the ducts and pipes of a building's services. Elements of function and structure appear on the exterior as color-coded ornament.

"You know I'm a whore," this expert self-promoter has repeatedly acknowledged, adding, "I'd work for the devil himself" in a 1973 interview. "I do not believe in principles, in case you haven't noticed," he said at a 1982 conference. Often hired as a "signature" architect to give a cachet of prestige to his commercial commissions, Johnson has no true signature other than his allegiance to trendiness.

At first, he was a passionate disciple of Mies van der Rohe, even joking his name was Mies van der Johnson. Working as his idol's assistant, Johnson designed interiors for the milestone Seagram Building (see page 134). In his Glass House, Johnson created the ultimate sleek Modernist box, achieving Mies's goal of "almost nothing."

Johnson is perhaps best known for his Post-Modern structures, like the AT&T (now Sony) Building (see page 141). This granite-clad skyscraper sounded the death knell for minimalist glass boxes. With its Classical loggia at the base and Chippendale top, it certified the marketability of Post-Modernism.

Johnson has been accused of being a shallow gadfly. His commercial jobs can be slapdash and garish, not to mention derivative. His elliptical Lipstick Building (1985) at 53rd Street and Third Avenue in Manhattan has a cheap look even though composed of rich materials.

"Post-ideological" is probably the best moniker for Johnson. As versatile as he is utterly without conviction, Johnson pulsates with the latest schemes and fads. Invariably called "the dean of American architecture," Johnson set the tone for architectural discourse for the better part of the century. "There is only one absolute rule today in the arts," Johnson said in 1987, "and that is change." On his ninetieth birthday, he was asked if he had words of advice. His answer: "Never, never, never stop what you're doing and rest."

HIGH-TECH:
INSIDE-OUT ARCHITECTURE

In a reversal of Modernist form-follows-function or form expressing structure, some architects show off technology as decor. From the 1960s, a High-Tech school of architects, primarily in the United Kingdom, embraced the concept of a building as a work of engineering art. The essence of the style is an up-front display of mechanical guts for aesthetic effect.

The premier example is Piano and Rogers's Centre Pompidou (1971–77). To create huge, flexible space inside, the architects placed a network of colored metal frames, pipes, corridors, and escalators outside the building's glass skin like an exoskeleton. Transportation systems, like stairs and elevators, are indicated in red; air conditioning and heat ducts are blue, water pipes are green, and conduits for electrical wiring are yellow.

Putting these complex systems in the foreground works better visually than functionally. High-Tech buildings don't grow old gracefully, since the labyrinth of pipes and ducts is difficult to clean and maintain. The Centre Pompidou (called the Beaubourg) was closed in 1998 for a complete overhaul.

The Italian architect Renzo Piano (b. 1937) is known for adventurous projects that challenge the limits of technology. His technically inventive engineering is evident in the New Metropolis (1997), a science center in Amsterdam. Its oxidized copper structure looks like a supertanker's prow rising at water's edge. Coming from a long line of building contractors, Piano gained a feel for hands-on design and construction techniques from his infancy.

Although some of his buildings showcase technology as ornament, others take a quieter approach. The Menil Collection building in Houston is calm and luminous. His Swiss museum, the Fondation Beyeler (1998) near Basel, is a spare, self-effacing cube. Simple and open, with glass walls and a transparent roof, the building is a radiant enclosure for art.

ROGERS: UTILITY CHIC. British architect Richard Rogers (b. 1933) has merged High-Tech with high-green. Concern for global ecology modifies his once-pure machine aesthetic, although he still emphasizes flexible internal space and space-age exteriors. Rogers's Lloyd's of London Market Building (1978–86) looks like a souped-up hotrod, with stainless-steel tubes and pipes on the exterior. Function seems to determine form and pervade every visible facet of the design but "sustainability" is its underlying goal.

Some of Rogers's energy-conserving tricks are as ancient as exploiting thermal mass in mud huts. An internal concrete ceiling absorbs cool night air and sheds it during the heat of the day, reducing the need for air conditioning. Siting in relation to the sun and triple-glazed skin for insulation also reduce

Lloyd's of London, Market Building, London, by Rogers, 1978–86
Elevators, stairs, pipes, and services are visible on the surface in this High-Tech building, which is extremely energy-efficient.

Neue Staatsgalerie, Stuttgart, Germany, by Stirling, 1984
Stirling led the movement away from Modernism's pure functionalism. His use of color and quirky historical references created dramatic forms very popular with the public.

artificial energy requirements. A glazed double skin reduces pollution and noise, and windows on the inner skin ventilate stale air. The entire building acts as a chimney, with airflow shedding heat in summer and trapping it in winter.

For sheer structural exhibitionism, Norman Foster (b. 1935) is tops. Known for creative architecture that works superbly, Foster devised his Hong Kong and Shanghai Bank (1979–86) of three slabs of different heights with functional and skeletal elements in full view. Giant trusses crisscross on the exterior to hold eight supporting masts together. Computerized systems for heating and ventilating, lighting, communications, and acoustics ensure smooth function.

The bank's full-height atrium is a crowning achievement in a building of such size. An external bank of mirrors acts like a sun scoop, reflecting light into mirrors inside that beam sunlight through the atrium to the plaza floor far below. The building is made of prefabricated glass and steel components with materials derived from aerospace technology.

STIRLING EXAMPLE. James Stirling (1926–1992) began as a Brutalist and High-Tech exponent. Without losing his techno flair, Stirling dallied with Po-Mo design, juicing up his buildings from the 1970s onward with a range of historic references. Enlivened by bright colors and undulating walls, Stirling's work is both monumental and casual.

Called "Big Jim" for his physical girth as well as his prominence in architecture of the 1980s, Stirling never wanted to be pigeonholed. "I, for one, welcome the passing of the revolutionary phase of the Modern Movement," he said. "Architects have always looked back in order to move forward." Diverse elements, like bright green mullions on windows and a blatantly Post-Modern arcade behind Classical statues, hold "an architectural conversation." The resulting mix expresses the conflicting facets of contemporary urban life.

Stirling's masterpiece is his addition to a Stuttgart museum called the Neue Staatsgalerie, a hodgepodge of High-Tech and Po-Mo. Stripes of polished gold sandstone and brown travertine and sweeping ramps unify the vast whole, punctuated by pipe railings in electric blue and fuschia. Green-framed windows weave in and out like Borromini's Baroque walls. Stirling called it "a collage of old and new elements."

Stirling believed that architecture could embody passion. In his buildings, innovative forms and psychedelic colors convey his intensity yet still relate to their context.

NEO-MODERNISM: KEEPING THE FAITH

Since 1965, when Modernism was pronounced dead, a few hard-liners have tried to keep geometric abstraction alive. Architects like Richard Meier, Charles Gwathmey, I. M. Pei, Tadao Ando, and Arata Isozaki continue to use sleek International Style surfaces, highlighting pure space and form. But they face a problem. When what used to be radical went from reviled to revered, and then deteriorated to old-hat, how could its disciples resuscitate it? Neo-Modernists, for whom applied ornament remains blasphemy, had to look in a new direction.

Among the younger generation, the Swiss partners Jacques Herzog and Pierre de Meuron (both born 1950) have kept the torch burning by opting for radical simplicity. Their compositions, like a 1998 California winery fronted by a wall full of loose rocks inside metal mesh, are powerful understatements, rich in texture and sensual beauty.

JAPANESE SIMPLICITY. Japan has proved especially receptive to Modernism's appeal. Kisho Kurokawa (b. 1934) merged Western Modernism with Japanese tradition in his Hiroshima Museum of Modern Art (1988). Linked pavilions with roofs like Edo storehouses are simplified forms that create a charged atmosphere.

Arata Isozaki (b. 1931) also synthesizes East and West, using computer-assisted design (CAD) to create his architecture of cubes and arches. His Fujimi Country Club (1973–74) is a string of continuous barrel-vaulted volumes in the shape of a question mark. The calligraphic quality of the design lends an enigmatic air to what looks like pure form.

Tadao Ando's favorite material is exposed concrete, but he achieves a sensuous effect by casting it in severely geometric forms open to nature. Ando's Children's Museum (1988–89) in Himeji, Japan, has a purity of form, color, and materials, transforming ordinary materials and reduced forms into a spiritual experience. Coupled with a shallow pool and waterfalls, the museum creates a magical site for play.

The Milanese architect Aldo Rossi (1931–1997) distilled forms to their essence, injecting a suggestive dimension through shadow games. "Original without being novel" is how the Pritzker Prize citation described his work. Rossi used severe geometric shapes (cones, cylinders, squares) in sequence to restore order to the chaotic, postwar world.

Il Palazzo Hotel, Fukuoka, Japan, by Rossi, 1989
Rossi's simplified geometric shapes achieve a surreal, haunting effect.

Rossi's compositions often have a surreal quality, recalling the spooky shadows and raking light of Giorgio de Chirico's paintings. Distorted proportions, wacky juxtapositions, obsessive repetition, and closed-off walls register a jolt of the unknown. His Il Palazzo Hotel has a stripped-down, Neoclassic facade of sumptuous marble columns and green copper lintels. The absence of windows is unexpectedly powerful, haunting. "While I may talk about a school, a cemetery, a theater, it is more correct to say that I talk about life, death, imagination," Rossi wrote.

I. M. PEI: PYRAMID POWER.

Born in China in 1917, the American architect I. M. Pei is one of the best-known architects in the world. He has never abandoned his Modernist fixation on bare geometric masses and continues to design variations on his signature glass pyramid. Pei's extension to the National Gallery of Art, the East Wing (1978), is a composition of triangles and wedges that comes alive inside its lobby. A Calder mobile sways in the overhead space, enlivened by a torrent of sunshine pouring through the 60-foot-high skylight.

Although he admitted, "I prefer jazz," Pei gave the Rock and Roll Hall of Fame (1995) in Cleveland a pyramidal glass tent as entry and asymmetric, cantilevered masses for drama. His Miho Museum (1997) in Kyoto may be the most exalted space of his career. A glazed, tubular-steel spaceframe bathes the interior in natural light. Slatted louvers create bars of shadows, transforming the lobby into a striated crystal.

Pei designed the aboveground entrance (1983–89) to the Louvre Museum in Paris (see page 162) as a 71-foot-high glass pyramid. An inverted glass pyramid extends into the underground interior, converting what could be a dark dungeon into a radiant pool of light. Nothing could be more of a contrast to the sturdy stone structures of the Louvre than Pei's immaterial pyramid. The counterpoint of royalist froufrou and Modernist clarity has striking impact.

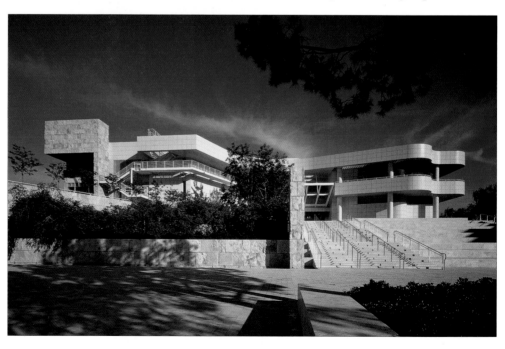

J. Paul Getty Museum, Los Angeles, by Meier, 1997
Located on a hilltop near the ocean, the $1 billion museum complex attempts to embrace both nature and culture. The brightness and openness of the travertine-clad campus recall the horizontal emphasis of early California Modernists like Schindler and Neutra. Meier displays his International Style obsessions, like gridded geometric forms and layered spaces enlivened by natural light.

MEIER: WHITE CASTLES.

Eskimos have countless words for snow, and Richard Meier's architectural vocabulary encompasses hundreds of shades of white. His hallmark is the Euclidean white box—sleek, slick, and shining like an ice palace. The formal purity of the International Style roars to life in Meier's hands.

Like some remnant of Le Corbusier, Meier's structures seem to exist as autonomous objects, making no effort to integrate with their surroundings. Their machinelike clarity and industrial materials, like steel pipe railings and glass blocks, reinforce the impression of precision and underlying geometric order.

Meier (b. 1934) does more than just refine Modernism to crisp perfection. His complex manipulation of masses, carving space and light almost palpably, produces an energized interplay between outside and inside. Meier called it a "dialectic of open and closed." Space and natural light circulate expressively through irregular forms in gridded layers.

Meier's 1997 masterpiece, the Getty Museum, shines like a temple complex on the Acropolis, high above the Los Angeles freeway. The buildings, with their ribbon windows, off-white cladding, and pipe-railed stairs, are virtual quotations from the International Style canon. "Beauty molded by light" is how Meier describes his work.

Villa dall Ava, St. Cloud, Paris, by Koolhaas, 1991
Irregular forms and slanted lines show Koolhaas's Deconstructivist tendencies.

Lerner Hall Student Center, Columbia University, New York, by Bernard Tschumi/Gruzen Samton, 1999
According to Tschumi, "Architecture is not only about form but what a building does." In this design, translucent glass ramps act as a circulatory system for the campus. Tschumi describes the vast glass court between two masonry wings as "an in-between space, a place of freedom and invention to be appropriated by its users." The openness of the crisscrossing ramps promotes social and academic interaction and builds a sense of community among students.

NEW FORMALISM: ARCHITECTURE AS SCULPTURE

Complex curves used to be confined to nature. Then came computer-driven design and manufacturing, which straightened out curve-related technical problems. With great success, software developed to design Mirage fighter jets has been adapted to three-dimensional architectural modeling. This breakthrough freed designers' imaginations, permitting sculptural architecture to blossom.

Computer programs churn out detailed designs and plans—even for unconventional geometric forms. Contractors consult sophisticated 3–D computer models that illustrate irregular shapes. Detailed precasting guidelines help fabricators. Digital design allows the architect uncompromising control and a streamlined construction process at reasonable cost. Cyberspace is transforming living and working space.

After the minimalism of Neo-Modernism and abstraction of Deconstructivism, sculptural architecture brought liberation. Functionalism took a backseat to the search for new forms undreamed of in the history of our built environment. Pioneering architects like Koolhaas, Frank Gehry, and Eric Owen Moss dream up idiosyncratic forms that look like nothing so much as giant sculpture.

ARCHITECTS' HOMES

An architect's own home, as Charles Gwathmey says, "is a laboratory in progress." It's where architects try out ideas and build their dreams with the most tolerant of patrons—themselves.

His clients, disgruntled at his total control of their residences, down to designing the hostess gown and napkin rings, sometimes called him Frank Lloyd Wrong. But in his own refuge, Taliesin East, Frank Lloyd Wright got everything right. The 37,000-square-foot complex is a premier example of organic architecture. Nestled on the edge of a hill and built of local limestone, laid in courses like natural strata, the house is a spur of the landscape. Interior walls are plastered with sand from the riverbank, and wood shingles were stained the color of native tree trunks at dusk. Blurring the boundaries between inside and out, a 40-foot "birdwalk" cantilevers into the trees like a branch.

If Wright's house was an homage to nature, Philip Johnson's paid tribute to Mies van der Rohe. The Glass House, inspired by Mies's 1947 design for the Farnsworth House, is anorexic architecture, all skin and bones. Johnson wrote, "A pure cubist form with no traditional sense of a house or of shelter, [the Glass House] represents Modernism taken as far as it could go." The 1800-square-foot rectangle, anchored by a brick cylinder that pulls everything together, allows 360-degree views, with nature the only wallpaper.

Frank Gehry took an ordinary house and made it into a funky collage of off-kilter fragments. Crude elements like raw plywood, corrugated metal, exposed studs, and a kitchen floor paved with asphalt give the house an unfinished, punk look. Although intensely eclectic, the final effect is of counterpoint, not chaos.

Frank Gehry house, Santa Monica, California, remodeled by Gehry, 1978

GEHRY: THE ART OF ARCHITECTURE.

Canadian-born Frank O. Gehry (b. 1929) is the most original contemporary architect working today, a leader in the creation of habitable sculpture. Gehry designs buildings as if he were a painter. Putting art back into architecture, he groups novel shapes in what seems like a haphazard jumble but with underlying unity. "Artistic expression," he has said, "is the juice that fuels our collective souls."

Gehry's early work, shaped by the Southern California environment where he practices, evinces a chicken-coop aesthetic. His buildings give the impression of an offhand work in progress. The exterior might look like a shattered whole, but inside, the units merge into a smooth spatial sequence. Gehry called it "cheapskate architecture" because he used handyman's-special materials like corrugated metal, plywood, and chain-link fencing. "I'm confused as to what's ugly and what's pretty," he said, refusing to snub utilitarian materials. His concerns, according to Gehry, are "cheapness, destruction, distortion, illusion, layering, surrealism."

NOT SO DUMB.

Gehry's own house reflects this provisional approach, stressing the process of disassembly and change. In 1978, he took what he called "a dumb little house with charm" (a Dutch colonial tract house in Santa Monica) and remodeled it to look like a freeway accident.

Quirky shapes at bizarre angles and unorthodox materials like his trademark cyclone fencing add layers of overlapping planes. The old house is visible through its envelope of junky fragments. "I tried to see Los Angeles for what it was," Gehry said. The house shows the confused, unresolved nature of modern life, as well as the ethos of a "city without a center." Although his source material is Pop culture, Gehry gives the banal an aesthetic spin.

**Guggenheim Museum, Bilbao, Spain, by Gehry, 1997
In His Own Words.**
Frank Gehry commented on the rolling curves of his work, "It's not just space—it's a kind of sculpture." Taking "the license to be outrageous and to explore is the way to get someplace." At Bilbao, "I took the soft shapes a notch further," he says, "almost taking shapes into a liquid state like a waterfall." He aims for "ephemeral" form, where "you won't be able to hold any form in your mind. It will constantly change, depending on your angle of view."

The improvised appearance of his structures is not a stylistic tic but an obsession. His forms grow out of the fray of life to express its flux. Gehry's personal symbol is a fish (which he renders as everything from a giant sculpture to a conference room or a lamp). The fluid forms of his buildings leap and flow like a fish swimming upstream against the tide of convention.

The California Aerospace Museum (1984) in Los Angeles introduced his concept of a "village of forms." Disdainful of facile harmony, Gehry fractured the design into an assemblage of separate forms to reflect the diversity of society, but with overall compositional unity.

His Vitra Chair Museum (1989) in Weil-am-Rhein, Germany, is a collage of half-domes, wedges, and crescent shapes, as if a wheel of cheese were sliced with a scythe. Gehry described the skewed masses' effect as "frozen motion."

In His Own Words

"You can climb all over this building," says Antoine Predock, adding, "Architecture is processional and ceremonial. I think of a building as a cinematographic experience of still frames. A building should encourage the search, the exploration in all

fields. Buildings should raise questions and become polemics in themselves.

"A building should engage all the senses. I go out of my way to maximize enriching possibilities and evoke a kinesthetic response to volumes and an intellectual comprehension of space.

"I am an eclectic in my own right. I enjoy being a *voyeur* and a participant in contemporary culture. It's all up for grabs. The notion of a drive-in movie screen inspired me here. I start with geology, go through culture and historical moments. My self-imposed mandate is to absorb all these things. It's all woven together, all part of the encounter with a place."

He continues, "You try to do a building that fuses new energies and sensibility. You try to advance the whole picture. My obligation to capital 'A' Architecture is to create a timeless aspect, a transporting building, without historicizing."

Nelson Fine Arts Center, Arizona State University, Tempe, by Predock, 1989

BILBAO: THE PINNACLE.

Philip Johnson called Gehry's Guggenheim Museum (1997) in Bilbao, Spain, "the greatest building of our time," and he may just be right. The curvaceous structure, with its shining scales of quilted titanium panels, has been compared to a basketful of fish or an exploding flower. Gehry used computer design for working models and final production drawings matched to the manufacturing process. He built the unique forms on time and within budget.

During its first year, 1.36 million people visited (three times the forecast), demonstrating the power of great architecture as a tourist attraction. Gehry's commission was "Build something spectacular!" and he delivered the goods. The titanium coat (bought for a song when Russians were dumping military stockpiles) changes color under different light conditions, from silver to purplish gray or gold. The building's forms seem to mutate as one circles the structure, unfolding a dynamic panorama of vistas.

Exploring the inside is also an adventure. The boat-shaped largest gallery (450 feet long, with no central supports) extrudes like a whale's tail under a bridge. What looks like fragmented, earthquake aesthetic from the outside is a promenade of delight inside.

3535 Hayden Avenue, Culver City, California, by Moss, 1996
Eric Owen Moss's aggressive architecture combines incongruous industrial materials and raw forms in a "junkyard" aesthetic.

PREDOCK: DESIGNING THE FACE OF A PLACE. The work of Antoine Predock (b. 1936) of Albuquerque, New Mexico, fits no neat category. His most salient trait is a drive to connect with the spirit of a landscape. Since his early designs were for desert areas, he built adobe houses that evoked not only the region's history, but its geology. Inspired by the Southwest and Spanish heritage, his work refers to native landscapes in an abstracted form that defies easy analogy.

Predock's American Heritage Center and Art Museum (1986–93) in Laramie, Wyoming, is a volcano-like cone clad in metal. With a smoke hole at the top and an interior timber frame like lodge poles of a teepee, the building looks both ancient and space-age. Nicknamed "Tony Corona" for the halo of white hair surrounding his face, Predock comes across like a New Age shaman of the desert. His buildings are eco-sensitive, using passive heating and cooling and indigenous materials, laden with vernacular references.

A building should be, Predock has said, "a ride." He activates the senses with the sound of running water, the scent of herbs, tactile surfaces, and his wizardry with light and shadow. More than Mr. Adobe, Predock is an avid recycler of Pop culture. He has based forms on UFOs, the Stealth bomber, even the outline of Bart Simpson's hair. The roofscape of his Nelson Fine Arts Center has a pseudo-Mayan pyramid to suggest a mountain, as well as an auditorium fly-tower like a drive-in movie screen. Images are projected on it at night. Predock calls the design, which features pavilions for viewing sunrise and sunset, an "altered atmosphere."

Predock is sometimes minimalist but always allusive and enigmatic. Searching to express his acute sense of place, he creates ambiguous rather than signature forms. "I think of architecture as abstract landscape," he said. "It's kind of like landscape in drag."

In His Own Words

"My mandate was to make a specific connection to the Jeffersonian tradition," says Robert Stern. "I had to balance the desire to create a space within the Jeffersonian vein with a place with its own identity. My major concept was the continuity of the past in the present. My own notion of what it means to be modern is to have a computer on a desk, which is a nice eighteenth-century piece of woodwork.

"I'm a long-time critic of architecture as a measure of the *zeitgeist*. Others should be less worried about the *zeitgeist* and more worried about the traditions entrusted to them. [People are] sick and tired of buildings that are expressive of technology or the autobiography of an architect but not of the place."

Darden Graduate School of Business Administration, University of Virginia, Charlottesville, by Stern, 1996

THE ANNOTATED PYRAMID

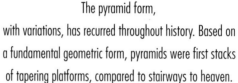

The pyramid form,
with variations, has recurred throughout history. Based on
a fundamental geometric form, pyramids were first stacks
of tapering platforms, compared to stairways to heaven.
The stepped pyramid of Zoser, by the first known architect, Imhotep, is the oldest surviving stone structure.
It resembles not only Babylonian ziggurats but Mayan temples built several continents, an ocean, and eons away.

Mayan stepped pyramids
(with nine receding stages of banked earth
and rubble) were mostly solid rock. The Pyramid of the Sun has a base the size of the
Great Pyramid of Egypt. Steep flights of stairs
mount to the top, where priests performed
gory rituals of human sacrifice.

In the twentieth century, architects have revived the archaic pyramid form as an image of modernity.
Built of glass to stress not solidity but lightness and transparency, I. M. Pei's clean, crisp geometry achieves maximum
contrast to the Baroque masonry buildings surrounding it. Argentine architect Emilio Ambasz designed a glass conservatory
in San Antonio, Texas, of warped green pyramids. In 1998, Philip Johnson proposed a deconstructed pyramid for
New York City, proving the ancient form has not yet crumbled to dust.

Clockwise from lower left: Pyramids at Giza, 2570–2500 B.C.E.; Ziggurat Ur-of-the-Chaldees, c. 2000 B.C.E.; Stepped pyramid of Zoser, Saqqara, by Imhotep, c. 2700
B.C.E.; Temple I, Tikal, Guatemala, c. 687–730 C.E.; Louvre entrance, Paris, by Pei, 1983–89

NEW URBANISM: MILES OF SMILES

New Urbanism, also called Neo-Traditionalism, has the admirable goal of promoting communal bonds through city planning. The name is a misnomer, however, since the philosophy is neither new nor urban. Neo-Trad communities are unabashedly suburban, and architectural styles are a pastel version of old favorites like Tudor, "colonial," or Victorian.

The basic concept is of a mixed-use village, where work, residences, and commerce intermingle, instead of being divided into distant zones. The ensemble is laid out on a pedestrian scale, with plenty of greenery, public parks, front porches for sociability, and picket fences for old-timey appeal. Drawing on a romanticized image of small towns in a pre-automobile era, the communities have houses on small lots close to the street and homogeneous designs redolent of apple-cheeked children, moms in aprons, and omniscient dads warbling, "Honey, I'm home."

The godparents of the movement are a husband-wife duo, Andres Duany and Elizabeth Plater-Zyberk. Their first New Urbanist enclave, Seaside, a town developed in Florida in the 1980s, is like a stage set for the film *It's a Wonderful Life.*

In the United Kingdom, Prince Charles has sponsored a similar movement. In 1984, he launched a "crusade" to achieve three Cs: "Community architecture, Classicism, and Conservation." Several architects in England, like Leon Krier and Quinlan Terry, took up the Prince of Wales's banner, producing buildings that revive past styles without Post-Modern irony. Poundbury in Dorset (built from 1988) is a new town of modest houses designed by Krier. Housing, shopping, and work coexist in a compressed area, prying people out of their cars, which strangle most cities.

Seaside, Florida, by Duany and Plater-Zyberk, begun 1981
This designed community seeks to recapture small-town values through pedestrian-centered amenities and mixed-use development.

Some architects have bought into the call for pre-Modernist structures, plumping them down not in designed communities but wherever a new building is commissioned. Allan Greenberg turns out meticulously detailed Neo-classic reproductions, especially for U.S. government buildings. The monumental Harold Washington Library Center (1992) in Chicago by Thomas Beeby is a fitting descendant of H. H. Richardson's massive libraries. Its red-granite, rusticated base, rich ornament, and sculptured gargoyles declare serious civic ambition.

New York architect Robert A. M. Stern began as a Post-Modernist, then—with his graceful, Neo–Shingle Style residences—veered into nostalgia. His summer "cottages" on the East End of Long Island are so faithful to their nineteenth-century models, they blur the line between authentic and reproduction. Stern achieves an upscale, Ralph Lauren image that is even more luxurious than the original. "Counterpointing in a dialogue across time," he calls it. His Darden Graduate School of Business Administration for the University of

Hearst Castle, San Simeon, California, by Morgan, 1919–47

At a time when women were barred from architecture schools and discouraged from entering the profession, Julia Morgan (1872–1957) was the first woman accepted at the École des Beaux-Arts. She had her own office from 1905 to 1940, designing more than seven hundred homes in northern California. Morgan spent decades supervising the design and construction of William Randolph Hearst's pleasure palace. After twenty years and $8 million, Morgan had produced one of the world's most lavish private residences. The 104-foot Neptune Pool, Hellenistic temple, and Classical colonnade show the stage-set nature of this eclectic showplace. Morgan, the first female engineering graduate of the University of California, Berkeley, could have kept adding on forever. Hearst ran out of funds before she ran out of ideas.

Virginia (see page 161) almost manages to outdo Thomas Jefferson's pavilions in refinement and elegance.

DISNEY DESIGN: THE MOUSE THAT ROARED.

The most generous patron of contemporary architecture in the 1990s was Michael Eisner, chairman and CEO of the Walt Disney Company. Eisner commissioned more than $1 billion worth of buildings for Disney's Neo-Trad Florida town, Celebration, for corporate structures, and for theme parks around the world. "Starchitects" like Graves, Venturi and Scott Brown, Gehry, Predock, Stern, Johnson, Isozaki, Rossi, and Moore were the beneficiaries of Disney largesse.

Robert Stern's Casting Center in Orlando is one of the most successful examples of Disney decor. It's also a hoot. A diaper pattern of pale colors evokes the facade of the Doge's Palace in Venice. Trefoil tracery in the shape of Mickey Mouse's head (empty, one notes) adorns the parapet. In response to those who criticize Disney commissions as ersatz, Stern replies, "Disney is fun!" Michael Eisner himself called it "entertainment architecture."

Disney structures show a tendency that infects more serious architecture at the end of the century. Like a Texas cowboy who is all hat and no mustangs, architecture has become more packaging than substance. Examples of this "jokey-tecture," like malls, casinos, hotels, and even noncommercial structures like academic buildings and libraries, merge architecture with spectacle.

Many buildings by name designers plagiarize motifs from the past to wow viewers with vulgar excess. Michael Graves's Dolphin and Swan Hotels for Disneyworld are over-the-top, stage-set architecture, more artifice than originality. Exaggerated size and color, spatial gimmicks, and silly theatricality are a recipe for the empty calories of archi-tainment.

In Graves's design for Disney's headquarters building (1991) in Burbank, California, 19-foot, cast-concrete caryatids of the seven dwarfs, with Dopey as the central figure, support a central pediment. "I've tried to walk the line between the whimsical and the jokey," Graves has said, "to navigate between the chasm of the cute and the abyss of easy irony."

CHERCHEZ LA FEMME: THE INVISIBLE FEMALE ARCHITECT

In 1998, 18 percent of the 55,000 registered U.S. architects were women. Only about 7 percent headed their own firms. (In the United Kingdom, women comprise 9 percent of architects, while in Spain, Germany, France, and Iceland the percentage varies from 10 to 16 percent.) They don't call a building an erection for nothing. Studs still frame the architectural world, run by the Old Boy System.

Working against the odds, women who have gained worldwide recognition include the Italian Gae Aulenti, Itsuko Hasegawa (the only active woman architect in Japan), and Denise Scott Brown of Philadelphia. Some gaining increasing notice are Maya Lin, Elizabeth Plater-Zyberk, Laurinda Spear, Zaha Hadid, and Patricia Patkau. Coming to the fore are Rebecca Binder, Victoria Casasco, Judith Scheine, Katherine Diamond, Sarah Susanka, and Deborah Berke.

Before the feminist movement of the 1960s, women were often the forgotten partners whose husbands or bosses got all the credit. Catherine Bauer channeled her energy into planning and architectural criticism while her husband, William Wurster, got the big jobs. Ray Eames was never as well known as her husband, Charles. Marion Lucy Mahony did most of Frank Lloyd Wright's drawings and much of the furniture design.

Now the pattern is for husband-and-wife teams to collaborate, sharing credit and design tasks. Co-heads of firms include Lella and Massimo Vignelli, Frances Halsband and Robert Kliment, Diana Agrest and Mario Gandelsonas, Laurie Hawkinson and Henry Smith-Miller, Margaret McCurry and Stanley Tigerman, Marion Weiss and Michael Manfredi, and Billie Tsien and Tod Williams.

Among the most sought-after team players are the husband-wife combo of Arquitectonica, Bernardo Fort-Brescia (b. 1951) and Laurinda Spear (b. 1950). Designs of the Miami firm mix fiery color with fearless geometry. At the center of their Atlantis (1982) condominium tower in Miami, they carved out a four-story opening. The void of this "sky court" contains a fire-engine-red spiral stair, blue whirlpool, and palm tree. Hot Caribbean meets cool Modernism. "We start from the premise that you should have a certain emotion when you see it," Spear has said of her work. Their expressive shapes mix fantasy and cutaway surprise, as in their International Swimming Hall of Fame, with its profile like leaping dolphins.

The Jacobite Manifesto

Jane Jacobs, although not an architect, was the most influential woman in changing the look of city architecture. Her book, *The Death and Life of Great American Cities* (1961), did for historic preservation what Rachel Carson's *Silent Spring* did for environmental conservation. Jacobs pointed out the virtue of diversity, from both economic and aesthetic perspectives. Standing up against the big boys of Modernism, she revealed the disaster of urban renewal's mass housing projects. Jacobs proved the chaotic disorganization of city life was more humane and, ultimately, more livable. Her manifesto kicked off Post-Modernism, with its preference for variety over uniformity, small rather than big.

NEW BLOOD 101: THE SHAPE OF THINGS TO COME

Most architects don't have the opportunity to build major structures until in their fifties, so *wunderkinds* are few. But it's possible to identify up-and-comers who are pushing the parameters of design.

In California, Thom Mayne (b. 1944) and Michael Rotondi (formerly partners in Morphosis) and Eric Moss (b. 1943) are known for astonishing work. Their buildings, in a distinctive industrial aesthetic, appear harsh, brooding with power.

In Moss's warehouse complexes in Culver City (see page 160), he transforms common materials like bolts into light fixtures or sewer pipes into columns. Philip Johnson dubbed Moss a "jeweler of junk." Samitaur (1990–96) is a poured-concrete, sculptural building that "looks like a freeway designed by a drunk," as Moss has said. His structure called "The Box" (1990–94) has a rooftop appendage that looks like a bucking bronco.

For Rotondi (b. 1949), architecture is a subversive craft that should redefine space. The goal of Morphosis was to "celebrate the complex." Mayne has said, "I start with complete blackness." The process is as interesting as the product and should produce architecture that reverberates. Mayne's disparate fragments form a collaged composition of rough cubic forms in tough materials. In one Santa Barbara home, Mayne fused architecture and landscape so seamlessly, a road runner dropped in to visit.

BREAKING NEW GROUND. Mexican architect Ricardo Legorreta creates sculptural designs saturated with intense color. His Visual Arts Center (1998) in Santa Fe is composed of red blocks with lurid desert colors like pink, purple, and charcoal. The linked units, Legorreta said, were "inspired by the concept of a little pueblo." Subtle, primal forms by Steven Holl (b. 1947) create a mystical space in his contemporary art museum, Kiasma (1998), in Helsinki. The two wings of the building are a collage of curves, grids, voids, and solids that interact with light and water to bend space and the viewers' perceptions.

French architects like Jean Nouvel (b. 1945), Christian de Portzamparc (b. 1944), and Dominique Perrault (b. 1953) are designing some of the most imposing monuments at the end of the century. In the United States, Costa Rican–born Carlos Jiménez inflects Modernist simplicity with Latin American and Southwest tradition. His Lynn Goode Gallery (1991) in Houston has a steel-paneled yellow facade with four gray recessed bays, creating a syncopation of open and shut.

At the Dominus Winery (1998) in Yountville, California, Swiss partners Jacques Herzog and Pierre de Meuron reinvented Modernist geometry with a sensual twist. They started with a basic oblong box, then—through a surprising choice of materials—transformed it from banal to boffo. The walls consist of wire cages, loosely filled with a jumble of rocks. Sunlight filters through baskets of stones to cast dancing shadows inside and out, animating the facade with visual texture. Solid as a rock it's not. Unexpected, sensational, and fun it is.

What's contemporary about contemporary architecture is not a matter of chronology but of making us see our environment anew. More than tacked-on special effects or pretty confections, design should reflect where we are, what we think and feel. If it is to outlast the moment, it should force us to think, feel, and see things we haven't experienced before.

"It's important that a building be strong, provocative," said Charles Gwathmey, "so that we take risks, extend ourselves, and engage each other." The best contemporary architecture investigates new areas, turning our prejudices upside down and letting the fresh breeze of the future blow open the doors of our minds.

GLOSSARY

A

Agora Open space in a Greek city used as a general meeting place.

Aisle Walkway of church parallel to the nave, separated from it by piers or columns.

Ambulatory Passage surrounding the choir of a cathedral; circulatory corridor created by continuation of the side aisles.

Apse In Christian basilica, usually a semicircular terminating chapel at the end of a long rectangular church.

Aqueduct Ancient Roman structure to bring water from distant source; consists of elevated masonry or brick arches supporting a water conduit.

Arcade Series of arches supported by columns or piers.

Arch Vaulted wall opening that can span large spaces.

Architrave Lower part of a classical entablature, which rests directly on the capital of a column.

Arcuated Method of construction based on the arch shape.

Art Deco Style of decoration and architecture characterized by aerodynamic ornament, 1925–30s.

Art Nouveau Style of fluid, sinuous lines based on natural motifs, popular in Europe, 1895–1906.

Ashlar Hewn or squared (smoothly finished) stone cut in regular rectangular blocks, or a masonry wall of finely dressed stone.

Atrium Central courtyard flanked by wings of a building.

B

Baluster Row of small spindles or posts (often vase-shaped) that supports a rail.

Balustrade A protective fence formed of balusters and rail, or parapet, either functional or ornamental.

Band windows A horizontal series of uniform windows that appear to be a continuous strip.

Baptistry Part of a church used for baptism.

Basilica In Roman Empire, a long building with narrow side aisles, wide central aisle ending in apse, covered by wooden truss roof; in early Christian architecture, a church with multiple aisles and a longitudinal nave higher than the side aisles, lit by clerestory windows.

Batter The receding upward slope of a wall or structure.

Battlement A parapet built with indentations, usually atop defensive wall of a castle.

Bauhaus Radical German school of architecture and design (1919–32) that produced Modernism.

Bay Vertical segment of a building, usually divided by columns or windows from adjacent bays.

Beaux Arts Formal Neoclassical style taught in Paris in the nineteenth century.

Blind arcade, arch, or window Elements of an arcade, arch, or window applied to a wall without any opening; used for decorative purposes to articulate a facade.

Bracket Horizontally projecting support for an overhanging weight such as a corbel or cantilevered balcony; a support under eaves often more decorative than functional.

Brutalism Style where rough constructional materials are exposed, derived from the use of poured raw concrete (*béton brut*) by Le Corbusier.

Buttress A projecting structure for support to give stability to a load-bearing wall; reinforces high walls and counteracts lateral thrust.

Byzantine Term used for eastern Christian art of Constantinople and Byzantine Empire of the fourth to fourteenth centuries.

C

Campanile Freestanding bell tower in church complex or Italian town.

Cantilever Horizontally projecting beam or part of a structure supported only at one end.

Capital Top, decorated part of a column or pilaster; crowns the shaft and supports the entablature.

Caryatid Sculpted female figure used as a column to support horizontal lintel.

Castellated Characterized by battlements or turrets, like a medieval castle.

Cella Windowless main chamber of Greek temple containing statue of the cult image.

Chevet East end of church, including side aisles, choir, ambulatory, chapels; chancel.

Choir Area beyond the nave in Christian church, between crossing and altar at east end.

Classical Style denoting the architecture of ancient Greece and Rome.

Clerestory Upper part of a cathedral nave containing windows.

Coffering Recessed panels in a ceiling, used to decorate the surface or lighten the weight of a dome or vault.

Colonettes Slender columns, usually turned; used more for visual interest than for support.

Colonnade Line of arches or columns bearing a horizontal entablature, as in St. Peter's Square in Rome.

Colossal order Also known as giant order, a system where columns rise from ground floor through two or more floors.

Column Vertical, round pillar that supports an arch or entablature.

Compressive strength Ability to sustain load (compression or squeezing forces) without fracture.

Corbel Bracket or stone projecting from the face of a wall to support a cornice, beam, or arch.

Corinthian order Most ornate of the Classical Greek orders, used extensively by Romans; capital is decorated with stylized acanthus leaves.

Cornice Ornamental molding atop a building or wall; a horizontal strip projecting from a wall to differentiate horizontal sections of a building.

Crenellation Battlement; parapet with alternating indentations (embrasures) and raised portions (merlons).

Crossing Square or rectangular area created by intersecting transept wings and nave of a church; sometimes surmounted by a tower.

Curtain wall Non-load-bearing skin that clads the outside of a modern building.

D

Deconstructivism Term derived from French literary-philosophical movement to indicate exploded, off-kilter architectural shapes of the 1980s.

Doric order Oldest and simplest of the Classical Greek orders, with heavy columns and plain, saucer-shaped capitals.

Dormer A vertically set window placed on the inclined plane of a roof.

Drum Cylindrical structure supporting a dome.

E

Eave Projecting overhang at bottom edge of a roof.

Elevation Drawing showing a vertical face of a building, either an interior or exterior wall.

Entablature The whole of the parts of an order between the column capital and the roof or pediment; divided into three parts: architrave (which rests immediately on the column), frieze (next over the architrave), and cornice (uppermost part).

Entasis Slight convex curve on Greek columns to overcome the optical illusion of concavity that would result if the shafts were straight.

Expressionism German artistic movement typified by bizarre, sculptural buildings and utopian philosophy, 1910–24.

F

Fan vault Vault composed of concave conoidal sections springing from the corners of the vaulting compartment, often decorated with ribs that radiate like the spokes of an umbrella.

Finial Ornament at the top of a spire, pinnacle, or gable.

Flamboyant style Extremely ornate late Gothic style with flamelike stone tracery and elaborate carving.

Fluted Carved with ridges or flutes (regularly spaced vertical, parallel grooves on the shaft of a column or pilaster).

Flying buttress Arch or half-arch commonly seen on the exterior of Gothic cathedrals; used to support high stone walls by counteracting lateral thrust, transmitting force to exterior support.

Folly Decorative pavilion, usually in the form of a Classical or medieval ruin, designed to enhance a landscape and inspire poetic nostalgia.

Forum Roman market and assembly place for political gatherings.

Frieze Horizontal band containing sculpted ornament on a wall.

G

Gable Triangular wall section at the end of a double-pitched (gabled) roof.

Gallery Roofed promenade or corridor; upper story over an aisle in church architecture.

Gingerbread Superfluous and intricate ornamentation; often ornately curved wood (bargeboard) characteristic of Carpenter Gothic style.

Gothic Medieval architecture characterized by pointed stone arches, rib vaults, stained glass, and flying buttresses.

Groin vault Also known as a cross vault, a compound vault formed at the perpendicular intersection of two barrel vaults.

H

Half-timbering A building in which the principal supports and frame are of exposed timber, with the interstices filled in with plaster or masonry; characteristic of Tudor style.

Hall church Church with a longitudinal plan in which aisles are the same height as the nave, with a single roof covering both nave and aisles; plan designed for sermons more than liturgy.

Hellenistic Style developed in the kingdom of Alexander the Great (in Greece and northern Egypt) between 323 and 27 B.C.E.; characterized by rich ornament and sculpture.

High-Tech Style dating from the late 1970s, which displays the technology, structure, and utilities of a building as a decorative element.

Horseshoe arch Arch shaped like a horseshoe, characteristic of Islamic architecture.

Ionic order Order of Classical Greek architecture in which a capital consists of two opposed volutes or scroll forms.

International Style Term devised by Hitchcock and Johnson to describe European Modernist buildings between the two world wars.

K

Keystone Central stone of an arch, which locks wedge-shaped voussoirs in place.

L

Lancet Narrow, pointed arch.

Lantern Structure on top of a roof with open or windowed walls; circular or polygonal turret, usually on top of a dome.

Loggia Arcaded walkway or covered but open hall commonly seen on Renaissance palazzos.

Lozenge Diamond-shaped decorative motif.

M

Mannerism High Renaissance style that exaggerated Classical forms to achieve a more individual (often eccentric) interpretation.

Mansard roof A curb roof, the lower slope of which approaches the vertical and often contains dormer windows, while the upper slope is nearly flat; a hallmark of Second Empire style.

Masonry Wall construction using materials such as stone, brick, or adobe.

Mastaba Ancient Egyptian tomb with walls that slope inward as the height increases.

Minaret Tall, slim tower attached to a mosque from which the muezzin calls the people to prayer.

Modernism Socially progressive movement in the early twentieth century that championed undecorated, cubic, functional architecture.

Molding Continuous decorative band, either carved into or applied to a surface to ornament or articulate a facade.

Mosque Islamic place of worship, usually consisting of a courtyard surrounded by arcades and a colonnaded prayer hall.

Mullion Vertical post or upright strip that separates and often supports a series of windows, doors, or panels.

N

Nave Long, main section of a church whose walls rise higher than the flanking aisles.

Neoclassicism Beginning late eighteenth century, a revival of formality and purity of Classical architecture after excesses of Baroque and Rococo periods.

O

Obelisk Tall, four-sided stone pillar, tapered and crowned with a pyramidal point, invented by the Egyptians.

Order Term for any of several styles of Classical architecture characterized by the type of column used; ancient system of form and proportion.

Oriel A bay window that projects from the outer face of a wall, of various kinds and sizes; characteristic of Queen Anne style.

P

Palladian window Three-part window with a large arched central opening and flanking rectangular side lights; also called Serlian motif.

Parapet Low wall or railing along the edge of a roof or balcony.

Pavilion Part of a building projecting from the rest; an ornamental structure in a park or garden.

Pediment Wide, low-pitched gable forming a triangular space above the facade of a building in a Classical style; a triangular crowning element over doors, windows, niches.

Pendentive Concave spandrel leading from the right angle of two walls to the base of a circular dome.

Pergola Horizontal trelliswork supported on columns forming an arbor.

Peristyle Colonnade surrounding a courtyard or building in an ancient residence or temple.

Perpendicular style English version of High Gothic style (c. 1330–1580) with extreme rectilinear accents in tracery, walls, and windows.

Pier Solid supporting member, rectangular or square, usually very sturdy.

Pilaster Shallow pillar or squared-off column attached to a wall, with base and capital projecting from wall.

Pilotis French word for thin, free-standing stilts at ground-floor level to hold up first floor, especially in buildings by Le Corbusier.

Pinnacle Thin pointed turret; decorative element on Gothic buildings that crowns a spire or buttress.

Plan Layout of a building drawn in a horizontal plane showing arrangement of rooms.

Plasticity Sculptural quality of a building, giving the appearance of being modeled from a ductile material.

Plinth Base of a column, pedestal, or statue.

Podium Low base or platform.

Polychromy Use of multiple colors in decoration of architecture or sculpture.

Porte cochère Large covered entrance porch, sheltering carriages while passengers descend.

Portico Covered porch or entrance on a building's facade, usually crowned by pedimented roof supported by Classical columns.

Post-and-lintel Method of construction in which vertical posts support horizontal lintel, or beam.

Post-Modern Eclectic style that originated in the mid-1970s as a reaction against Modernism; appropriates elements and colors from many historical periods, adding notes of whimsy and irony.

Pylon Towerlike gate in Egyptian temple complex; thick walls slant inward.

Pyramid Tomb structure for Egyptian pharaohs with sloping triangular sides, built on square plan and converging at a single point.

Q

Quoin Distinctive units of brick or stone that accentuate the corners of a building.

R

Reinforced concrete Mixture of sand, aggregate, and cement, given additional tensile strength by inserting steel rods within its mass.

Rib Load-bearing structural element outlining a ceiling vault.

Rococo Ornate decorative style characterized by delicate forms, light colors, and floral arabesques.

Romanesque Medieval style that revived Roman elements like the round arch and basilica.

Rose window Prominent circular window in Gothic cathedral, decorated with tracery.

Rotunda Circular or polygonal structure usually capped with a dome.

Rustication Masonry cut with deep joints; blocks either smooth, textured, or roughened.

S

Section Diagram showing a vertical slice through a building.

Setback Receding silhouette in which upper stories of a tall building are stepped back from lower levels; expedient designed to allow more light to reach street between skyscrapers.

Shaft Main vertical part of a column between the base and capital; can be smooth or fluted.

Skeleton frame Freestanding frame of iron or steel supporting the weight of a building, on which the floors and outer walls are hung.

Spandrel Triangular space between adjacent arches and below horizontal molding above them.

Stoa Covered open gallery facing agora in Classical Greek architecture.

String course Narrow, continuous ornamental molding on the facade of a building; horizontal cornice that visually separates floors of a building.

Swag Ornamental motif resembling a piece of draped cloth.

T

Tectonics Load-bearing structure of a building in which individual technical and formal elements are organized into a uniform artistic whole; science or art of construction.

Tensile strength Capable of resisting rupturing forces that stretch or pull apart structural elements.

Terra-cotta Fine-grained, red-brown fired clay used for roof tiles and decoration (literally means "cooked earth").

Thrust Lateral horizontal force within a wall created by the weight of arches or roof structure, wind pressure, gravity.

Trabeated System of construction in which posts or pillars support a beam or lintel.

Tracery Curved, branchlike mullions of a stone-framed window; ornamental pattern of perforations in a screen, windowpane, or panel; especially lacy openwork at top of Gothic windows.

Transept Horizontal wings perpendicular to the nave and choir, which gives the church plan form of a cross.

Transverse arch Arch that separates one bay of a vault from adjacent bays.

Trefoil Three-lobed design resembling cloverleaf.

Triforium Narrow wall passage open to the nave, above the first-floor arcade and under the clerestory windows in Gothic churches.

Truss Rigid frame of timber or metal pieces forming triangular units.

Turret Small, slender tower, usually at the corner of a building and containing a circular stair.

V

Vault Arched ceiling of masonry, brick, or wood.

Veranda Open gallery or porch covered by a roof.

Vernacular Referring to indigenous or traditional building styles.

Volute Spiral-shaped, scroll-like ornamental motif on Ionic capital.

Z

Ziggurat Stepped pyramid structure with ramps characteristic of Babylonian and Assyrian architecture.

INDEX

Page numbers in *italics* refer to illustrations.